TEEN TRENDS

A NATION
IN MOTION

REGINALD W. BIBBY
DONALD C. POSTERSKI

Stoddart

To
Armand Mauss and Jim Berney:
mentors, colleagues, friends

First published in 1992 by
Stoddart Publishing Co. Limited
34 Lesmill Road
Toronto, Canada
M3B 2T6

Canadian Cataloguing in Publication Data

Bibby, Reginald W. (Reginald Wayne), 1943-
  Teen trends : a nation in motion

Includes bibliographical references.
ISBN 0-7737-5531-4

1. Teenagers - Canada.   I. Posterski, Donald C., 1942-   . II. Title.

H0799.C2B52 1992   305.23'5'0971   C92-094961-4

Cover Design: Brant Cowie/ArtPlus Limited
Typesetting: Tony Gordon Ltd.
Printed and bound in Canada

Stoddart Publishing gratefully acknowledges the support of the Canada Council, Ontario Arts Council, and Canadian Publishing Centre in the development of writing and publishing in Canada.

06-0816

CONTENTS

PART II / NEW POSSIBILITIES

PREFACE

Teen Trends represents an effort to provide Canadians with a clear picture of where young people are headed, along with sound thoughts on how we might respond to what is taking place.

As such, the goal has been not only to produce a book that is academically solid, but one that discusses the implications of the research with parents, professionals, and other adults who have a special interest in youth. The attempt to reach a broad audience is not without its perils. Academics invariably want more theory, more technical information, more sophisticated statistical analyses, more cross references. Meanwhile, practitioners are usually not content to stop with description, wanting to move on to application.

Committed as we are to good scholarship and good communication, we have tried for balance. For those readers looking for theory, the book is grounded in classic sociology's assertion that the key to understanding individuals is understanding the social environments from which they come. Accordingly, we view Canadian young people as products of an ever-changing Canadian culture. Just as Canada is a country under construction, young people are in the process of building their lives out of the materials our society is giving them.

Regarding the description-application issue, we've found that most Canadians want both. People usually see the research findings as interesting and intriguing. But invariably they proceed to the obvious question "What can we do about it?" *Teen Trends* is the result of an attempt to combine Bibby's trend research expertise with Posterski's extensive work with youth in producing a book rich in both information and implications.

The statistical reporting is presented in a straightforward manner. The references, the methodological specifics, and other technical information have been placed at the back of the book. Rejecting the role of grim-faced clinicians, we have let our individual writing styles express our personalities, with the hope of not only being understood but enjoyed.

Teen Trends has been made possible by three key participants. First, we wish to thank the Lilly Foundation for providing the funding for the latest 1992 national youth survey, as well as the most recent 1990 national adult survey. The willingness of such American friends to help Canadians better understand themselves says much about the goodwill that exists south of the border. Second, we are extremely grateful for the overwhelming co-operation of some 200 high schools and CEGEPs across Canada in the form of school boards, principals, guidance counsellors, and other personnel, resulting in an astounding 93 per cent response rate. Third, our debt to the 4000 students who took the time to fill out our questionnaire is enormous. We have tried hard to represent them well.

Others have played significant roles. The University of Lethbridge, with the assistance of the Lilly Foundation, freed Bibby for three semesters to complete the 1990 and 1992 surveys, carry out the data analyses, and work on the book. Such generosity is matched by few universities anywhere. Posterski received valued staff and other resource support from World Vision Canada, of which he is Vice-President for National Programs.

A large number of individuals played roles in the carrying out of the survey and in the preparation of the manuscript. They include Joan Morin, Jules Lehouillier, Dianne Erickson, Michele Therrien, Suzanne Lehouillier, Nickina Bullock, Dave Bibby, Tine Skovbye, Chuck Ferguson, and Bruce Cameron. We particularly appreciate the superb contribution made by senior research associate Reg Bibby, Jr., in co-ordinating much of the survey specifics, including sampling, data collection, coding, and data entry. We again have enjoyed working closely with Stoddart's managing editor Donald G. Bastian, a long-term associate and friend, and thank copy editor Maryan Gibson for her skilled and insightful input.

Finally, we thank Jozefa, Beth, our families, and our friends for their support and patience in what has been a demanding but gratifying project.

REGINALD W. BIBBY
DONALD C. POSTERSKI

INTRODUCTION

Life is dynamic. The world and everything in it are in a constant state of motion. It's true of the physical world, true of all living things. Without movement, there is no life. Our very concept of time assumes movement. And in a fraction of a second, the future absorbs the present, leaving behind the debris of the past for storage in archives, photo albums, and memory banks. Because life is in motion, nothing is impossible; few things are ever final. Then again, nothing is a sure thing. Except movement. Life is movement. Maybe that's why young people like to move, why children can't sit still. They're full of life.

TEENAGERS IN MOTION

We stressed the idea in *The Emerging Generation*, pointing out that life involves constant emergence, continuous becoming. We don't merely get old; we constantly are becoming something new. The teenage years, however, are novel in that they represent a time of multidimensional emergence. Following a decade of being treated as premature adults — regarded as inferior experientially, physically, intellectually, socially, emotionally, and spiritually — teenagers become full-fledged adults. A multidimensional transformation signals their farewell to childhood.

The central argument of the book was that such a time of intense motion involves far more than one's own initiative and abilities. Young people do not evolve in a social vacuum. Others profoundly influence the process, most notably parents, friends, teachers, and the media. For some, clergy, coaches, and group leaders have significant roles. To varying degrees, these primary people promote emergence — but they also block it. Some do much to help teens grow up; others try to keep them forever young. It is our strong belief that the teen years can be enjoyable years for all those involved *if* adults can succeed in finding a balance between providing direction and providing room — giving emerging young people the help they need to move into adulthood, while having the good sense to give them increasing room to become our equals.

To look at teenagers is to see youth in motion. But it is to see much more.

A NATION IN MOTION

A 15-year-old from London, Ontario, told us wryly, "Most people my age have no idea what is going on. This survey was unnecessary. The opinions of underdeveloped minds should not make a difference. But I'm glad you received my opinions to show you that all is not lost."

More than a few adults are inclined to think of young people as "just kids," and dismiss their thoughts and ideas. These adults need to think again. To look at teenagers is to see the kind of young people our country is turning out. In a very real sense, they are at the leading edge of our culture. Through the media and the school, they are being exposed to our dominant cultural ideas. Consequently, they are not just kids going through a phase. Young people provide us with an invaluable mirror of who we currently are, as well as offer us something of a window on what we are becoming.

These days, our country can benefit immensely from such mirrors and windows.

Life in Canada has been dynamic. Our nation has been anything but static. Like many of our societal counterparts around the world, we've been moving and moving fast since our inception in 1867. Ongoing change has characterized our 125 years of history.

The conspicuous fact that we are still in search of ways of binding the country together has disguised another fact — that we've been engaged in a very robust and creative struggle to determine how we, as people with diverse backgrounds, can flourish together on common geographical turf. But while unity has been a primary concern, it has hardly been our only concern. We've been moving forward quickly as a nation — passing through the agricultural and industrial eras, becoming part of the modern age of information. Along the way, we've been making endless adjustments, developing and revising our institutions and culture, our ideologies and outlooks, our policies and programs.

It's been paying off. Our standard of living and overall quality of life is the envy of much of the world. But that's just so far. The tape is still running. Life is still moving. There's much to maintain, much to improve.

In the last half of this century, the federal government, led by the innovative Pierre Trudeau, embarked on an ambitious attempt to enhance Canadian life. Considerable effort has been given to defining and enhancing the roles of Quebec, women, cultural minorities, and natives in national life. Symbols of the efforts include the Official Languages Act (1969), the Royal Commission on Women (1967-70), the multiculturalism policy (1971), the Charter of Rights and Freedoms (1982), and ongoing attempts to revise the Constitution to everyone's satisfaction.

Today, in the midst of much confusion about who we are and what we are becoming, there is much to be gained by looking at what amounts to "the net effects" of our efforts to create a more just society. Young people can help to provide such a view.

OUR INFORMATION BASE

Our method has been to engage in conversations with teenagers through a series of national surveys. In 1984, in an attempt to address the problem of limited information on youth, we carried out what we believe was the first comprehensive national survey of young people in Canada. The results were published in *The Emerging Generation*. The 3600 high school students between the ages of 15 and 19 who participated were in the school system in the 1970s and early 80s. The themes of the just society were in the process of being launched; our 15-year-olds that year were born the year the Official Languages Act was passed.

In 1992, we completed another large-scale survey of youth, involving almost 4000 high school students across the country. These teenagers were born between 1973 and 1977, and began school between 1979 and 1983. (For methodological details, see Appendix.) They are the first "Charter Generation." In addition, they are the first generation to live in the space age, to welcome cable television, to live among computers, to be part of a society with an economy increasingly based on service and information. Their parents are the first generation to have to adjust to the extensive fragmenting of the family, the marginalizing of religious institutions, and the personalizing of morality.

In looking at change, we have done more than compare young people with themselves; we have also compared them with adults. Bibby has been monitoring social trends since the mid-1970s through a unique series of Project Canada national surveys carried out in 1975, 1980, 1985, and 1990, with more than 6000 adults participating. The adult and youth surveys included many similar items, making it possible to explore change between Canadian adults and youth in an unusually large number of areas. We have made some use of a third national youth survey that we completed in 1988 for the Canadian Youth Foundation. Designed somewhat differently from the 1984 and 1992 surveys, this study involved face-to-face interviews with some 2000 15- to 24-year-olds.

We're hearing, then, from about 15,000 Canadians, young and old, from British Columbia to Newfoundland. The unique design, involving longitudinal data and interlocking teen and adult surveys, provides information that is without precedent in Canada.

Together, the surveys provide an invaluable look at the kind of young people we were producing in the early 80s compared with the early 90s. What has become apparent is that significant changes have taken place over the decade. Some will confirm readers' expectations. Some will come as a surprise. Some patterns will be disturbing.

A NOTE ON PREDICTING THE FUTURE

Our claims concerning the strength of our data are not matched by our claims of being social psychics. Precisely because of the speed of time, even the most gifted observers of social life are really looking at the past rather than the present, trying to make sense of what the future has left behind. In reality we are just a few steps ahead of historians and archaeologists.

What makes social forecasting particularly tough is that life tends to defy prediction. History repeats itself — but only in the most general of ways. Unfortunately, even here, such cycles are spotted in retrospect rather than in advance. And so it is that the best futurists and forecasters — from the Alvin Tofflers to the Daniel Bells — are superior to the psychics only because they do a better job of reading present patterns, earning their keep when those patterns stay in place for a few more years. We can identify key developments and players, point to demographics and psychographics, venture a guess or three about what should happen. Occasionally we look like geniuses. Often we look ridiculous.

By carefully identifying short-term trends, however, it's possible to get a reading on where we are going in the immediate future. Most important, an improved understanding of the current flight plan makes it possible to become engaged in the rerouting process, positing alternative possibilities to the directions in which our young people and country seem to be headed.

WHAT WE HOPE TO ACCOMPLISH

There is considerable good news in our findings. Canada's parents, along with our much maligned institutions — including the federal government — have been doing some things very well. We've been making progress. The authors are not among those who think that life would be improved if we could do the impossible and return to the illusory "good old days." At the same time, the findings suggest that some significant problems exist. They call for positive responses.

Accordingly, the first half of the book, written by Bibby, attempts to provide us with a clear reading of what is happening to young people and why.

In the second half of the book, Posterski responds to what is taking place. Building on the survey findings and his extensive experiences with youth and the people involved in their emergence, he discusses with parents, educators, the media, clergy, counsellors, and adults more generally how life might be enhanced for young people, ourselves, and the rest of the country.

As two people who love life and believe it can be a great experience for everyone, we favour working with people to enrich life rather than against people to make it more difficult. We consequently have little interest in merely assailing everybody, including our institutional leaders.

We think it is important to offer sound critiques. But we also believe that critiques should be followed closely by efforts to find ways to move life forward and upward. Such an approach is preferable, we think, to the common alternative of attacking and conquering.

We also believe that the dynamic nature of life is a source of hope. Because the old is constantly being replaced by the new, the present will soon be transformed. Creation is ongoing. For those who make the mistake of trying to cling to what is disappearing or gone, the constancy of change produces no little anxiety. For others, the dynamic nature of life brings with it the possibility of new beginnings, enhancement, growth. Where there's life, there's hope.

We are not only interested in data but also in dreams. Our dream is that an improved understanding of what is, combined with our efforts to respond to what we know, will advance life for all Canadians.

PART I /
NEW DIRECTIONS

S*ignificant changes are taking place in the lives of Canadian young people. In some familiar areas, such as values and religion, the prevalence of familiar patterns can obscure important new departures. In other areas, the new developments are far more obvious.*

- *Chapter one examines some extremely noteworthy yet subtle departures from dominant patterns in five areas of life — relationships, values, marriage, sexuality, and religion.*

- *Five readily observable trends that are having a profound impact on young people are presented in chapter two. These new developments are taking place in the areas of information, problems, choice, justice, and expectations.*

- *Our analysis of the findings has revealed that there are two particularly distinctive departures from the prevalent national patterns. Chapter three examines those variations as they are found among Quebec youth and young women.*

- *Chapter four addresses the question of what it all means, critically assessing what the trends say about Canadian life — what we are doing right and what we are doing wrong.*

Old patterns are changing; new patterns are emerging. Canada will never be quite the same.

1

FIVE OLD PATTERNS
THAT ARE CHANGING

1. RELATIONSHIPS ARE STILL SUPREME —
BUT FOR FEWER PEOPLE

The contest isn't even close. What young people value more than anything else are relationships. They want good interpersonal ties and they want to be loved. As documented by our new survey, some 85 per cent report that friendship is "very important" to them, while 80 per cent place high value on "being loved." One 15-year-old from Calgary sums up the situation succinctly: "I think the greatest value in a teenager's life is friendship." In the words of a Vancouver 18-year-old, "Friends will do anything for one another." A grade-11 student from Niagara Falls comments, "It's important to have people to confide in and lean on. It keeps your sanity."

And where do young people turn for these personal relationships? Some 93 per cent say that their friends are the source of "a great deal" or "quite a bit" of enjoyment. In the words of one Vancouver 18-year-old, "Friends will do anything for one another." About 70 per cent specifically cite a girlfriend or boyfriend. Yet, for many, best friends include members of the opposite sex who are not boyfriends or girlfriends in the romantic sense. One 15-year-old female from the small Ontario town of Listowel explains:

> I have as many boyfriends as I have girlfriends. I have one really good
> friend and he's a guy. A lot of people can't understand how we can be so

open with each other. I guess we are both good listeners, and we care about each other.

The enjoyment derived from relationships with family members falls noticeably behind. Some 67 per cent of young people say they receive a high level of enjoyment from their mothers, while 60 per cent say the same about their fathers. Brothers, sisters, grandparents, and pets — yes, *pets* — are the source of "a great deal" or "quite a bit" of enjoyment for roughly one in two teenagers. A 16-year-old from Montreal, for example, says he receives little or no enjoyment from either his mother or father. He adds, "What I enjoy most is my dogs." An 18-year-old female in the same city is not quite so hard on mom and dad. "When something big goes wrong," she says, "I want to talk to my friends, my dog, and my parents."

Young people want gratifying relationships. They want companionship. They want individuals in their lives who care about what's happening to them. Nothing is rated more highly. But there's an important qualifier.

THE RELATIONSHIP ASTERISK

The numbers who say relationships are supreme are down somewhat from a decade ago. Between 1984 and 1992, the proportion of teens who view friendship as "very important" has dropped from 91 per cent to 84 per cent, while those who place a similar level of importance on being loved has slid from 87 per cent to 80 per cent.

Further, the percentage of young people who indicate they receive high levels of enjoyment from their mother has declined from 78 per cent to 67 per cent over the last decade, with the figure for fathers also slipping — from 71 per cent to 60 per cent.

The drop may appear to be an insignificant blip on the statistical screen. But lest cynics blame the differences on sampling error, we would remind readers that our highly representative samples are unusually large, consisting of over 3500 teenagers each; our margin of error is no more than about two percentage points. It appears something is indeed happening "out there." We think the drop is one of many indicators of an increasing emphasis on the individual over the group in Canadian society.

THE IMPORTANCE OF FRIENDS							
"What I enjoy the most is . . ."		"When something big goes wrong, I want to tell—"			"When something great happens, I want to tell—"		
Friends	26	Friends		61	Friends		47
Sports	19	Family		22	Everyone		35
Sex	7	Mom	10		Family		15
Music	6	Dad	2		Mom	5	
Partying	3	Other fam	10		Dad	1	
Reading	2	God		2	Other fam	9	
Family	1	Teachers/Couns	<1		Others		3
Other	36	Others		15			
TOTALS	100			100			100

In %s

Variations Regionally, Quebec young people are somewhat more likely than other young Canadians to say that they enjoy relationships of all kinds. The differences between males and females in enjoyment of social ties are small, but more females tend to derive enjoyment. There are few differences among racial groups in enjoyment sources, with the exception of dating; perhaps reflecting the opportunity to do so, 60 per cent of teens from visible minorities say they receive a high level of enjoyment from dating, compared to 75 per cent of whites. As one 15-year-old black female from Etobicoke succinctly notes, "I feel left out sometimes."

THE CALLOUSNESS MYTH

Sadly, because some adults do not have particularly good relationships with teens, they help to fuel the widespread stereotype that young people are callous and detached, not willing or even wanting to experience warmth and affection. Many mothers and fathers long for earlier days when their children could be hugged and wanted company and caring. Then, sons and daughters seemed so much more open, expressive, and responsive. Now, according to the stereotype, adolescents just aren't interested. They've changed.

Nothing could be further from the truth. Such propaganda may be a salve for parents who are not connecting well with their teenagers. But it is out of touch with relational reality.

Canada's young people continue to place tremendous value on

good relationships. Ideally, they should be able to experience them with everyone; there are no inherent, built-in limits. In practice, however, most young people find those good ties only with their friends.

Many have additional valued ties with their pets. The relational role animals play should not be overlooked or underestimated. There is a family pet in 50 per cent of Canadian households, with most of these being dogs (28 per cent) and cats (25 per cent), although birds and fish (five per cent each) are also out there in fairly large numbers.[1] Our youth survey shows that in those one in two homes with pets, the percentage of teens who report high levels of enjoyment from them (68 per cent) is actually *higher* than what they report for mothers and fathers or siblings or grandparents.

MIRRORING ADULTS

In valuing relationships so supremely, young people are following in the footsteps of their parents and other adults. The ongoing Project Canada adult surveys — conducted every five years since 1975 — have shown there is nothing Canadians regard as more important than relationships.

The 1990 survey, for example, found that 82 per cent of adults give a "very important" rating to family life, 81 per cent to being loved, and 77 per cent to friendship. Some 80 per cent say they receive high levels of enjoyment from their children, friendships, and marriage. The tendency for moms to outdo dads in the gratification department carries over into adulthood. British Columbia's phone system, for example, expected to handle about 750,000 calls during the course of 1992's Father's Day, about 350,000 fewer than those for Mother's Day. "Traditionally," said a BC Tel rep, "dads receive fewer calls than moms." The same is true for greeting cards. One Vancouver store manager offered this explanation: "Fathers contribute a lot to nurturing kids, but most people are more sentimental about their mom."[2]

By way of comparison, 63 per cent of adults regard a comfortable life as "very important" while 50 per cent give a similar high rating to a rewarding career. Pets, incidentally, receive a high enjoyment rating from 41 per cent of all adults, with the figure jumping to 66 per cent among those who have dogs, cats, and the like.

Few of us are able to experience optimum living for long without having good social ties with family, friends, and colleagues. Psychiatrist William Glasser goes as far as to say that "at all times in our lives we must have at least one person who cares about us and whom we care for ourselves." If we don't, says Glasser, "we will not be able to fulfill our basic needs."[3] Young people are no different from the rest of us.

Worth noting, however, are the signs that there has been some devaluings of social ties, as well as a discernible decrease in enjoyment received from parents. In isolation, the modest changes may seem insignificant. But as we will see, they are consistent with a more general pattern of accelerated individualism in Canadian life.

2. VALUES ARE MUCH THE SAME — EXCEPT INTERPERSONALLY

Every generation worries that the next generation won't turn out as well as the previous one. Listen to this lament: "Children today are tyrants. They contradict their parents, gobble their food, and terrorize their teachers." Sound like a recent observation from someone in your community? For the record, the words were spoken by Socrates, some four centuries B.C.!

Even comparisons with the recent past suggest that adult anxiety levels have not subsided much. A 1965 Gallup poll found that 76 per cent of Canadians believed there should be a curfew in their communities for youths under 16.[4] In late 1990, 68 per cent of Canadian adults complained, "In general, values in Canada have been changing for the worse." Not to be outdone, virtually the same number of teenagers in our 1992 national survey — 67 per cent — agreed with them.

One 16-year-old female from the small community of Papineauville, Quebec, for example, maintains that "the young generation is on its way to rejecting all that our ancestors tried to build." She signed her questionnaire, "A student who is afraid of the future, for her children, and also her grandchildren." Another 16-year-old female, from the Northwest Territories, comments:

I believe that my generation has different values and morals than our parents' generation. My views are different because a lot of traditional values proved to be failures for me.

A 17-year-old male from the B.C. community of Pemberton also expresses concern:

I would just like to say that the teens of today make me sick. They don't care about the future or the present. That attitude has got to change, or Canada is going to go nowhere.

There's no doubt about it: each new generation brings with it anxiety about the future. Fortunately, the anxiety is seldom justified. We have frequently cited the excellent summation of educator Anthony Kerr: "I have a pretty fair idea of history over the past 25 centuries," he says, "and cannot recall a time when the old were fully satisfied with the young." Yet, for all the hand-wringing, notes Kerr, "the world has gone on, apparently getting no worse."[5]

Most of the qualities adults say are important to them are also solidly endorsed by today's young people. The news will undoubtedly come as a relief to many. As with relationships, however, an important footnote is needed: there are signs that some time-honoured interpersonal values are not being endorsed to the extent they were as recently as the early 1980s.

WHAT TEENS WANT

When it comes to what young people want out of life, freedom and friendship rank first and second respectively, cited as "very important" by about 85 per cent of young people. Significantly, the highly related values of being loved and having choices follow closely behind. As noted, there has been a slight decline in the past decade in the proportion of young people who say that they highly value friendship and being loved.

Some 75 per cent of teenagers also place considerable importance on being respected. Central to becoming full-fledged human beings, with the same status as adults, are freedom and respect. Young people, emerging from the domination of parents and teachers, youth leaders and clergy, crave the opportunity to live life increasingly free of the control of adults. They also want to be treated as equals.

On the heels of friendship, freedom, and respect come the material goals of success and a comfortable life — highly valued by around 70-75 per cent of 15- to 19-year-olds. In a society in which living standards are high and affluence widespread, young Canadians want to live well.

From here on, the news is less encouraging and, in places, a bit troubling. The ideal of social compassion gets mixed reviews. On the positive side, six in 10 teenagers say that concern for others is "very important" to them. On the negative side, four in 10 do not. Our country has done a reasonable job of "institutionalizing" caring. It is inappropriate, officially, for individuals, groups, or organizations to be indifferent to people. But it appears the idea has only partly caught on.

Reflecting the reservations many teenagers have about their parents, about six in 10 place a high value on family life. Against the standard of what ideally might be, life at home is often less than highly gratifying for both young people and parents.

A number of other characteristics and areas of life are ranked even lower on the teenage value ladder. About one in two say that being a Canadian is very important to them, slightly below 1984. The figure for teens outside Quebec is about 50 per cent, inside Quebec 30 per cent.

Only about 25 per cent of the nation's young people give a "very important" rating to such values as popularity and recognition. This is not to say teens don't value the acceptance and applause of those they consider significant, that is, acquaintances or peers whose ideas and opinions are important to them. It's just that these "reference

VALUED GOALS OF TEENAGERS AND ADULTS

% Viewing as "Very Important"

	YOUTH		ADULTS	
	1984	1992	1985	1990
Freedom	84	86	89	85
Friendship	91	84	83	77
Being loved	87	80	83	81
Having choices	–	79	–	–
Success in what you do	78	76	66	64
Being respected	–	75	–	
A comfortable life	75	70	66	63
Concern for others	–	62	–	63
Family life	65	60	84	83
Being a Canadian	50	45	68	61
Recognition	42	28	34	29
Cultural-group heritage	–	24	23	24
Being popular	21	22	9	–
Religious-group involvement	–	11	–	20*

*Religious group heritage.

groups" or "reference individuals," to use sociological terms, do not constitute the entire student body. Sometimes it's the case that a small group of close friends are significant. In other instances, it may be a school subculture, these days carrying such names as "jocks," "freaks," "preppies," "skaters," and — in larger cities — "skinheads" and gangs.[6] For some, the reference individuals are not even necessarily their own peers. One articulate 16-year-old male from Brantford, Ontario, expresses this point well:

> *Actually, I don't really care whether I am well-liked or not. I get along, generally, with business people and adults better than with people my own age. But, then again, most people my age are not too bright. And, whether or not people my own age like me, I don't care, since it will be the successful business people who will take an interest in me, and whom I'll have to impress.*

Despite our strong national emphasis on Canadians cultivating their cultural heritages, only 24 per cent of teenagers say that their cultural-group background is "very important" to them. The figure is down about five percentage points from 1984. Among adults, the figure is also 24 per cent.

For many, national background appears to be little more than a part of family history and has not been particularly nurtured. Responses such as "I have no idea," "I don't know," and "a wide variety" were common, along with qualifiers such as "I think." These individuals were among the more than four in 10 teens who offered no specific information on the item. In responding to the question about her cultural-group background, a 16-year-old female from Edmonton expresses things this way:

> *I've asked about it, but my ancestors came to Canada so long ago that my relatives say it doesn't make any difference.*

Then there is the problem of people having complex combinations of national heritages. One wonders, for example, who the much-maligned WASPs in fact really are. By way of illustration:

- A 17-year-old woman from Halifax informs us that her cultural group background is Jewish and English, and she lists her religion as Unitarian.

- A male, also 17, from a small community north of Edmonton, lists his ancestral groups as "Swedish, Italian, North American Indian, French, German."
- A 15-year-old from Fort Frances says her background is "English, Scottish, Irish, and native."
- A 17-year-old from Bedford, Nova Scotia, says her cultural ancestry is Jewish, Dutch, and German; her religion is Baha'i.

There are certainly exceptions. One 15-year-old who lives on an Alberta reserve, tells us that his ancestry is "Indian — we own Canada," and adds that his heritage is "very important" to him. Others with a wide variety of cultural backgrounds indicate they are significant. Still, for about four in five young people, they are not.

Even less important to teens is religious-group involvement, viewed as highly significant by only 10 per cent of the nation's 15- to 19-year-olds. In the words of one 16-year-old male from St. Catharines, Ontario, "I am Catholic, but I don't care much for religion." Another male from Vancouver, also 16, reveals, "I believe in God but don't go to church. I am partly Christian."

It seems that relatively few young people associate religion with "good times."

One 15-year-old female from Verdun, Quebec, describes religious services this way:

> *They are dull. The priests put you to sleep. I like religious services in the United States. There they move and the music is entertaining.*

For some young people from groups where, historically, religion has been important, commitment has waned, but group identification remains significant. Such is the case with a 17-year-old woman from Montreal, who indicates that her heritage is important, but religious involvement is not, and adds, "I am Jewish, but I do not believe in religion."

Variations While there is considerable uniformity in values across regions, the variations that do exist tend to involve Quebec and gender. Quebec youth are less likely than teenagers elsewhere to place high value on the individualistic traits of freedom, success, and a comfortable life, along with being popular and recognition. Young females are considerably more likely than young males to place importance on friendship, being loved, being respected, and concern for others. Differences by race are minor.

An examination of the Project Canada findings for adults as of late 1990 reveals a very similar ranking of values. The major exception is family life; it receives a top ranking for adults, in sharp contrast to its moderate placement by teenagers. Changes from 1985 are modest, being largest for friendship, being a Canadian, and cultural group heritage.

GETTING THERE: VALUED MEANS

In addition to valued ends, we have also probed the importance young people give to the "means" of living out life. Such values point to the interpersonal "norms" that people see as important as they pursue their goals.

There is some evidence that, between the early 1980s and 1990s, a slight shift has been taking place. On the one hand, at the top of the charts, more than seven in 10 teenagers continue to say that cleanliness is "very important" to them. At the bottom, only four in 10 continue to say that they place a high value on imagination and creativity; generosity is similarly valued.

However, long-standing interpersonal values show signs of decreasing endorsement:

- The proportion of teens who indicate that honesty is "very important" to them has dropped from 85 to 70 per cent since 1984.
- The proportion who give a top rating to politeness has fallen from 64 to 53 per cent.
- Forgiveness is now highly valued by 59 per cent — down slightly from a decade ago.
- The percentage of young people who regard working hard as "very important" has plummeted from 69 to 49 per cent.
- Teenagers who place a high value on intelligence has declined from 63 to 56 per cent.

In short, the major goals Canadians seemingly have valued for some time — relationships, freedom, success, comfortable living — continue to be viewed as "very important" by most young people. But many long-revered interpersonal values, including honesty, forgiveness, politeness, and hard work, are showing signs of being applauded by decreasing numbers of teenagers. The concern of an 18-year-old from London, Ontario, may be warranted: "Morality is losing its importance. Our governments need to be giving more attention to morality and values." A 17-year-old from the small community of Walkerton, Ontario, is even more pointed: "I think the world is a selfish and cold-hearted place to be."

Combined with the slight decline in the importance accorded friendship and being loved, such findings suggest that social life — while still very important to most young people — is nonetheless not being valued to the extent it was even in the fairly recent past.

The importance of the individual, as opposed to relationships and the group, has been on the ascent. Some of the changes are not going unnoticed. Regarding hard work, for example, in January 1992, Japanese Prime Minister Kiichi Miyazawa joined his house speaker, Yoshio Sakurauchi, in saying that America is losing its work ethic. He commented that the belief "in producing things and creating value has loosened too much in the past 10 years or so" in the United States.[7] Our survey findings indicate he could have included Canada.

Variations Examinations by region, community size, and race reveal differences involving Quebec and females. Quebec teens are less likely than young people elsewhere to place high value on many of these interpersonal values, including cleanliness, forgiveness, intelligence, and working hard. Young women are more likely than young

---

**VALUED MEANS OF
TEENAGERS AND ADULTS**

% Viewing as "Very Important"

	YOUTH		ADULTS	
	1984	1992	1985	1990
Cleanliness	79	72	75	69
Honesty	85	70	96	89
Humour	–	69	–	–
Forgiveness	66	59	75	55
Intelligence	63	56	61	58
Politeness	64	53	70	62
Working hard	69	49	67	58
Creativity	–	45	–	38
Imagination	42	–	41	41
Generosity	–	40	–	52

men to value cleanliness, along with honesty, forgiveness, politeness, and generosity.

It is not just a coincidence that the importance Canadian *adults* place on many of these same interpersonal traits has also declined since the mid-80s. Fewer men and women across the country are placing a high value on such traits as honesty, cleanliness, politeness, and hard work. Particularly noteworthy is the plunge in the salience assigned to forgiveness — from 75 per cent to 55 per cent in only five years! We believe this is an extremely important finding, and will examine it further in chapter four.

THE ENJOYMENT MYTH

The perception that values have changed would, by itself, provide reason for adults to be anxious about the life-styles of teenagers. But two factors have dramatically heightened that anxiety. The first is the life experiences today's parents had when they themselves were teenagers, primarily in the 1960s and early 70s. Many encountered the sexual revolution and expanding drug culture first-hand. Now they fear their teenagers may be doing some of the things they and/or their friends were doing. The second source of accelerated worry lies in the explosion of technology in recent decades. Revolutionary changes have taken place in sight and sound, global communication and travel. Sex and drugs, plus the visual and audio explosion, plus the freedom provided by travel, add up to high-flying life-styles. Or so it would seem to many a mother and father.

They're wrong. For all the anxiety, the survey findings suggest that the primary sources of enjoyment for most teenagers are pretty much the same as they were in the past. The number-one source of enjoyment is friends, with music a close second.

The importance of relationships is reflected in the enjoyment young people say they receive from boyfriends, girlfriends, and dating. The freedom theme is evident in some seven in 10 teenagers, who report they receive a high level of enjoyment from their own room; it's hard to feel autonomous without one's own space.

We need to point out that humour is highly valued by Canadian teenagers. They enjoy laughing, and are not lost for wit. In the midst of telling us the future looks grim because of environmental and economic problems, one 15-year-old male from Pointe Claire, Quebec, for example, concludes his remarks by saying, "People should practise safe sex, eat more veggies, and listen to lots of Led Zeppelin." A female of the same age from a small Ontario community notes, "I feel that this community is in trouble if it doesn't shape up — economically, lawfully, and environmentally. Other than that, I feel that Canada's full of warm, loving, wary citizens!" A 16-year-old from Halifax tells us, "I get depressed about school, grades, and arguments with my parents — which happen a lot. What I enjoy the most," she adds, "is laughing."

In a middle range of enjoyment is sports, an important source of enjoyment for 80 per cent of young men and 55 per cent of young women. The surveys suggest that close to four in 10 females and just over four in 10 males participate in non-team sports. Team-sport involvement is more popular among males (50 per cent versus 30 per cent). Regional and racial variations are small.

About 60 per cent of male teens and 30 per cent of females say they actively follow sports. The NHL is closely followed by 44 per cent of teenagers, major league baseball by 33 per cent. Reflecting aggressive marketing in recent years, a surprising 28 per cent say they closely follow the National Basketball Association. Among the major pro sports, football comes in fourth, with the National Football League followed by 26 per cent of teens, the CFL by 22 per cent. By the way, when asked in an early 1992 Gallup poll which of the two pro football leagues they prefer, 28 per cent of Canadians said the CFL, 21 per cent the NFL.[8]

The importance of professional sports in the lives of many young people can be seen in this comment from a 16-year-old Winnipeg male, who has nervously watched as the rumours fly that the NHL Jets may be moving and the CFL Blue Bombers might not have a league to play in:

The government needs to put more money into Canadian sporting teams such as the CFL and Canadian hockey teams. If we lose these, we lose a lot of our culture and pride. A successful franchise brings in money to the city, as well as attention from other countries.

In his concluding remarks, a Hawkesbury, Ontario, 15-year-old tells us that "Mulroney should be fired, we need to find a way to eliminate the national debt, and we need to bring back the death penalty." He then abruptly shifts gears as he adds, "The Canucks will win the Stanley Cup, Eric Lindros will never play for Quebec, and the Ottawa Rough Riders will take the Grey Cup." Sports is a significant part of the everyday lives of very large numbers of teenagers.

Television continues to be an important daily activity for most of the nation's young people. More than 80 per cent of 15-year-olds report they watch television at least two hours a day (35 per cent four hours or more). Less than three per cent indicate they rarely or never watch the "tube." Some six in 10 say they receive "a great deal" or "quite a bit" of enjoyment from television — about double the figure for adults. The figure for video viewing is 58 per cent. The apparent disparity between hours watched and enjoyment continues to point to the fact that television is a background activity for many Canadians, young and old. In the words of one 15-year-old from the Northwest Territories, who says she watches only about one hour a day, "I'm too busy to watch TV, but I listen to it when I do homework."

Variations TV and video viewing, and enjoyment tend to be slightly higher in Quebec, as well as among young males and females and members of visible minorities. According to Statistics Canada, these regional and gender patterns are also characteristic of adults. While Canadians watched an average of 23.4 hours of TV a week in 1989 — essentially the same as 10 years earlier, viewing was highest in Quebec at 25.7 hours and lowest in B.C. at 21.6 hours. Probably reflecting employment outside the home, the gender pattern for adults was different from that of teens. Men watched an average of 22.1 hours, women 26.7 hours.[9]

In contrast to television and videos, the number of teenagers who say they enjoy reading stands at only about 40 per cent. Approximately 50 per cent of females and 30 per cent of males claim to be frequent readers.

Enjoyment of cars requires some qualification. Just under 40 per cent of all Canadian teens — 44 per cent of males and 30 per cent of females — say they receive a high level of enjoyment from their various vehicles. But among those who have cars, the enjoyment level is much higher — 77 per cent, with the figures for males and females 80 per cent and 75 per cent respectively. Typical of such males is a 17-year-old Westmount, Quebec, male who comments, "What I enjoy most is cruising in my car."

At the bottom of the joy rankings are activities that tend to be adult-driven — school, jobs, youth groups, and in last place, religious

SOURCE OF ENJOYMENT FOR TEENAGERS AND ADULTS*

% Indicating Receiving *"A Great Deal"* or *"Quite a Bit"* of Enjoyment

	YOUTH		ADULTS
	1984	1992	1990
Friendships	95	93	92
Music	93	89	81
Your stereo	69	73	–
Dating	77	73	–
Your boyfriend or girlfriend	70	69	–
Your own room	–	68	79*
Sports	71	67	45
Television	68	61	53
Your VCR	–	58	–
School	54	43	–
Reading	–	41	–
Your car	36	37	–
Your job	44	33	57
Youth groups	27	28	–
Your religious group	24	15	32

* House or apartment.

groups. They are organized and staffed by adults and, like it or not, exist in large part to serve adult agendas. We will pick up on this pattern in greater detail in chapter four.

WHAT ABOUT DRUGS?

Further to fears, there is no question that drugs are readily available to teenagers. Some 65 per cent of young people say that if they wanted to use drugs, it would not be difficult to obtain them; 10 per cent say it would be difficult, while the remaining one in four don't know — presumably they have little interest in using them. Very significantly, there isn't much difference in accessibility by gender, race, region, or community size. Drugs are available everywhere. As one 17-year-old female from a small southwestern Ontario community put it, "I have been offered every kind of drug and liquor. These things are so easy to get."

But despite the fact that teens can readily obtain drugs, most don't bother. For all the publicity, illicit drug use has, in fact, been *decreasing* in Canada in recent years.

Use of the legal drug nicotine has also been decreasing. Regular cigarette smoking dropped from 30 per cent in 1984 to 26 per cent in 1988, and is currently at 20 per cent; 65 per cent say they don't smoke. A recent Statistics Canada survey of 15- to 19-year-olds — in school or not — has placed the number of smokers at 23 per cent.[10]

Weekly alcohol use, has also dropped slightly in the past decade, from 23 per cent to 18 per cent, with 25 per cent saying they never use alcohol at all. A major study carried out by Statistics Canada in March 1989 found the level of alcohol use among all 15- to 19-year-olds to be virtually identical — at 74 per cent.[11]

Incidentally, among Canadian adults, regular smoking stands at about 33 per cent, down from 47 per cent in 1975 — but still considerably higher than among teenagers. Alcohol is used by about 75 per cent of adults, virtually unchanged from 1975, but up from a 1943 level of 59 per cent.[12]

Just four per cent of 15- to 19-year-olds say they are using marijuana or hashish weekly or more, down slightly from six per cent in 1988 and down significantly from approximately 15 per cent in 1984. Another 14 per cent are occasional users, while some 82 per cent say they never use marijuana. Other illegal drug use remains low, at two per cent.

Detailed drug surveys in Ontario corroborate our national findings. The Addiction Research Foundation found that, in 1989, 14 per cent of 15- to 19-year-old students used cannabis, down from 32 per cent in 1979. The Ontario survey also found that the use of cocaine had dropped from 5.1 per cent in 1979 to 2.7 per cent in 1989. Crack use, probed for the first time in 1987, was around one per cent in both 1987 and 1989.[13]

The observation of a grade-11 student from the northern community of Thompson, Manitoba, seems to be fair:

Adults think there is a major problem with drugs and teens. There usually isn't. I mean, if you go to a party, people are not going to come up to you and force them on you. It is usually only the addicts that the adults notice. I don't do drugs, by the way.

Reflecting their limited use of drugs, few are looking for more liberal drug laws. While one grade-10 student from Vancouver writes that "marijuana should be legalized because it doesn't lead to heavy drug use," his view is not shared by most. Only 27 per cent of teenagers feel that the use of marijuana should be legalized, virtually the same proportion as in 1984 (28 per cent).

We do not mean to downplay the seriousness of drugs when they are abused. Illicit drug use certainly still exists. One 16-year-old woman from rural Manitoba reminds us:

Substance abuse is a huge problem in my high school. I'd say that about 65 per cent of the people in grades 10, 11, and 12 have tried drugs, and about 15 per cent are steady users. There isn't enough for teenagers to do, so most of them do drugs or drink. Many of my friends drink every weekend.

An 18-year-old from Richmond, B.C., comments:

Everyone drinks and many engage in sexual activities. Most teens have tried drugs some time in their lives. I'm starting to see the long-term effects it has had on my life.

A 16-year-old native female from Saskatoon says:

There should be more rehab centres in Canada for kids on drugs or alcohol. I find nowadays that sobriety is really important to teenagers.

Yet the dominant downward pattern of drug use is encouraging, especially when we remember that young people are living in a culture where alcohol use is taken for granted, smoking is common, and the use of prescription drugs is rampant. A Statistics Canada study, for example, found that, in a typical month in 1989, almost one in 10 women between the ages of 55 and 64 outdid men in taking a tranquillizer such as valium.[14] In such a drug-pervasive cultural milieu, any decrease in use is welcomed.

Incidentally, given the ready accessibility of drugs on the one hand and the lack of use on the other, the federal government's approach to dealing with drug abuse is puzzling, to say the least. In 1987, at a time when drug use was declining, the government declared that it was going to get more aggressive in fighting abuse, and pumped about $200-million into a five-year program that included a strong emphasis on border enforcement. In late March 1992, Revenue Minister Otto Jelinek claimed the government has been making substantial progress in its efforts to stop the flow of illegal drugs into Canada, and announced that it was boosting the budget by about 20 per cent to $270-million for the next five years. While approximately two-thirds will be spent on prevention, treatment, rehabilitation, and research, almost one-third is earmarked for border enforcement. "Whether you like the government or not, you must applaud this initiative," Jelinek said.[15]

DRUG ACCESSIBILITY AND USE

In %'s

"If you wanted to use drugs, how difficult would you say it would be for you to obtain them?"

	1988	1992[*]
Extremely difficult	13	5
Fairly difficult	13	5
Not very difficult	38	26
Not difficult at all	36	64

[*]"Don't knows" eliminated to permit comparisons with 1988.

% Indicating "Weekly or More"

	1984	1988	1992
Some marijuana or hashish	12	5	4
Other illegal drugs	5	2	2
Smoke cigarettes	30	26	20
Drink beer, wine or other alcohol	23	21	18

Our findings on high accessibility and low use suggest that the applause should be less than the government expects. A policy that seems to hold more promise is one that attempts to control the importation of drugs, yet recognizes they will always be available and instead places its major attention on dealing with the societal ills that make drug abuse attractive, along with treatment in those cases where drugs are abused.

Variations Differences between marijuana use and other illegal drug use are minor by region and race, but drug use is marginally higher among males than females. Cigarette smoking varies little by region, although the number of young people smoking weekly or more is slightly higher in the Atlantic region (28 per cent) than elsewhere (about 20 per cent). Smoking is somewhat more characteristic of females (22 per cent) than males (19 per cent). The aforementioned Statistics Canada survey of all 15- to 19-year-olds places the number of female smokers at 24 per cent, male 22 per cent.[16] Alcohol use is also more common among males (22 per cent) than females (15 per cent), and in Quebec (23 per cent) than in other regions (17 per cent). Differences in smoking and alcohol use by community size and race tend to be small.

WHAT ABOUT SEX?

Yes, the anxiety is warranted. Sex has become fairly commonplace among Canadian young people, something taken pretty much for granted as an enjoyable part of life. As one 18-year-old woman from Richmond, B.C., calmly puts it, "What I enjoy most are skiing and sex." A 15-year-old from the Quebec City suburb of Ste-Foy adds, "What I enjoy most is making love and playing hockey."

There are some significant things happening in the sexual realm that we will turn to later. For now, let's be frank about what teenagers are doing on dates.

Since the early 80s, we have been asking young people what they regard as appropriate physical behaviour when people on a date "like each other." There has been little change over the past decade. Kissing on the first date is approved of by 82 per cent, necking by 52 per cent, petting by 33 per cent, and sexual intercourse by 12 per cent. Within "a few dates," the approval levels go up to 99 per cent for kissing, 96 per cent for necking, 86 per cent for petting, and 56 per cent for intercourse.

Such views, combined with the threat of AIDS and the ongoing tendency of moms and dads to be reluctant "to let go of their children," do not make for easy feelings among parents. A December 1991 Gallup poll found that about five in 10 adults think that today's young people should have less sexual freedom than they themselves had. About four in 10 maintain that they should have the same amount of freedom, while just one in 10 feel they should have more.[17]

Variations There is little difference by region in the kissing and necking instances. However, Quebec young people are far more likely than their counterparts elsewhere to approve of both petting (95 per cent) and sexual intercourse (70 per cent) after a few dates.

Differences between young men and women are very pronounced. Although males and females are almost equally likely to approve of kissing on a first date, gender differences increase with the level of physical intimacy. In the case of necking, and certainly petting, young females are more inclined than males to say such behaviour is appropriate only after a few dates; about 20 per cent of females do not approve of petting at all. As for sexual intercourse, the gap widens. While about 75 per cent of males approve of sex within a few dates, only 40 per cent of females hold such a view.

In comparing teenagers in 1984 and 1992, what is particularly striking is that there had been virtually no change in attitudes over the past decade *for either males or females.* One might go as far to say that the sexual revolution has had a powerful impact on the premarital attitudes and behaviour of young men. But a majority of young females continue to disapprove of premarital sex, unless there is a strong relational bond. We will return to this issue shortly.

IN OUR IMAGE

Canadian young people are largely mirroring Canadian adults in placing supreme value on friendships, enjoying music, saying "no" to illicit drugs, and, especially in the case of females, tying sex to significant relationships.

Ask adults who lived out their teenage years in the 50s, 60s, or 70s what they enjoyed most in their teens, and the answer is uniform: friends and music. In fact, even today, adults cite music as their second major source of enjoyment — following relationships with children, spouse, and friends. Young people in the 1990s follow the same pattern. Technology has altered the environments and improved the sound. But the two big sources of enjoyment are still the same.

The national adult surveys have also found that most Canadians are opposed to the use of illegal drugs and think that sex should be associated with meaningful ties. For the most part, teenagers agree.

In many ways, by adult standards, the value picture for Canadian young people looks pretty good. A female grade-10 student from Calgary sums up the situation accurately — and graphically:

> *I think teenagers deserve more credit! My dad thinks all teenagers are bad asses — you know, into drugs, sex, and crime. We're not all like that. I mean, sure there are a lot of bad teenagers out there, but there are also "a lot" of bad adults out there.*

An Etobicoke 16-year-old seems equally on target:

I feel that teenagers have a good idea of what and who they are. Sure they are a little crazy and want to have fun. But this is the best time for it, because pretty soon we'll be planning careers, family, etc. All teenagers are a little rebellious, but it is just a part of growing up, and learning about responsibility.

However, the auto manufacturer's well-known slogan, proclaiming, "Times change — values don't," is only half-correct. The same "good picture" conclusion concerning valued goals does not apply to valued means. Interpersonal values appear to be changing. Yet, here again, the data on changing adult values in the interpersonal area indicate that young people are only reflecting the dominant emphases on individualism found in the adult world.

In the past year or so, Canadian journalists have followed their American counterparts in arguing that so-called "baby boomers" — those born in the two decades after the Second World War — have abandoned the "me" emphasis of the 1980s and are now less materialistic, spend more time with their families, and have become more generous.

The Wall Street Journal ran such a story on Americans in June 1991. One Canadian reprint of the article carried the headline, "Lower Boom on Expectations," with the subhead, "The recession has again taught Americans that small can be beautiful. But while belt-tightening is in, so is volunteerism and helping the poor."[18] In keeping with the common practice, however disturbing, of ignoring cultural differences between our two countries, the media on this side of the border pounced on the idea and applied it, warranted or not, to Canada. Just over a year later, in April 1992, Canadian Press dispatched a story across the country that informed people from Newfoundland to British Columbia that the "Me Generation" was changing its focus. Canadians, we were told, were altering their approach to life. Just by coincidence, the writer used as evidence belt-tightening, volunteerism, and donations to charities.[19]

The problem with both stories is that neither offered hard data. Instead, they were built on unsubstantiated rhetoric, a handful of illustrations that supported the thesis, and the usual selectively edited quotes from "experts."

We suspect that such talk about the abandonment of self and the renewed concern for others tells us more about the life-stages of writers and editors than it does about our culture as a whole. *Our data support no such acceleration of interpersonal values. We find, in fact, just the opposite.* As trend analyst Faith Popcorn has summed up so well, "Me-ness" is still in. "But it's a *nicer* narcissism now."[20]

Before we all join journalists in declaring that even Socrates was not always right, we might be wise to let his words regarding the contradicting of parents, the gobbling of food, and the tyrannizing of teachers ring down from yesteryear. Socrates' concern with interpersonal relations, including manners, may well have renewed significance for Canadians in the 90s.

3. MARRIAGE AND PARENTHOOD ARE STILL IMPORTANT — BUT OPTIONS SEEM ENDLESS

The reality of divorce has understandably led some observers to conclude that disenchantment with marriage is on the rise. About 14 per cent of Canadian adults indicate they've been divorced. However, the divorce rate has increased significantly in recent decades. Whereas just over 10,000 Canadian marriages ended in divorce in 1968, by 1990 the figure was almost 10 times higher, at close to 100,000. Almost a quarter of the marriages that took place in the 1960s ended before their twentieth anniversaries.[21]

More young people than ever before are consequently experiencing the reality of divorce first-hand. Approximately one in four teenagers say their natural parents are either divorced or separated. Indicative of the pervasiveness of this phenomenon is the finding that the proportion of teens from Roman Catholic homes where divorce or separation has occurred (18 per cent) is now about the same as that of Protestants (19 per cent) and people of other faiths (19 per cent); the level for teens from homes where a parent claims no religious affiliation is higher (34 per cent).

The latest survey has found that Canadian youth nonetheless are anything but disillusioned with marriage. Some 85 per cent say they expect to get married. And that's just a minimum figure. Obviously, many of the remaining 15 per cent will change their minds, probably pushing the figure to more than 90 per cent. The proportion who plan to marry is essentially unchanged from 1984.

Reflecting traditional patterns, almost nine in 10 of the marriage-bound plan to have "a church wedding." In view of the fact that only two in 10 of teenagers currently are weekly service attenders, such a finding may come as something of a shock to more than a few religious leaders. As a 17-year-old from Lac La Biche, Alberta, put it when asked to describe the nature of his religion, "I'm leaving myself open so that when it comes to marriage, I'll take on that religion."

There's no doubt the dramatic increase in divorce has meant more teens than ever before are finding themselves having to adjust to changes in family life.

Comments such as the following illustrate some of their experiences:

- My parents are married but they live separately. I live with my mother.
- My father is remarried; my mother remarried but is now divorced.
- Mom never married my real father; she is now in her second marriage, though.
- They just never got married. It is like they are married.
- He's not my natural father, but he's the only dad I know.
- My natural mother and father never married. I live with my mother and stepfather.
- I live with my mother, but I don't know my natural father.
- I live with my parents and they live together. But they're actually separated, and each has a partner.
- I live on student welfare. My parents are divorced and are both alcoholics. The police thought it would be best for me to live alone.

One 15-year-old female from Alberta states candidly:

I think that Canada's families are falling apart. When I think of my friends (over 20 of them), none of them have a happy home life. There is always a big problem — not much love from either of their parents.

However, such disillusionment with marriage itself is not widespread among young people. Some 86 per cent of those who plan to marry say they expect to stay with the same person for life. This figure includes 89 per cent of the teens who come from homes where their natural parents are still married to each other, and 78 per cent of those are young people whose parents have not stayed together. A 15-year-old from a small community near Grande Prairie, Alberta, maintains that "people should stay married." His admonition is the hope of many teens.

They also feel strongly about marital fidelity. Their openness to premarital sex is matched by their opposition to extramarital sex. Only 10 per cent approve of such relations, representing no increase from 1984.

Teens who have experienced happy homes are inclined to want to have the same experience for themselves in adult life. Those whose home lives have not been as positive seem determined to have better home lives.

WHO TEENS CURRENTLY ARE LIVING WITH

In %'s

	Mother and Father	Mother Only	Mother and Stepf	Mother and Mpart	Father and Stepm	Father and Fpart	Father Only	Other	Totals
NATIONAL	71	10	5	2	2	1	3	6	100
Roman Catholic	77	9	4	2	1	1	2	4	100
Protestant	74	8	6	2	1	1	2	6	100
Other	68	15	3	1	3	1	2	7	100
None	60	14	9	3	3	1	5	5	100

*Stepf=stepfather; Stepm=stepmother; Mpart=male partner;
Fpart=female partner.

PENDING PARENTHOOD

In addition to marriage plans, 84 per cent of the country's teenagers anticipate having children. This figure represents a slight decline, from 92 per cent in 1984 to 87 per cent in 1988. The drop is not the result, as some might suspect, of more young women aspiring to careers and therefore not wanting to have children. The drop has been similar for males, as well. The trend seems to be consistent with a tendency toward greater individualism, including more personal freedom — a cultural theme we have already seen reflected in both the devaluing of relationships and the decreasing endorsement of a number of interpersonal characteristics.

There is little reason to believe that the desire to have children will continue to decrease significantly, especially given recent renewed cultural reinforcement for being a parent. Summing up 1991 "fads, fashions, and fetishes," a colourful unnamed Canadian Press writer offered these thoughts:

Suddenly it was chic to be great with child. High-profile pregnant women were popping up all over the place . . . Demi Moore was near birth and baring . . . Deborah Norville of NBC's Today Show, *Mary Hart of* Entertainment Tonight *and actress Ann Jillian publicly paraded their pregnancies, while newscaster Connie Chung repeatedly reported her unsuccessful attempts at motherhood. Two high-profile TV characters dealt with on-screen pregnancy — Murphy Brown . . . and* Married with Children's *Peg Bundy.*[22]

With 1992 have come the proud announcements of the likes of Jack Nicholson, Rod Stewart, Burt Reynolds, and Warren Beatty that they are fathers. In Nicholson's words, "Us guys can still roll, can't we?"[23] Parenthood is in.

Following the completion of their education, about 95 per cent of both males and females say they intend to pursue careers. A finding that has considerable significance for future employers is that, eventually, some 35 per cent of Canadian young women plan to stay home and raise their children for at least a few years. Perhaps surprisingly, 30 per cent of young males say they have the same hope. Presumably, the two sets of aspirants will not be married to each other!

CHILDREN WITHOUT MARRIAGE

While one 16-year-old from Willowdale, Ontario, sums up the thoughts of many when she says, "I would like to get married and raise a family," there are large numbers of Canadian teens who think somewhat differently. They are found in the largest numbers in Quebec. In that province, a slightly lower proportion of teenagers (79 per cent) plan to marry, and a slightly higher proportion (87 per cent) plan to have children. The resolution of this apparent contradiction lies in a further important finding: Quebec teenagers — at 82 per cent — lead the nation in saying they approve of people having children without being married. Significantly, however, 64 per cent of young people in the rest of Canada also agree with that assertion, making for a national average of 70 per cent.

We must emphasize that agreeing it's all right for people to have children without being married may say more about tolerance of diversity than it does about personal preference. One 15-year-old male from Victoria, after condoning the idea, is quick to add, "But *I* wouldn't do it!" A 17-year-old from Halifax also strongly agrees with the concept of people having children without being married, but she says by way of postscript, "I hope women having kids can support them." Another female of the same age who lives in a small Manitoba community is in agreement with the idea of having children without being married. She, too, tacks on a qualification: "I wouldn't plan it that way. I think there should be a future of possible marriage."

Still, there is little question that such sentiment about children outside marriage represents a significant departure from the prevalent view of marriage and children that characterized Canadians, young and old, in the past. The change, by the way, is not being resisted by females: 73 per cent approve of unmarried people having children, compared to 67 per cent of males. It also is not the result of different attitudes being held by newcomers: only 58 per cent of teens who were born elsewhere approve of the unmarried bringing children into the world, compared to 71 per cent who were born in Canada.

The role of the media in legitimizing such a range of marriage and parenthood possibilities should not be underestimated. If any number of marriage and parenthood possibilities are good for the stars of television, the rock stage, the playing field, and the screen, why shouldn't they also be good for the fans?

MARRIAGE AND PARENTAL PLANS OF TEENAGERS			
% Indicating "Yes"		1984	1992
EXPECT TO:			
Get married	NATIONALLY	85	85
	Males	84	84
	Females	86	86
Have children	NATIONALLY	92	84
	Males	91	83
	Females	93	84
APPROVE OF:			
An unmarried couple living together	NATIONALLY	–	88
	Males	–	89
	Females	–	87
Having children without being married	NATIONALLY	–	70
	Males	–	67
	Females	–	73

WHAT ABOUT COHABITATION?

Part of the public's confusion about the popularity of marriage seemingly has been due to a misreading of the meaning of the increasing tendency of young Canadians — and older Canadians — to live together. Cohabitation has been interpreted by many as representing an alternative to marriage. In reality, cohabitation sometimes *precedes* marriage, sometimes takes place *between* marriages, and sometimes *follows* marriage. But it seldom is a substitute for people *ever* marrying.

There's little doubt that living together has been on the rise. Statistics Canada reports that, as of 1981, only 350,000 Canadian couples were living common-law. By 1991, the figure had soared to about one million.[24] In percentages, that's 12 per cent of all couples living common-law in 1990, double the six per cent figure for 1981.

Among 15- to 19-year-olds who were living as couples in 1990, 82 per cent were not married, up markedly from 50 per cent in 1980.[25] Moreover, acceptance of cohabitation is common among teens. The 1992 survey reveals that 88 per cent of the nation's youth believe, "It is all right for a couple who are not married to live together." There is little variation by region, gender, or race.

Additional Statistics Canada data make it clear that, for most Canadians, cohabitation is not replacing marriage. Rather, it tends to take three forms:

Premarital cohabitation As of 1990, 63 per cent of all Canadians living together had never been legally married. Some 35 per cent were divorced or separated, and the remaining two per cent were widowed. Obviously marriage is still a strong possibility for many of the single 63 per cent.

Between 1984 and 1990, the percentage of adults who had married at some point in their lives decreased from about 74 per cent to 71 per cent. But the drop, acknowledges Statistics Canada, occurred almost exclusively among people younger than 40. All this may mean is that young people are postponing marriage, rather than rejecting it.

Supportive of such an assertion is the Statistics Canada finding that, in 1990, despite the fact that almost 30 per cent of adults said they had lived in at least one common-law relationship during their lives (almost 10 per cent had lived in two or more), only eight per cent currently were. The drop from 30 per cent to eight per cent indicates that most move on to marriage, to the person they lived with or someone else.

Postmarital cohabitation   For people involved in the remaining 37 per cent of common-law relationships, living together is a postmarital experience. Interestingly, between 1984 and 1990, the age category where the greatest proportional increase in common-law ties took place was the 40-49 cohort. While living with someone, many will stay "single" indefinitely.

Intermarital cohabitation   However, obviously many divorced men and women will remarry. It's important to note that cohabitation is highest for divorced men and women younger than 35 and decreases steadily thereafter, suggesting that cohabitation frequently is a temporary situation. A single snapshot at one point in time, especially if that point is early in people's lives, fails to tell the entire cohabitation-marriage story.

For many in this category, there is no great sense of urgency to get married. They've been through it before and need to have a good reason to go through the "legal work" to get into something they went through a lot of "legal work" to get out of. When asked about the possibility of getting married, a common response is, "Why bother?"

Clearly some will remarry, occasionally with fanfare, more often unobtrusively. Jay Leno, in describing his feelings about taking over from Johnny Carson in May 1992 after being a guest host for five years, used an analogy that sums up how many appear to feel about marriage after cohabitation:

> *It's like living with a girl for four or five years and deciding to get married. It's no big deal to you, but your relatives slap their foreheads and say, "Thank God, it's legitimate."* [26]

In the case of the majority of teenagers, cohabitation certainly is acceptable. Yet, it is not a substitute for marriage. The survey findings leave little doubt that most both *plan to eventually marry, and plan to stay married.*

A REFLECTION OF HOPE — AND INDIVIDUALISM

For all their marital problems, Canadian adults have continued to marry and remarry, believing that optimum relationships are possible. And although they often encounter difficulties with their children, they nonetheless have continued to have them, if in smaller numbers. Cohabitation is increasingly common among adults, but for most is a premarital or postmarital experience.

Most teenagers are not abandoning the hope of a happy marital relationship, complete with children and fidelity. Their marriage-and-family dreams appear largely to reflect the dreams — if not the actual experiences — of their mothers and fathers. Clearly, many are wanting fairly traditional family life experiences as they look to the future.

But large numbers are feeling pretty flexible about marriage and children — open to an increasing range of possibilities that our society has deemed legitimate. Everyone is increasingly free to marry, cohabit, or not marry; continue a marriage or terminate it; have children in marriage, outside marriage, or not have them at all; engage in marital sex, nonmarital sex, or be celibate; be heterosexual, homosexual, or both.[27]

Illustrative of "the new possibilities" is the experience of a 16-year-old from a small Ontario community. Her natural parents are together, but she has chosen to live with her boyfriend. She views herself as a committed Christian, and attends services about once a month. She informs us, "I am expecting within the next three months." But her pregnancy has not altered her plans. She expects to marry and to pursue a career. While finances are a concern, she tells us, "I'm hoping that when I marry the baby's father, we will have a better chance at handling the costs" and that life in general "will be better by the time my child is my age." Her relationship with her parents is strained.

Teenage pregnancy is not the choice of large numbers. It is, however, indicative of ever-increasing life-style choices — some of which are greying the hair of adults.

The findings show that today's young people greatly value the idea of enduring relationships and, in most instances, the idea of having children. But they also feel they have almost an unlimited number of choices as they go about the business of putting the family package together.

4. SEXUALITY HAS BEEN TRANSFORMED — BUT THE REVOLUTION IS OVER

Teenagers might be expecting to postpone marriage. But the vast majority are not expecting to postpone sex. Currently, approximately

55 per cent of 15- to 19-year-olds are sexually active. Regional variations are minor, with activity slightly greater in the Atlantic provinces (62 per cent), followed by Quebec and Ontario (57 per cent), and the West (about 50 per cent).

However, the surveys do not show that sexual involvement has become separated from relationships for large numbers of young women and many young men. Some 87 per cent of teenagers say they approve of sex before marriage when people *love* each other — slightly above the level of adults (80 per cent). But that teen figure drops to 64 per cent for premarital sex when people *like* each other — 77 per cent in the case of males, 51 per cent for females.

The findings should also serve as a reminder to adults that about two in 10 teenagers still disapprove of sex before marriage. One outspoken 15-year-old from Saskatoon states: "I'm proud to say I have never been sexually involved, and I try to influence my friends in the same way." A grade-10 student from Vernon, B.C., says that "abstinence is the only way" and complains that "family-life education only excites young people too early."

Still, like teenagers in the 80s, young people of today give every indication of engaging in sex on a level probably never before matched in Canadian history. Today's teens, however, appear to be better informed than any of their predecessors. Approximately 85 per cent of 15- to 19-year-olds have taken sex-education courses, compared to only 40 per cent of adults. Further, about nine in 10 maintain that they are fairly knowledgeable about birth control.

Reflecting both information and fairly extensive sexuality programs, three-quarters of those who are sexually involved claim to be using available devices. While often chastised for not using birth control, teenagers do express some complaints of their own. For example, one 17-year-old male from Nova Scotia — where the availability of birth-control devices in public places has been hotly debated — comments that "condoms should be made more available to young people." He points out that an old scenario familiar to many is still taking place: "It's embarrassing to go up to the cashier with three people behind you."

The results of improved information and increased use of birth-control methods is showing. Statistics Canada data for the period 1975 to 1989 indicate that teenage pregnancies declined during those years from 53.4 per 1000 teenage girls to 44.1.[28]

That is hardly to say that naivety is a thing of the past. One 17-year-old from a small Ontario town tells us:

Everything revolves around my boyfriend. He's the most important thing in my life and I love him. And, yes, I have made love to him. He doesn't use condoms because we make love — we don't just have sex.

Variations Although they do not lead the country in premarital sexual behaviour, Quebec teens are far more likely than those elsewhere to approve of premarital sex, regardless of whether "love" (93 per cent) or "like" (86 per cent) is involved. As for racial groups, east Indian and Pakistani teenagers, followed by Orientals, are less inclined than others to approve of premarital sex. Orientals are considerably less likely than other groups to be sexually *active*, while east Indian and Pakistani youth are also somewhat less active.

Gender differences are pronounced, particularly in attitudes toward premarital sex when love is involved. The sexual revolution of the 60s has not severed sex from valued relationships for at least one in two young women and one in four young men. That is not to say that female teens do not enter into such relationships and proceed to sexually indulge. Close to 50 per cent of females acknowledge they

PREMARITAL SEXUAL ATTITUDES AND BEHAVIOUR BY REGION, GENDER, AND RACE:		
In %'s		
	APPROVE IF LOVE	APPROVE IF LIKE	SEXUALLY ACTIVE
---	---	---	---
NATIONALLY	87	64	55
British Columbia	85	58	51
Prairies		80	53
Ontario	87	57	56
Quebec	93	86	58
Atlantic	86	57	62
Males	88	77	62
Females	86	51	49
Whites	88	64	57
Blacks	86	59	57
Natives	85	63	63
Orientals	80	57	26
E. Indian-Pakistani	72	51	42

are currently sexually active, only slightly below the 60 per cent figure for young males.

THE AFTER-EFFECTS OF THE REVOLUTION

Let no one be mistaken: there was a genuine revolution in sexual thinking and behaviour in the 1960s. By 1975, 90 per cent of Canadians between the ages of 18 and 34 said they approved of premarital sex, in sharp contrast to only 65 per cent of people 35 to 54 and just 43 per cent of those 55 and older.

However, once in place, the 90 per cent figure for 18- to 34-year-olds has not really increased. Today it remains essentially the same, at 92 per cent. But with the aging of the population, what was 65 per cent among 35- to 54-year-olds in 1975 is now 82 per cent; and among those 55 and older, the 43 per cent figure of 1975 now stands at 59 per cent. As the population further ages, it is conceivable that, by the year 2000, close to 90 per cent of Canadians will approve of premarital sex, while a durable core of some 10 per cent will continue to be opposed to such behaviour.

The sexual revolution changed the way Canadians viewed sex outside marriage. But, having succeeded in transforming attitudes and behaviour about sex, the revolution has long been over. What we have witnessed in the past decade or so is the transmission of the new sexual values from first-generation revolutionists to their offspring. The reason the national figures of acceptance have risen over the past twenty years is not because young people are becoming more permissive than their parents. Rather, the protests of grandparents troubled by the changes have — with their passing — been relegated to history.

WHAT ABOUT HOMOSEXUALITY?

In response to the increasing cultural legitimizing of homosexuality, the proportion of young people who approve of homosexual relations has increased since the early 80s from 26 per cent to 38 per cent. The comparable figure for adults is 34 per cent. Approval of homosexuality is highest among teens from Quebec (54 per cent) and B.C. (42 per cent), and among young women (47 per cent versus 28 for males). There are no differences by race.

Many teens exhibit hostility, disgust, and fear when responding to items about homosexuality. One 17-year-old male from a small town in northern Saskatchewan who disapproves of homosexuality comments, "That is where diseases come in. It would be different if they had their own island."

Even young people who approve of homosexual relations show signs of frequently only tolerating such an orientation, rather than regarding it as a viable alternative to heterosexuality. As one 15-year-old Toronto female puts it, homosexuality is all right "if that is what they believe. If two people of the same sex really love each other, they are entitled to the same respect that heterosexual couples receive."

The belief in the normalcy of heterosexuality remains widespread among young people. The observation is not based only on our present findings. In reviewing the results of their 1990 national survey of students in grades eight to 10, researchers Janelle Holmes and Eliane Silverman wrote, "So pervasive is heterosexism that very few young women [or men], even in the anonymity of the questionnaire, raised the subject of homosexuality and gay relationships."[29]

Here, as with sex outside marriage, the revolution in attitudes has been showing signs of levelling off. Between 1975 and 1990, there was a modest increase in the proportion of adults who say they approve of homosexuality — from 28 per cent to 34 per cent. In the adult instance, the mild increase appears to reflect a liberalization of attitudes that followed on the heels of the 60s' sexual revolution. By 1975, some 42 per cent of 18- to 34-year-old Canadians approved of homosexuality, compared to only about 25 per cent of 35- to 54-year-olds and just 16 per cent of people 55 and older.

But the acceptance of homosexuality has plateaued. The endorsement level of today's under-35 group stands at 43 per cent, the same as in 1975. The young adults of 1975 have now graduated into the 35-54-year-old cohort, and at 40 per cent continue to stand in sharp contrast to Canadians 55 and older, who endorse homosexuality to the tune of only 16 per cent.

With the aging of the population, it is conceivable that, shortly after the turn of the century, the national approval figure for homosexual relations in Canada will increase to around 40 per cent. It is not at all clear, however, that the approving proportion will climb much higher than that in the predictable future.

Although teenagers do not tend to approve of homosexuality, they mirror adults in the belief that homosexuals should not be denied civil and social rights. Currently, 72 per cent of young people maintain that "homosexuals are entitled to the same rights as other Canadians," up from 67 per cent in 1984. The figure for adults is somewhat higher at 81 per cent, compared to 70 per cent in 1980. One 15-year-old female from a small B.C. community who strongly disapproves of homosexual relations expresses her view this way: "A person's sexual preference has nothing to do with whether or not they are treated as humans." A male of the same age from Calgary has a similar outlook. He strongly disagrees with homosexuality, but maintains homosexuals are entitled to the same rights as others, adding, "They should not be judged by their sexual behaviour."

In March 1992, dozens of demonstrators showed up outside the pavilion where the Academy Awards ceremony was taking place to protest against what they considered negative gay stereotyping by Hollywood in the soon-to-be-released *Basic Instinct*, and in three Oscar-nominated films: *The Silence of the Lambs, JFK*, and *Fried Green Tomatoes*. A spokeswoman for the activist group Queer Nation declared:

> *We see ourselves [in movies] as freaks, killers, psychopaths, and perverts. We see ourselves as lonely victims. We see ourselves made to reflect straight anxieties about sexuality and gender.*[30]

There is good reason to believe that Canadians generally, whether young and old, do not support negative stereotyping of homosexuals any more than they support the negative stereotyping of other social groupings. However, our survey findings suggest that the numerical

SEXUAL ATTITUDES				
% Agreeing	YOUTH		ADULTS	
	1984	1992	1985	1990
Sex before marriage is alright when people LOVE each other	80	87	77	80
Sexual relations between two people of the same sex is sometimes alright	26	38	29	34
Homosexuals are entitled to the same rights as other Canadians	67	72	76	81

majority's acceptance of homosexuals is a long way from being matched by their acceptance of *overt* homosexuality. One 16-year-old from the Northwest Territories seems to sum up the feelings of perhaps the majority: homosexuality is all right "if they keep it to themselves."

WHAT ABOUT ABORTION?

In the midst of great controversy, the number of legal abortions that have been carried out in Canada has risen from 11,000 in 1970 to 66,000 in 1980 and to 94,000 in 1990. As of 1990, for every 100 births, 23 abortions were performed in Canada and 40 in the U.S. Among teenagers around the same time, 36 in 100 pregnancies ended in abortions.[31]

Almost 90 per cent of teenagers take the position that it should be possible for a woman to obtain a legal abortion when rape is involved — virtually the same proportion as adults. One Regina 17-year-old offers this personal note:

> I believe abortions should be legal because I got pregnant from rape. I've lived through the pain of being a pregnant teen, and it's hard to handle.

A 16-year-old from a conservative northern Alberta community tells us, "I used to be pro-life. But this summer my friend got pregnant and I think her decision to have an abortion was the right one."

Teenagers also appear to be open to legal abortion in situations where a mother's health is seriously endangered or there is a possibility of a serious defect in the foetus.

However, young people do not tend to favour what amounts to "abortion on demand." Only 41 per cent agree that a woman should be able to obtain a legal abortion "for any reason" — a figure almost identical to that of adults. Among them is a 15-year-old male from Duncan, B.C.:

> I think abortion should be allowed to a point, like if a woman has been raped. But if it's just some woman out having fun, then, no!

A 15-year-old female from rural Ontario offers qualified approval: "I feel abortion should be legalized. Everyone makes mistakes."

Among the 10 per cent who do not approve of abortion under any circumstances is this 15-year-old female from Pembroke, Ontario:

I am pro-life, and believe a child should never ever be aborted. If my mother had had an abortion, I would not be here today.

Differences in attitudes toward abortion are minor by gender, race, and region, except for a slightly higher level of opposition in the Atlantic provinces.

Contrary to popular perception, teenagers clearly mirror adults when it comes to abortion attitudes. Teenage females are frequently also misrepresented when it comes to actual behaviour. In 1990, 20 per cent of the women who had hospital abortions were younger than 20. But 54 per cent were in their 20s and 24 per cent were in their 30s; two per cent were older.[32] Looked at another way, approximately one in five of the women who had abortions were teenagers. Yet only about two in 100 teenage women had abortions.[33]

These overall survey findings on the attitudes toward abortion of both teenagers and adults defy the prevalent perception that Canadians are split almost evenly into pro-life and pro-choice camps. Younger and older Canadians who take a pro-life position to the point of being opposed to abortion of any kind make up approximately a five to 10 per cent minority in Canada — roughly the same proportion, incidentally, as in the mid-1970s.

But this is hardly to say that the remaining 90 per cent of Canadians are pro-choice. When rape or the health of the mother or unborn child is *not* involved, the populace has significant reservations. For example, the adult surveys have found that if an abortion is sought because of inadequate income, being single, or simply not wanting to have a child, support for the availability of a legal abortion drops to about 50 per cent. As noted, abortion "for any reason" has the support of only 40 per cent of Canadians, old or young.

If pure pro-lifers — who are opposed to abortion under any circumstances — make up 10 per cent of the population, pure pro-choicers — who favour abortion for any reason — constitute a 40 per cent minority. Most Canadians, some 50 per cent, do not take a black or white stance. Their positions are highly situational.

For all the controversy and publicity that has surrounded the abortion issue, the youth and adult surveys show that attitudes have remained virtually unchanged over the past two decades. Moreover, there are virtually no differences in abortion views by age. And while differences do exist by education and religious involvement, it is important to keep in mind that these are relative differences within the two categories. Neither a majority of Canadians with university degrees, nor a majority of Canadians who are not involved in religious groups, hold the pro-choice position. Conversely, pro-life advocates do not include a majority of weekly church attenders or a majority of people who have not graduated from university.

These findings suggest that aging, education, and secularization will not significantly alter the proportional sizes of the pro-life, pro-choice, and situational camps in at least the immediate future.

ABORTION ATTITUDES				
% Agreeing				
	YOUTH		ADULTS	
	1984	1992	1985	1990
It should be possible for a woman to obtain a legal abortion when a female has been raped	86	88	86	90
It should be possible for a married woman to obtain a legal abortion when she does not want to have any more children	39	–	46	48
It should be possible for a woman to obtain a legal abortion for any reason	–	41	37	38

A NOTE ON EXTRAMARITAL SEX

The 1960s' emphasis on sexual liberation included a movement to free up marriage, enabling married partners to engage in sex with other people. Terms like "swinging," "open marriage," and "group marriage" were tossed freely about, and more than a few observers were seeing monogamy as a thing of the past.

In 1975, 21 per cent of Canadians said that extramarital sex either was "not wrong at all" or only "sometimes wrong." There was reason to believe that a radical change might be taking place.

It didn't happen. The percentage of Canadians now maintaining that extramarital sex is "not wrong" and only "sometimes wrong" has dropped slightly to 17 per cent. Significantly, only 18 per cent of current 18- to 34-year-olds hold such a view, down from 28 per cent for that age group in 1975. Presumably many people found that such behaviour simply didn't work all that well.

For the record, a 1992 U.S. survey found that less than one in three married men said they would "play around," even if they had a guarantee they would not get caught.[34] The fact that no such guarantee exists clearly reduces that figure in practice — to about one in four. In Canada, asked in early 1992 how important certain features are for a "successful marriage," the trait cited by more men and women (94 per cent) than any other was "faithfulness."[35]

Young people, in disapproving of extramarital sex, are reflecting adult attitudes, and in some instances, their negative experiences.

ADULT SEXUAL ATTITUDES BY AGE GROUPS: 1975-1990					
% Approving					
	Premarital Sex		Homosexual Relations		Extramarital Relations
	1990	1975	1990	1975	1990	1975
NATIONALLY	80	68	34	28	17	21
18-34-year-olds	92	90	43	43	18	28
35-54-year-olds	82	65	40	25	19	23
55 & older	59	43	16	13	11	23

THE MYTH OF THE IMPACT OF THE AIDS SCARE

The extensive publicity given to AIDS, compounded by such revelations as NBA star Magic Johnson's testing HIV-positive, has had a profound impact on the perception that the disease is now a serious problem. Almost 80 per cent of today's teenagers regard it as "very serious," up slightly from about 75 per cent in 1988.

What is less clear is whether the disease is having a significant impact on the *sexual behaviour* of young people. When we asked teenagers about the influence of the reality of AIDS on the "people they know," about 53 per cent said their acquaintances are less likely to engage in sex, 73 per cent maintained they are tending to have fewer partners, and 95 per cent said such people have been more inclined to use condoms.

It nonetheless is a big jump from what one *thinks* others are doing to what one is *personally* doing. When we asked about their own behaviour, focusing on the 55 per cent who are sexually active, two in three said they have altered their sexual habits. This compares with one in three teenagers in 1988, and one in three single adults in 1990. Concern and personal modification are higher among females than males. Alteration of one's own habits is lower in Quebec than elsewhere.

These findings indicate that the threat of AIDS is having an impact on a growing number of young people. But it certainly is not contributing to an overall decrease in sexual activity. Approximately the same proportion of teenagers (55 per cent) are engaging in sexual intercourse now as in 1984. The response to AIDS has hardly been "no sex." Abstinence has not risen in popularity.

We also know that only three in four teens who are engaging in sex are using some form of birth control, with these forms varying considerably. This means that more than one in four sexually active young people — perhaps closer to two in four — are *not* using condoms as a means of engaging in "safe sex." Among them is this 16-year-old from northern Manitoba who, when asked if AIDS has influenced her sexual habits, says, "No — my boyfriend and I don't use condoms."

Such findings suggest that, for large numbers of teenagers, the AIDS scare is still something "out there." They see it as a big problem, one leading lots of people to respond with caution. To be sure, some teens are definitely influenced by its presence. One female grade-10 student from Calgary tell us, "I don't like having sex because I had a close call with almost contracting the AIDS virus." Another grade-10 student from Pembroke, Ontario, says that the fear of AIDS has contributed to her virginity: "I almost went all the way, but go scared because even a condom is not 100 per cent safe when it comes to AIDS." A 17-year-old female from Halifax, who is an avid fan of both pro basketball and Magic Johnson, says, "Magic Johnson's contracting the HIV virus has opened my eyes. Safe sex was not really a priority for me in the past, but it will definitely be in the future." And a 16-year-old female from Victoria comments:

> *I am not sexually involved at the present time, but I have AIDS on my mind constantly. I don't think that anyone who is not married should have sex with AIDS and all the STDs [sexually transmitted diseases] around.*

But in the minds of many teenagers, they themselves have little to worry about, especially if they are involved with people they trust and care about. Perception is frequently not being met with precaution. In the blunt words of a 16-year-old female from New Brunswick, "AIDS is very serious, but it does not stop young people from having sex." More disturbing is the fatalistic attitude of this 16-year-old from a small Ontario community, who says that AIDS has not influenced her own sexual habits: "We are all going to die sometime."

Much of the reason for the lack of precaution at the personal level would seem to be due to the disparity between what the media say and what young people see happening around them. Here are some brief facts on AIDS, provided by Statistics Canada:[36]

- As of August 1991, there were about 5246 known cases of AIDS in Canada. Only 261 (five per cent) of these people were women.
- However, merely two per cent (about 100) of these AIDS cases involved people younger than 20, and more than half of these cases (62) were babies who were born with AIDS.
- True, say experts, the period from infection to the onset of symptoms often takes as much as six years. Yet, 87 per cent of Canadian men who have contracted AIDS have put themselves at risk through homosexual activity.
- For another five per cent, the key link has been blood products or injected-drug use. Just five per cent of the cases have been related to heterosexual contact, with more than half of these involving people from countries where AIDS is endemic, such as Haiti.
- To date, the total number of males who have contracted AIDS through heterosexual relations stands at about 100 — two per cent of all men with AIDS. Approximately 20 of these males are younger than 30.
- As for the 261 Canadian women, about six in 10 have contracted AIDS through heterosexual activity, half of these through heterosexual activity with a person from an endemic country.
- This means that a total of about 80 Canadian women had contracted AIDS as a result of having sexual relations with men born in Canada and other non-endemic countries. The figure includes some 25 women younger than 30.

The threat of AIDS to young people may well be real. But the figures to date are missing. So far at least, AIDS is affecting very small numbers of people in very specific parts of the population, especially not heterosexuals engaging in limited or no sexual behaviour. Consequently, when Magic Johnson says, "It happened to me, it could happen to you," young people listen — although they would be naive if they didn't question how comparable the basketball star's sex life is to theirs. When they see television highlights of American AIDS co-discoverer Dr. Robert Gallo telling a Vancouver conference in early 1992 that "AIDS is the first truly global epidemic, existing everywhere except Antarctica,"[37] they take note. Still, the observation seems foreign to their everyday experience. One southern-Alberta health worker sums up the situation aptly: "AIDS awareness is not a problem among young adults, but convincing them to heed the warnings is. They tend to have the attitude that it won't happen to them."[38]

Experts convinced that AIDS represents a serious problem for teenagers need to keep the issue in front of young people, complete with data. The observation of this 17-year-old female from the small Quebec town of Papineauville seems sound:

I believe that ongoing publicity about AIDS will gradually help us to be more careful, using condoms and being cautious about our number of partners.

	NAT	MALE	FEM	BC	PR	ON	QUE	ATL
RESPONSE TO AIDS								
% Agreeing								
See as "very serious" problem	77	71	82	75	77	78	74	83
People you know:								
Less likely to engage in sex	53	51	55	58	54	55	49	54
Likely have fewer partners	73	69	78	74	74	71	77	71
More likely to use condoms	95	94	95	93	94	95	96	94
AIDS has influenced own habits of sexually involved: "YES"	67	63	71	68	71	71	55	74

THE LEGACY OF THE REVOLUTION

There are few topics that send chills down the spines of parents more than the sexual activity of their adolescents. Today's teens, particularly females, are typically tying physical involvement to significant relationships. But fall in love and like they do. And in more than one in two cases, they are engaging in sexual intercourse.

It is a situation that we adults have created. What we are witnessing in the 90s is the outcome of a sexual transformation that our generation put in motion. Today's young people are not sexual innovators. They simply are sharing in the legacy of the revolution.

Overall, these findings for young people and adults suggest that Canadians continue to have strong beliefs about what is appropriate and inappropriate sexual behaviour. Moreover, the trend data show that the nation is not necessarily ever-changing its endorsement of diverse behaviour. Widespread approval of premarital sex hits a wall at the 90-per-cent mark, the acceptance of homosexuality at approximately 40 per cent, the endorsement of extramarital sex at about 20 per cent, abortion on demand at about 40 per cent.

Freedom in the sexual realm in Canada appears to have surprisingly rigid limits.

5. RELIGIOUS INVOLVEMENT IS STILL DECLINING — YET SPIRITUAL INTEREST SEEMS TO BE RISING

When it comes to religious and spiritual issues, the findings point to an anomaly. Organized religion is in serious trouble with young people. In contrast, the spiritual realm has been anything but abandoned by teenagers.

RELIGIOUS INVOLVEMENT

During the past decade, the bleak situation facing Canada's religious groups in the early 1980s has deteriorated further. Today, just 18 per cent of the country's 15- to 19-year-olds indicate they are attending religious services on a weekly basis — down from 23 per cent in 1984. What's more, those who attend every week drops from 19 per cent for 15-year-olds to 13 per cent for 19-year-olds.

This doesn't mean that young people are abandoning organized religion altogether. Some 80 per cent of teenagers continue to identify with Canada's religious groups; that is, they'll say they are Protestant, Roman Catholic, Muslim, and so on. When asked if they anticipate turning to religious groups for ceremonies relating to birth, 80 per cent say "yes." In the case of weddings, the number increases to 85 per cent; in the case of funerals, it increases again to 90 per cent. Further, 23 per cent say they regard themselves as "committed Christians" while another three per cent maintain they are committed to other religions — appreciable figures, although down from a total of 39 per cent in 1984.

But the tough reality facing the country's religious organizations is that religion is being strongly marginalized by the vast majority of Canadian youth. Only about 20 per cent think it is important to live out religious faith in everyday life, and a mere 10 per cent say they regard religious group involvement as "very important," down slightly from 14 per cent in 1988. As one 18-year-old from a small Ontario town puts it, "I'm a religious Catholic. However, some things the church teaches I'm sceptical about. I like to be free to think for myself." She differs from the position of the church, for example, in approving of premarital sex, abortion, homosexuality, and parenthood outside marriage.

Further, as we saw earlier, just 15 per cent report they receive "a great deal" or "quite a bit" of enjoyment from religious groups — the lowest of any area of Canadian life probed, and down from 24 per cent in 1984. True, the enjoyment figure does rise to about 50 per cent for teens who are weekly attenders. But such a finding draws mixed reviews. It's an improvement on 15 per cent, but it's also a serious indictment of religious groups, given that it also means 50 per cent of the most active young people get little or no gratification from involvement in organized religion! Among them is this wry 17-year-old from Ottawa who claims to attend services every week. "I enjoy going to mass," he says. "I'm very comfortable there . . . I often sleep."

One cannot help but suspect that attendance for at least some of these young people is not particularly voluntary — that apparent commitment is sometimes tainted by coercion. A grade-10 student, an Anglican from a small New Brunswick town, tells it like it is: "My parents make me go." Among other "involuntary attenders" is this 16-year-old female from the small Quebec city of St-Georges who describes herself as a Roman Catholic, but adds, "I consider myself a Christian and I practise regularly (2-3 times a month). But I do not go by choice."

Beyond attendance and enjoyment, young people are no more optimistic about the future of organized religion than they were in the early 80s. In 1984, 19 per cent of young people thought that organized religion would gain in influence by the year 2000. As of 1992, the figure stands at 16 per cent — just below the figure for adults (19 per cent).

To read the religious situation accurately is to remind everyone there is a core of religiously committed young people — perhaps as many as 20 per cent of teenagers. For example, a 16-year-old male from Burnaby, B.C. comments:

> *Because I am a Roman Catholic, I am a hopeful person. I want to do my best to see the earth cleaned, the debts paid, and the world live in peace. But most of all, I hope to see religion return to the hearts of people, right and wrong be pointed out, and people become moral again.*

From the Yukon comes these words from a 16-year-old Pentecostal female who attends services every week: "I am a believer in Jesus Christ. I believe he died and rose again for my sins." A 17-year-old female from Niagara Falls simply says, "I'm glad I'm Catholic." A 16-year-old from Halifax who says she attends synagogue about twice a month comments, "I think that maintaining my Jewish identity throughout my life is extremely important."

INVOLVEMENT IN AND ATTITUDES TOWARD ORGANIZED RELIGION *In %'s*			
	YOUTH		ADULTS
	1984	1992	1990
Identify with a group	85	79	90
View self as committed	39	24	26
Attend weekly	23	18	23
Receive High Level of Enjoyment	24	15	32
Religion: Will Gain Influence	19	16	19

The committed, however, constitute a minority. Overall, the findings do not add up to a pretty picture for Canadians who value participation in organized religion.

Variations Involvement and interest in organized religion is consistently low regardless of region, community size, gender, or race. Things are particularly bleak in Quebec and our larger cities, and among males and whites. Again, however, we would emphasize that differences are fairly small.

SPIRITUALITY

But let's not misread the situation. Paradoxically, young people are having severe difficulty relating to organized religion precisely as they exhibit a strong interest in the things that religion has traditionally focused upon — the supernatural, spirituality, meaning, morality, and ethics. While religious involvement is being seen as "very important" by only about 10 per cent of teenagers, 46 per cent are giving that rating to the *quest for truth*, and 24 per cent to *spirituality*. Time and again, young people express an openness to things spiritual, and disinterest in things organizational. To illustrate:

- I believe in God, but I don't think I have to go to church to prove it. — *a grade-12 student from Toronto*
- I'm Jewish, and consider myself religious, but I only attend services for weddings and funerals. — *a 17-year-old female from Pemberton, B.C.*
- I am a non-practising Catholic, but I am interested in spirituality. — *a 17-year-old male from St-Georges, Quebec*
- I don't go to church, but I believe in God and pray. — *a 16-year-old female from Watson Lake in the Northwest Territories*
- My religion is an individual interest in spirituality, not really religion. — *a 17-year-old female from Montreal*
- I have no belief in religion, but I enjoy studying all the varieties because spirituality is interesting, if not realistic. — *a 17-year-old male from Bedford, Nova Scotia*
- I have strong beliefs in God but nothing I believe in complies with any religious organization — *a grade-12 student from London*

Something is seriously wrong.

Teenagers readily acknowledge that they have spiritual needs. They continue to raise questions about the meaning and purpose of life. They believe that some things are morally right and that others are morally wrong. In short, teenagers still have a keen interest in areas of life that the gods have historically addressed.

THE SUPERNATURAL

More specifically, belief in supernatural phenomena — God, the divinity of Jesus, supernatural forces, including the evil variety — remains high. One in three think they have experienced God. More than half give credibility to ESP, astrology, and psychic phenomena.

Two in three believe in life after death; one in three think they will be reincarnated.

Indicative of the fascination with the supernatural and unknown realms is the prevalence of such themes in rock videos and movies. Popular movies in recent years have included *Ghost, Field of Dreams,* and *The Golden Child.* Significantly, no less than eight of the 10 top-grossing films of all time have pronounced supernatural or science-fiction themes. They include *The Exorcist, E.T., Raiders of the Lost Ark,* and the *Star Wars* trilogy.[39]

Variations in teenage interest in "the transempirical" are modest by regions, community size, gender, and race. Across the country, the evidence is conclusive: teenagers are intrigued by things supernatural. We would go so far as to suggest that, with the help of the media, interest in supernatural phenomena has never been greater.

There obviously are some teens who discount things "non-empirical." Among them is this 16-year-old male from a small Ontario town: "Religion is a fault of the weak. 'Religion' should be belief and faith in one's self, rather than in a fabricated supernatural being." However, he is in a numerical minority. A female of the same age from St. Catharines sums up what seem to be more prevalent sentiments this way:

> *I personally don't believe in having a certain religion because you don't know for sure that one is any better than the other. I just believe that there is something spiritual up there and I believe in my heart, not because of what others tell me.*

A 15-year-old native from Regina comments, "I believe there is a God, but not the one in the Christian religion. I also believe in spirit guides." And a very reflective 17-year-old woman from Glace Bay, Nova Scotia, has this to say:

> *There are some aspects of Christian belief with which I agree, others with which I disagree. I believe that if you are good in this life, your next life, in another dimension, will be better. I believe that there are other dimensions parallel to ours. When we die, we travel to another dimension. This could explain supernatural occurrences, etc. I believe in meditation, yet not involving a God. For me, meditation centres on music, nature, visions, etc. I'm not a blind believer, but not quite a staunch agnostic. I consider my "unorganized religion" a combination of all religions.*

SUPERNATURAL BELIEFS

% Agreeing

	TEENS	ADULTS
God exists	81	83
Divinity of Jesus	80	75
Some people have psyhic powers	69	59
Supernatural forces exist	66	–
Life after death	64	68
Evil forces exist	64	–
Astrology	53	34
Extrasensory perception	52	59
Contact with the spirit world	44	39
I have experienced God	34	46
I will be reincarnated	32	27

SOURCES: *Project Teen Canada* surveys, 1984, 1988, 1992; *Project Can90* adult survey.

SPIRITUAL RECEPTIVITY

Nearly 60 per cent of Canadian teenagers also indicate that they have spiritual needs. For most, such needs — however conceptualized — appear to be intermittent rather than ongoing; only about 25 per cent say that spirituality, as such, is "very important" to them. But even at that, it surpasses the apparent interest in organized religion.

Receptivity to spiritual issues certainly is expressed in a variety of ways, only some of which involve traditional ideas about religion, God, and so on. For example, one 15-year-old Métis female from Kamloops, B.C., says, "I believe that the only superior force comes from within us."

Questions of meaning and purpose also continue to be raised by most teenagers. Our 1984 survey found that only about 10-20 per cent of young people "never" reflect on issues such as life's origin and purpose, how they can find real happiness, and what happens after death.[40] As of 1988, some six in 10 were reporting that the question of life's purpose is of concern to them — about the same proportion, for example, who expressed concern about loneliness — seemingly signalling an opportunity for religion. One Jamaican-born 17-year-old from Toronto is particularly poignant in expressing his sense of purposelessness:

Life is a highway, and I don't have a car.
Life is a highway, and I don't know where we are.

I know life isn't easy, but I thought
it was supposed to be worth living.

Life is the worst institution of them all.

I hate life, but I'm afraid of death.

I wish I could trade in my life for a new one.

Young people also have a sense that, while many things might be of equal value and should be tolerated, there are some things that are better than others or morally right. For example, while almost seven in 10 say that "what is right or wrong is a matter of personal opinion," about six in 10 agree that "how we live will influence what happens after we die." Further, when confronted with the point-blank observation that "some things are right and other things are wrong," all but one in 10 teenagers agree. There is strong uniformity across the country's regions.

Canadian young people give evidence of believing in gradations of accuracy and moral virtue. Publicly, they affirm the notion that truth is an individual matter. Privately, they show signs of discarding such a generous posture.

WHAT ABOUT SATANISM AND WITCHCRAFT?

In the spring of 1990, three teenagers in Lethbridge, Alberta, committed suicide within a period of two months. The suicides were alleged to have satanic-cult connections. Fuelled by the local media, as well as the importing of "experts" to address packed public meetings, hysteria set in among parents across the city. Journalists descended from across North America, and for a few months the city of 60,000 received dubious international recognition as "the satanic capital of Canada." No charges were ever laid, and the RCMP seriously doubted all along the existence of cult ties to the suicides. Nevertheless, apparently inspired by the event, the national media joined regional media in preparing and disseminating numerous stories on teenage involvement in cults.

In the face of claims that significant numbers of teenagers are involved in satanism and witchcraft, it is important to have some good first-hand information, beyond relying on a relatively small number of cases and the impressions of various experts.

We brought the issue up with young people. Specifically we asked, "Among teens you know, how common is involvement in satanic groups or practices, as well as involvement in witchcraft groups or practices?"

Some 90 per cent say involvement in Satanic activities is either "nonexistent" or "fairly uncommon." One in 10 say such participation is "fairly common."

In the case of witchcraft activities, 93 per cent say that involvement is likewise either "nonexistent" or "fairly uncommon." Here again only about one teen in 10 reports that participation is something that's common.

We remind readers what these findings mean: approximately eight to 10 per cent of teenagers say that, among young people they know, involvement in these groups and practices is quite common. This does not mean that eight to 10 per cent of teenagers are participating. How many young people does this "awareness" translate into? Maybe three to five per cent, probably less.

Being intrigued is not synonymous with participation. Some 65 per cent of teenagers believe that evil forces exist. But that does not mean they themselves are involved in these "deviant" practices. Speaking about some activities on Vancouver Island, one 18-year-old from Nanaimo — who personally believes in the existence of evil forces — offers this brief opinion: "I live near a graveyard famous for 'evil' practices. These isolated incidents are pranks, no more."

Variations Our examinations show that, according to teenagers, involvement in either satanism or witchcraft is not appreciably higher or lower in any part of the country, in cities or small towns, among males versus females, or among whites or members of visible minorities.

What is apparent from our findings, though, is that participation characterizes a relatively small proportion of young people. We do not mean to imply that no one is involved. Some definitely are. One 15-year-old female with Roman Catholic parents, who lives in a small Quebec community, confides, "I used to participate in black mass."

We also do not mean to minimize the impact of satanism and witchcraft on some teenagers and their families. But as with new religious movements generally, at both the teen and adult levels, participation appears to be extremely marginal.

INVOLVEMENT IN SATANISM AND WITCHCRAFT						
"There has been some talk about young people having an interest in satanism and witchcraft. Among teens you know, how common is involvement in —"						
In %'s						
	NAT	BC	PR	ON	QUE	ATL
SATANIC GROUPS OR PRACTICES						
Fairly Common	8	8	10	8	7	10
Fairly Uncommon	32	33	35	36	22	39
Nonexistent	60	59	55	56	71	51
WITCHCRAFT GROUPS OR PRACTICES						
Fairly Common	7	8	8	7	7	7
Fairly Uncommon	28	26	33	30	21	32
Is Nonexistent	65	66	59	63	72	61

IMITATING THE REST OF US

The attendance decline for teenagers has not occurred in isolation from the rest of society. Canadian adults continue to embrace a wide range of beliefs, to express the need for spirituality, to raise the so-called ultimate questions, and to look for direction in relating to others.

Yet young people are becoming less and less involved in religious groups. At the end of the Second World War, almost 70 per cent of Canadians were attending religious services on close to a weekly basis. In 1975, some 72 per cent of Canadians said they had attended services weekly when they were growing up.

In the post-1960s, weekly adult attendance has dropped from 31 per cent in 1975 to a current level of 23 per cent — about the same level as that of teenagers. Significantly, in 1975, 37 per cent of parents with school-age children said they were exposing them to religious instruction outside their regular school day. By 1990, that figure had fallen to 26 per cent — only slightly above the adult and teenage attendance levels.

If current patterns remain constant, the weekly attendance level for adults will dip to about 16 per cent by the year 2000. Teenage attendance will also fall to about the same level.

But for all the problems of organized religion, there remains a considerable "market" for the things that have been central to religion over the centuries.

It seems to work this way. To live life is to raise questions about meaning, which frequently require answers that transcend what humans have to offer. The point of one's life, the mystery of death, the strange experiences that lack rational explanations, a desire to find significance, together result in a market that religion historically has serviced.

It's as if a society has a certain volume of spiritual interest that remains at a fairly constant — and high — level over time. During periods when organized religion is flourishing, such spirituality is not particularly visible, since it has found a home for its expression in churches and temples. During times when organized religion falters, spirituality does not disappear but, if anything, seems to rise. Why? Because without an institutional home, it becomes all the more overt and visible. Spirituality goes public. People who otherwise would be worshipping in churches and relying on the authority of tradition are writing and talking about their personal quests for meaning. Thus we have the appearance of spiritual interest rising precisely at a time when involvement in organized religion is declining.

In the light of the magnitude of the market for meaning and transcendence, it is only to be expected that a number of new "companies" will appear on the Canadian scene to fill the void left by traditional religious groups.[41] Among the new meaning-makers are the media. No one should be surprised to find the film industry capitalizing on the obvious voids in the meaning and supernatural realms, along with television, rock videos, New Age thought, and so on. What is more difficult to understand is why the responses of the country's long-standing religious organizations have, at least to date, been so inept.

2

FIVE NEW PATTERNS THAT ARE EMERGING

The five trends examined so far involve modifications of *existing* patterns in the areas of relationships, values, marriage, sexuality, and religion. The national youth-survey findings also point to five significant *new* patterns, which characterize the lives of Canadian young people. They are associated with information, problems, choices, justice, and expectations. As with the five trends just discussed, these five new patterns have readily identifiable sources in Canadian and American culture.

1. YOUNG PEOPLE HAVE NEVER BEEN MORE INFORMED — NOR MORE AMERICAN

It's a popular pastime to pan the educational system and to complain that, these days, young people are not as knowledgeable as their parents and grandparents were when they were teenagers.

The claim is nonsense. Today's young people are the best-informed teenagers in Canadian history. When it comes to a basic awareness of what's happening in the world, they leave their counterparts of the past three generations in the dust.

For starters, educational data show that, as recently as the late 1950s, only 15 per cent of Canadians had high school diplomas and a mere five per cent had university degrees. Today's teens already have more formal education than their grandparents and many of their parents. Moreover, they are starting university in far greater numbers than ever before.

But the main reason young people are so much better informed is not because of the traditional three Rs, but rather because of today's three Ts — television, technology, and travel.

Television has revolutionized perception. The endless array of channels available through cable has put young Canadians in contact with the entire world. In addition to catering to their specialized tastes, television provides them with a "headline knowledge" of what's happening around the globe. Names like Gorbachev, Mandela, and Hussein are recognizable to almost everyone. Events ranging from the demise of the Soviet Union to the summer Olympics in Barcelona have been at least glanced at and partially absorbed.

Critics who downplay the information young people are receiving from television haven't been taking a good look at the vast assortment of offerings available on the set lately. Groucho Marx once said, "I find television very educational. Every time someone switches it on, I go into another room and read a good book.[1] His comment no longer draws a laugh from those in tune with television.

Well-known Washington columnist Carl Rowan writes:

> . . . *I look at my privileged grandchildren and marvel at how much they learn from television. Three kids, age three to eight, who are not permitted to be TV junkies, astound me by displaying knowledge that they have gained from the wrongly assailed "boob tube." Looking at these kids, I know that television has to be part of any cure of the problems of education.*[2]

Technology has contributed to the information explosion by supplementing its television advances with such recent additions as the VCR, CDs, FAX machines, and, of course, computers, all of which make it possible to receive, process, and store information in ways completely unthinkable to teenagers in the 60s, let alone earlier.

Travel is another source of information. Today's young people are travelling outside their provinces in unprecedented numbers. The 1992 survey has found that about nine in 10 of Canada's 15- to 19-year-olds have been outside their home provinces. Eight in 10 have been to the U.S., while almost four in 10 have already travelled outside North America.

In large part, increased travel reflects what their parents have been doing. Between 1980 and 1990, the number of trips Canadians took to the U.S., stimulated increasingly by cross-border shopping, jumped by 90 per cent. In addition, trips to international destinations other than the U.S. doubled to more than three million. Consistent with our survey findings, Statistics Canada reports that, among Canadians under the age of 20, 32 international trips per 100 people were taken in 1989, up from 27 per 100 in 1980.[3]

Relative affluence and technology have combined to put Canadian young people in direct contact with other parts of the world. And so it is that just four per cent were unaware that there had been a GST debate and only 11 per cent had no familiarity with the Oka crisis. The mass slayings in Milwaukee caught the attention of 71 per cent of the country's teenagers, the Communist Bloc breakdown 63 per cent. On the other hand, just 42 per cent expressed familiarity with the Spicer Commission — perhaps because it did not strike a nerve with young people, as well as the fact that it received no play in the American media. The degree of awareness of these items was fairly uniform across community size, gender, race, and region. The only exception was Quebec, a point we will return to in chapter three.

One minor concession to critics: we are not saying the information teenagers have about events and issues nationally and globally is necessarily deep. But when it comes to broad general knowledge, today's teens dwarf previous generations.

HEADLINE AWARENESS OF TEENAGERS			
In %'s			
Very-Fairly Interested	Not Very Interested	Never Heard of It	TOTALS
The War in the Gulf	86	13	1	100
The GST debate	68	28	4	100
The Oka crisis	58	31	11	100
The Communist Bloc breakdown	51	22	27	100
The mass slayings in Milwaukee	46	25	29	100
The Spicer Commission	13	29	58	100

MADE IN AMERICA

For an ever-increasing number of Canadian young people — and adults — a primary source of information is American television. In 1952, when Canadian television was launched, there were already close to 150,000 TV sets in Canada drawing signals from the U.S., where stations had appeared in 1947. Currently, Canadians are spending about two-thirds of their viewing time on U.S. programs.[4]

The key new variable is cable television. Nonexistent in 1970, it now reaches some 75 per cent of Canadian homes. Packages include an average of about 15 U.S. channels. The offerings typically include that global hero of the Gulf War, CNN, and frequently the symbol of headline information in popular form, HNN (Headline News). American music and sports and channels are also plentiful.

And so it is that, in the course of watching an average of some three hours of TV a day, Canadians are gazing Stateside for two hours and viewing so-called Canadian programming for one hour.

The "so-called" is warranted. One hardly needs to be reminded that even the existing Canadian networks and local channels are swamped with U.S. programming, limited only by CRTC guidelines. Seemingly "pure" Canadian news programs on CBC and CTV draw liberally from American networks "feeds." Not to be outdone, Canadian sports programming typically inserts U.S. material. To watch something so apparently Canadian as a Sunday CFL game between the Saskatchewan Roughriders and the Hamilton Tiger-Cats on the CBC or TSN is to find NFL scores liberally spliced in. A cursory peak at American channels the same day reveals that no one south of the border is bothering to return the cordial scoreboard favour.

The net result of this kind of unequal television exchange is found well beyond Canadian enchantment with the NFL and American unawareness of the CFL. Gallup surveys in 1991 revealed that 93 per cent of Canadians knew that George Bush was the U.S. president, but only 13 per cent of Americans were aware that Brian Mulroney was our prime minister. Further, 90 per cent of Canadians were able to identify Washington as the U.S. capital, in sharp contrast to only 16 per cent of people south of the border who knew that Ottawa was our nation's capital.[5]

Incidentally, we are not in any sense overlooking or underestimating the motion-picture industry, along with its offspring, the video industry. Nor do we mean to imply the important role of the print media. Their impact on our culture is certainly significant. We're simply arguing that the marquee player here is television.

If Canadian nationalists — in reflecting on books, films, music, and other art forms — have worried in the past about our being inundated by American culture, then American television should be bringing on total nervous breakdowns. For television does far more than merely inform and entertain. It shapes our very sense of what is. It creates reality. How do we know that AIDS is a serious problem, that a Gulf war is being won, that George Bush is a hero, that nuclear war no longer is an urgent problem, that sexual harassment is becoming rampant, that George Bush is no longer a hero, that Mike Tyson is a villain? You know the answer.

American television is having a dramatic influence on how Canadians, young and old, construct and interpret the world, including the Canadian world. Our concerns, from the economy to drugs; our dreams, from success to travel; our heroes, from rock stars to politicians; our perceptions, of Canadians versus Americans — all are largely *made in the U.S.A.*

HEROES, AMERICAN-STYLE

In our latest survey, we asked young people about their "favourites" in a number of areas, including TV programs, singers, movie stars, pro sports, authors, TV newspersons, politicians, and world leaders.

In virtually every instance, teenagers chose American over Canadian. Tops in their respective categories were the likes of "Beverly Hills 90210 ," Guns n' Roses, Julia Roberts and Arnold Schwarzenegger, and Stephen King. Good grief — the Chicago Bulls of the NBA gave the Montreal Canadiens and Toronto Blue Jays a run for the money as the country's favourite team! And Wayne Gretzky failed to garner the most votes as teenagers' favourite athlete. That honour belongs to Michael Jordan of the Bulls. Gretzky finished second.

But that's not all. We've got some bad news for people like Peter Mansbridge, Lloyd Robertson, and Pamela Wallin. Although teenagers tended to cite more Canadian news personalities than Americans, when it comes to top vote-getters, the winner was Dan Rather of CBS, followed by Connie Chung of NBC. Oh yes — the favourite politician among Canada's teenagers? George Bush of that country across the border.

Particularly telling about the impact of the American media on Canada's young people are the findings of a late-1991 Gallup poll of U.S. teenagers between the ages of 13 and 17. The survey found that their favourite actress was Julia Roberts, their favourite actor, Arnold Schwarzenegger. The poll further revealed that, among teenagers, basketball is "the fastest-growing spectator sport" in the U.S.[6] It sounds remarkably Canadian.

Also telling is the extensive marketing of athletes such as Michael Jordan, and pro sports leagues, notably the National Basketball Association and the National Football League. Jordan's income from endorsements in 1991 is estimated to have been more than $20 million (U.S.). According to the *Globe and Mail's* William Houston, Jordan "has been called 'corporate America's $25-million spokesman' and 'the most powerful huckster in the world.' " In 1991, Jordan dropped Coca-Cola for an $18-million deal with Gatorade. He has close to 20 other accounts, most notably with Wheaties, Nike, and McDonald's.[7] All this is paying big dividends in Canada. Jordan's paraphernalia in the form of jerseys, jackets, sweats, and caps can be found across the country.

The popularity of similar L.A. Raider offerings is also readily visible to the Canadian eye. In fact, Raider jackets have become so coveted they are difficult to hang on to, as this Canadian Press news item reveals:

> *WINNIPEG (CP) — A 14-year-old Winnipeg boy was punched in the mouth and robbed of his football jacket this week, making him the city's seventh victim of thieves who target trendy sports clothing. "They said, 'Give me your jacket or you're dead,' " the boy said Thursday. The boy's father said he was furious about the theft Wednesday of his son's L.A. Raiders jacket. A 15-year-old boy was arrested.[8]*

Ironically, Canadian teenagers can lipsync the rhetoric about American impact on our culture. No less than 63 per cent of 15- to 19-year-olds with an opinion say they think Americans have "too much power" in Canadian life. In the words of one grade-10 female student from B.C., "We are becoming too American. They have too much influence over us." A 15-year-old male who was born in Montreal and now lives in Calgary comments, "It makes me mad when people in Canada depend so much on the U.S. and don't have confidence in Canada." A 17-year-old female from Yarmouth, Nova Scotia, is in a minority in protesting, "I think that Canadians are too quick to blame Americans."

We have even found that a full 76 per cent of teenagers agree that "the CBC is good for Canada," with support for the CBC endorsed by 79 per cent of anglophones and Radio Canada by 65 per cent of francophones. Most do not agree with one young Montrealer of Greek origin who complains that "the CBC is a national disgrace and should be abolished or completely privatized."

But despite the complaints about American influence and praise of the CBC, the song Canadian young people are singing is written and accompanied by Americans. In the summary of one 18-year-old woman from Vancouver, "Everyone seems to like the U.S.A. more than Canada."

TOP THREE FAVOURITES:		
In %'s		
#1	#2	#3
TV PROGRAM — Bev Hills 90210	Chambre en Ville	Cheers
SINGER/GROUP — Guns n' Roses	Metallica	Bryan Adams
MOVIE STAR — Julia Roberts	Arnold Schwarz.	Kevin Costner
PRO SPORTS TEAM — Canadiens	Blue Jays	Bulls
ATHLETE — Michael Jordan	Wayne Gretzky	Magic Johnson
AUTHOR — Stephen King	V.C. Andrews	Danielle Steele
TV NEWS PERSON — Dan Rather	Connie Chung	Tom Brokaw
POLITICIAN — George Bush	Brian Mulroney	Jean Cretien
WORLD LEADER — George Bush	Mikhail Gorbachev	Nelson Mandela

A good rule of thumb seems to be: all things being equal, the heroes for young Canadians are Americans. If a Canadian such as Wayne Gretzky or Bryan Adams is a hero, it's because he or she has made it big in American eyes — and has been so portrayed by the U.S. media, notably television. The same is true of historical figures. Until such time as the likes of our little-known first prime minister John A. Macdonald and heroes from our covert cowboy culture such as Kootenai Brown and Ernie Cashel[9] are given U.S. play, they will continue to bask in obscurity.

A number of young people are well aware of the lack of Canadian identity and tell us:

- Canadians have no real identity in the eyes of other countries. And without high international status in sports, entertainment, etc., we don't even have a lot of pride in ourselves — *a grade-10 student from Victoria.*
- Youth of today have very little or no pride in the accomplishments in Canada — *an 18-year-old from Regina*
- I love Canada very much and it bothers me that it is not getting enough support from the people who live here — *a 16-year-old female from Winnipeg*
- Canada should stop following the United States around. We are our own country — *a 17-year-old male from Brantford, Ontario*

The problem is, for all the apparent consternation, teenagers as a whole are "buying American," economically and culturally.

There's an important policy implication, by the way, for any Canadian entrepreneurs who want to promote Canadians as heroes or stars. Take, for example, the only indigenous major professional league we have — the Canadian Football League. It sounds strange to say, but it nonetheless is current-day reality: *to flourish in Canada, the league has to be recognized as significant by the U.S. media.*

Never mind that we kind of like our football up here, so much so that 3.5 million of us watched the 1991 Grey Cup game between the Argonauts and Stampeders — well above the 2.1 million of us who caught baseball's lavishly publicized All-Star Game right here in Toronto.[10] (If that surprises you, congratulations: you're a typical Canadian.) The fact is that, even if the Grey Cup game is important, we have the nagging feeling that it is "just Canadian," paling in the face of the Super Bowl.

When the CFL scores begin to appear regularly on CNN's late-night sports, Canadians will finally believe their league is world-class. When Americans say something is big, we tend to believe them. Anything less, in most Canadian eyes, is second-rate.

The same phenomenon, incidentally, applies to the American creation of Canadian problems. Mordecai Richler's observation about Montrealers applies to virtually all Canadians:

> *Montrealers, reading about their plight in Canadian newspapers or magazines . . . tend to dismiss doomsday scenarios as the mischief of indigenous hacks: made-in-Canada, therefore minor league, of no consequence. But a report run in the* Wall Street Journal, New York Times, *or the London* Daily Telegraph *or* Economist *predicting the breakup of our nation inevitably reverberates in our own press the next day and commands serious attention here, even an overreaction.*[11]

As usual, we have to add a qualifier: there is the occasional exception to even the above iron-clad rule. Take Bryan Adams. His album, *Waking up the Neighbours*, which included the hit theme from *Robin Hood* "I Do It for You," has sold more than seven million copies worldwide. "I Do It for You" was number one on the charts in 21 countries, including Canada, won the American Music Award as favourite pop-rock single, and was nominated for an Oscar.

However, at the 1992 Juno Awards, handed out by the Canadian Academy of Recording Arts and Sciences, Adams didn't fare nearly as well. He won the Canadian Entertainer of the Year award, which was based on fan balloting. He also was given a Special Recognition award by the board of directors. But Adams failed to win *any* awards in any category that required voting by the 1500 members of the academy. They gave the Best Single award to Tom Cochrane for his song "Life Is a Highway."

Peter Steinmetz, the president of the academy, had this to say:

> *Canadians have a terrible habit of eating their own. It's terribly unfortunate and I personally find it very distressing. I can't control it. I can't influence it, and it's frustrating. But it's reality.* [12]

Variations Provincially there is one exception to much of what we've been saying — Quebec. Teenagers there break with the rest of the country in being much more inclined to cite Canadian, and specifically Quebec favourites, in *all* areas probed. Canadians come out first in the cases of TV program, pro sports team, athlete, TV newsperson, and politician, and in each of the remaining categories get a much higher endorsement in Quebec than in the other regions.

FAVOURITES				
In %'s				
% CITING ANY	AMERICAN	CANADIAN	OTHER	TOTALS
TV Program	85	76	22	2	100
Singer/Group	73	60	16	24	100
Movie Star	64	69	12	19	100
Pro Sports Team	64	46	53	1	100
Athlete	58	51	41	8	100
Author	42	82	6	12	100
TV News Person	28	29	70	1	100
World Leader	23	44	6	50	100
Politician	19	22	72	6	100

OUR NATIONAL INFERIORITY COMPLEX

It is difficult to live in the same information range as a neighbour that views itself as second to none without getting an enormous inferiority complex.

For what it's worth, Canadian young people, exposed as they are to American thought, complete with American self-confidence, power, and energy, are buying the idea that Canadians tend to rate behind Americans when it comes to a number of valued traits. We're not talking here about stars; we're talking about average people in the two countries.

According to our teenagers, Americans are considerably more likely than Canadians to be confident and to take risks. One grade-11 student from Niagara Falls suggests that "our economy is so bad precisely because we are not risk-takers." Americans are also seen as far more patriotic, leading one grade-12 student from the small Manitoba community of Pinawa to say, "Canadians could learn a thing or two about patriotism from them." Americans are also more likely than Canadians to be viewed as being the world's best at what they do. In the words of one grade-10 Toronto student who aspires to live in the U.S., Americans "are the best at most of the things going on today."

Our teenagers do concede, however, that Canadians are probably just about as globally minded as Americans. Hold on, though: the concession is tricky to interpret as a victory for our side. Here, young people may well be torn between a sense that Americans seem very preoccupied with themselves and yet also seem intensely involved in world affairs. We Canadians, meanwhile, come across as rather moderate when it comes to self-absorption and moderate in our concern about things abroad. The net result is the judgment that the two countries end up about even in the globally minded contest.

Overall, the words of one francophone from Lennoxville, Quebec, may sum up the sentiments of many Canadian young people: "We are and will always be the little boy that tries to imitate the U.S. adult." The sense that "American is best" is pervasive. Americans are given better grades than Canadians in every region of the country.

A final bit of evidence? At the time the 1992 survey was conducted, President George Bush and Prime Minister Brian Mulroney were both doing poorly in their respective national opinion polls. Yet, 74 per cent of Canadian teenagers say that "Bush is doing a pretty good job as U.S. president," while the percentage who give the same "pretty good job" rating to Mulroney comes in at a whopping 19 per cent. Among adults, a Gallup poll released in February, 1992 found that 11 per cent approved of how Mulroney was "handling the job."[13] We rest our case.

TEENAGE PERCEPTION OF SELECT CHARACTERISTICS OF CANADIANS AND AMERICANS		
% Describing as "Very Well" or "Fairly Well"		
	AMERICANS	CANADIANS
Confident	91	66
Patriotic	89	47
Risk-takers	84	43
World's best at what they do	62	40
Globally minded	56	54
AVERAGE	76	50

A FURTHER LOOK AT THE THREE-R MYTH

In recent years, education critics have been particularly vocal in deploring the decline in the quality of education. At least two in-depth national literacy surveys have found that significant numbers of Canadians appear to have problems with basic reading, writing, and arithmetic that jeopardize their ability to participate fully in Canadian life.[14]

International studies have also turned up some gloomy findings that have been seen as indicative of Canada's competitive disadvantage in an increasingly global marketplace. One such report, examining school children in the western world, was released in February 1992. Based on 1991 data, it claimed that, in both science and math skills, Canadian students ranked ninth out of fourteen countries. Among the countries ahead of Canada were Korea, Taiwan, Switzerland, Hungary, Italy, and the Soviet Union. Those trailing Canada included the U.S., Scotland, Ireland, and Spain. One bright spot was Alberta, which ranked fourth in science and sixth in math.[15]

Alberta's glory was short-lived. One month later, a study was released comparing science and math curricula in Alberta with those of Germany, Japan, and Hungary. The study claimed that Alberta's schools rate among the best in North America. But they lag behind Europe's and Asia's finest. The failure to teach math and science early enough, said the report, will result in Canadian businesses becoming less competitive in global markets.[16]

Any effort to assess such concerns about the deterioration of the infamous three Rs, along with related science skills, needs to differentiate between (1) the Canadian population as a whole, and (2) high school graduates.

If we look at the population as a whole, then the three Rs match is no contest. The educational attainment levels of Canadians have been increasing consistently over our history and have particularly jumped since the 1950s. There is absolutely no question but that more Canadians than ever before are reading, writing, and carrying out basic mathematical tasks. They are also receiving introductions to the physical and social sciences.

If we are concerned about problems with the three Rs of today's high school graduates, compared to graduates of the past, the debate is not as easily resolved. Some of the issues can readily be sketched.

Given the high dependence in previous decades on the written word, it seems plausible that graduates in days past tended to have reasonably good literacy skills. They had to. Given, also, the need to rely on oneself to carry out basic to complex mathematical tasks, it is conceivable that high school graduates in previous eras were fairly proficient at math. Again, they had to be.

Today's young people don't have to be. We all know the situation well. Profoundly important technological advances in the field of communications have transformed how information is disseminated. The written word has been supplemented by sight and sound. The world and all that is in it is being conveyed directly to the eye and the ear. With increasing frequency, even the words in a best-selling book are lifted off the printed pages and placed on audio cassettes.

And math isn't what it used to be. Once unknown and once financially elusive calculators can be bought with spare change. Addition and subtraction, multiplication and division — not to mention square roots and other tough manoeuvres — can all be carried out in seconds with minimal mental effort. What's more, there are no errors. These days, even mathematics professors reach for their calculators when they're balancing their chequebooks.

Education does not operate in a cultural vacuum. What we need to store in our heads and what we can store on our shelves changes with the times. Today's technological realities call for significant revisions with respect to the emphasis that is given to reading, writing, and arithmetic. To read well but not view well, to write well but not hear well, to memorize formulas without knowing when to use the procedures, is to be less than literate in the 1990s.

Our concern with declining abilities in the three Rs needs to be tempered with our concern for how well today's young people are combining these old skills with the new means available to them as they attempt to understand the world. People who are computer literate in the 90s, for example, are in all likelihood in a better position than people at any time in history to access and work with information — even though their skills in the three Rs may be modest.

If our criterion for such educational success is information, today's teens are readily outdistancing previous generations. If our criterion for educational success is being able to deal creatively with that information, then the warning light that goes on may pertain not so much to the demise of reading, writing, and 'rithmetic, as to the often forgotten "fourth R" — reflection.

IN OUR IMAGE

In March 1992, Canadians were informed by Southam News that the Prime Minister's office spends close to $850,000 each year on news summaries. In his effort to find a provocative angle on the story, writer Ian Austen told the country that the outlay reflects the need to satisfy "the news addiction of Prime Minister Brian Mulroney and his staff."[17]

Nice try, Ian, but you missed the point. The PM and his associates know full well that the media, led by television, create reality for Canadians. If they are to understand how reality is being constructed across the country, it's essential they stay on top of what the media are saying. Hopefully the government has a substantial budget for reviewing television news summaries as well, including those of the American networks. A "news addiction?" Hardly. To be informed, government must keep in touch with the messages of today's media.

The information explosion has had a powerful impact on Canadians of all ages. The "three Ts" have expanded the worlds of countless people. Older Canadians, for example, many of whom never graduated from high school, have — in the era of cable television — joined young people in becoming more informed than any senior citizens in our country's history. They, too, have been gaining a "headline knowledge" of the world. If parents and grandparents seem more knowledgeable than they did twenty years ago, it's not just a figment of our imagination. Score a big contribution for television.

Changing technology and increasing travel have also been working to facilitate the expanding awareness of province and region, nation and globe. Through it all, the American influence on Canadians of all ages has been getting more and more pronounced. The fact that such an obvious pattern has gone unrecognized by the overwhelming majority of Canadians is merely the tip of the iceberg of a much greater shortcoming: the information explosion has not been matched with accelerated reflection.

Precisely because we are being showered with so much information, it is critically important that we learn how to screen information and to evaluate the merits of the myriad claims. Otherwise we become not only inundated but gullible. And when we become gullible, we also become highly vulnerable. As we will see shortly, Canada's teenagers are seeing and believing too much. Consequently, they're in danger of becoming overwhelmed by the negative portrayals of both the country and the planet.

2. YOUNG PEOPLE SEE PROBLEMS EVERYWHERE

I am worried about the problems of today. I do not like the new Constitution. I don't think natives should have their own government. I don't think that the French people should have special rights as well. I don't like the GST. I don't like the morals in our world today — I think that they are getting worse. I hate to watch the news and see what our world's coming to. — a grade-11 Alberta student

The world is going to have to do something about its problems, such as the environment and racism. If not, we might as well blow the world up now. — a grade-12 New Brunswick student

The old story says, if you cry wolf too many times, no one will believe there really is a wolf out there. But until we know for sure it's all a game, someone's crying wolf shakes us up more than a little.

Since at least 1976, Canada's dominant buzz-word has been *crisis.* The election that year of the Parti Québécois, the countdown to finalize the Meech Lake accord in 1990, and the 1992 efforts to produce a new Constitution have all been accompanied by claims that Canada is facing its most severe crisis in history.

In addition to the national political crises, we have seen a proliferation of interest groups since the 60s, each working hard to convince the country that their cause is urgent. Issues have been virtually unlimited and have included racial discrimination, gender inequality, aboriginal issues, the environment, sexual assault, child abuse, abortion, and the rights of the physically disabled, to name just a few. To get their points across, interest groups have frequently invoked the six-letter word: crisis.

The Canadian social landscape is characterized by crisis, crisis, crisis. By now it is clear that the country's unity crises are social creations that serve the interests of federal and provincial governments, along with a variety of interest groups. Unity problems and constitutional problems are created by us and will be solved by us — when we choose to solve them. Causes drawn to our attention by interest groups are often very valid and require responses. But the concerns to which groups are pointing are likewise *social* problems that have *social* solutions. We will solve them if and when we choose to solve them. These are not problems of extinction of the species or the earth's colliding with the sun.

Still, there's been a lot of yelling in Canada, a lot of grim-faced newscasts, a lot of morbid headlines, a lot of last-ditch efforts. One response is to ignore the noise; another is to become insensitive. Still another is to take the yelling seriously.

In Canada, there are signs that our young people do. They have similar social and personal concerns to the teens of a decade earlier; they want to experience optimum living. But having grown up in a Canada in crisis, complete with governments and interest groups working overtime to convince Canadians of the urgency of their causes, today's teenagers are far more likely than those of the early 80s to see serious problems virtually everywhere. The observation of one 16-year-old Quebec male from a small francophone community is just the tip of the perception iceberg:

> *The world is in a period of incredible social, political, and economic upheaval. And, in my opinion, it's only the beginning.*

A 17-year-old female from Vancouver sums things up this way:

> *The reason I feel doubtful about the future is because of all the doomsayers.*

SOCIAL CONCERNS

AIDS

As young people look at life in Canada, the issue seen by most as the greatest threat to their staying alive and living well is AIDS. It has been ranked number one by teenagers since at least 1988. Some 77 per cent view AIDS as a "very serious problem," up from 70 per cent just four years ago. Little variation in perception exists by region or race.

Females, however, are somewhat more likely than males to see AIDS as a serious problem (82 per cent versus 71 per cent).

There is little doubt that the perception that AIDS is a serious issue became more entrenched with Magic Johnson's November 1991 revelation that he had the HIV virus. As seen earlier, interest in the NBA has skyrocketed among Canadian teenagers: 28 per cent say they closely follow the NBA — second only to hockey and baseball. Always on the alert for local angles on news stories, within a month the Canadian media was circulating its indigenous AIDS sports story: in early December a Montreal newspaper broke the story that a Montreal woman claimed to have had sex with about 50 pro hockey players before she died of AIDS in 1989. Russ Courtnall, admitting that he had been no saint in the past, declared:

> *Society is losing its morals. I was scared enough to go get tested last year. I've been guilty . . . and obviously, that was the reason I got tested. It's not something you can ignore.*

Courtnall said he'd decided it's best for people to wait until they're married before they have sex.[18]

Our findings, discussed earlier, suggest that neither Johnson's announcement nor the Habs' anxiety seriously altered the sexual behaviour of Canadian young people or adults.

Similarly, in the U.S., November 1991 polls of adults and teens found no change in either their concern about getting AIDS or their inclination to favour abstinence over safe sex as a result of Johnson's disclosure.[19]

The findings show that AIDS is regarded as a very serious problem. The response of people young and old to AIDS, however, is another matter.

THE ENVIRONMENT

One of the premier concerns of young people is the environment. Some 70 per cent view it as an extremely serious problem, up from only 37 per cent in 1984. What's more, the same proportion say that the government should give high priority to recycling specifically.

In expressing concern about the environment, teenagers are not lost for criticism of adults. One 17-year-old male from Regina doesn't mince his words:

The young people of today are inheriting your earth and we are getting a BUM deal. Most youths are not so much worried about what is currently happening to them, as what is going to happen to them.

When teenagers reflect on Canada's role in dealing with global environmental issues, about 75 per cent maintain that our country should be highly involved. By way of comparison, 57 per cent think Canada should be actively involved in pursuing human rights legislation, and just 26 per cent favour our taking an active role in dealing with the world's population problems.

One 17-year-old from Pemberton, B.C., has this to say:

Canada should be absolutely, thoroughly involved with the conservation of our rainforests — not just with environmentalism. If the Canadian government sponsored tree-planting in the half-million acres of land available in the world, we could easily soak up all the CO_2 that is causing the greenhouse effect.

While variations in environmental concern are not large, Quebec teens, along with females and whites, express somewhat greater alarm than others.

THE MAJOR SOCIAL CONCERNS

% Indicating "Very Serious"

	TEENS		ADULTS	
	1984	1992	1985	1990
AIDS	–	77	–	48
The Environment	37*	69	51*	55
Child Abuse	50	64	51	51
Drugs	46	64	47	49
Teenage Suicide	41	59	29**	–

*In these surveys, the word "pollution" was used.
**In this survey, the word "suicide" was more generally used.

CHILD ABUSE, DRUGS, SUICIDE

Three issues that personally affect many young people — child abuse, drugs, and teenage suicide — follow close on the heels of concern about AIDS and the environment. In each of these three cases, there has been about a 20 percentage-point jump since 1984 in the proportion of young people who regard them as "very serious" problems. Here, females are considerably more likely to express concern than males. Regionally and racially, variations are small, except in the case of drugs, where members of visible minorities — except for Orientals — express greater concern than whites (73 per cent versus 63 per cent).

The seriousness of **child and sexual abuse** is reflected in the disclosures of teenagers in two areas. First, four in 10 report that they personally know someone who has been physically abused at home. The figure is considerably higher than the 17 per cent found by a May 1991 Gallup poll asking the same question of adults.[20] Second, four in 10 also say they personally are aware of someone who has been sexually abused. It is estimated by researchers that about two in 10 females and one in 10 males have been personally abused sexually.[21] One 15-year-old from Montreal adds reality to those numbers:

> *I have been a victim of violence by my stepfather. Nobody helped. I lived four months in hell until I left secretly to live with my grandmother. It happened three months ago, and I am still upset.*

An 18-year-old from St. Catharines who is now on her own tells us:

> *I was molested, but my parents don't know. I also was abused at home, before my parents split up. I don't talk to my mother and feel sad when I see my father. There's not much hope for my young brothers and sisters.*

We have already seen that **drug abuse** applies to only a minority of teenagers, despite the fact that access is widespread. Nonetheless, 62 per cent of young people report that they personally know someone who has a "severe alcohol or drug problem." To be sure, that someone could be an adult, as well as a young person. But the point is that drug abuse in one form or another is being experienced first- or second-hand by large numbers of teenagers.

Teenage suicide is also an issue that 15- to 19-year-olds don't merely read about. About 60 per cent say that they themselves know someone who has attempted suicide. One grade-12 student from Halifax tells us, "My friend came very close to committing suicide. She had the drugs and was ready to do it, but changed her mind that night because of us — her friends." A 16-year-old from a small community in southern Ontario discloses, "I have a cousin who has tried twice to commit suicide by slashing her wrists." A grade-12 student from rural Manitoba confides, "I have a close friend in a coma right now because he hung himself." It may sound morbid but it nonetheless needs to be faced: some young people regard suicide as a viable option for them. One extremely reflective 16-year-old girl from Montreal offered us these thoughts:

The more we live, the more life
is disgusting.

Life is black.
It's a black hole,
Dirt, an impurity,
A stain on polluted earth.

I would like to disappear
in a black hole
and come out
the other side
where all is beautiful.
No suicide.
No violence.
No pollution.
No war.
No black.

KNOWLEDGE OF SELECT BEHAVIOURS

"APART FROM what you read in the papers and see on TV,
do you yourself know anyone who . . ."

% "Yes"

	NAT	MALE	FEM	BC	PR	ON	QUE	ATL
Has been physically abused at home	42	29	54	46	47	44	33	42
Has been sexually abused	39	27	50	41	39	39	35	43
Has a severe alcohol or drug problem	60	53	67	56	61	56	65	67
Has attempted suicide	58	48	68	60	67	53	58	58

Variations Consistent with their greater tendency to perceive these three issues as serious problems, females are considerably more likely than males to express personal knowledge in these areas. Physical and sexual abuse is *less* likely to be cited by Quebec teens. Whites and natives are more likely than teens from other racial groups to express familiarity with all but sexual abuse, where levels are the same. If anything, reported knowledge of these kinds of behaviour is actually *higher* in Canada's smaller communities, rather than in cities of 100,000 or more.

Caution needs to be used in interpreting these findings. The fact that 50 per cent of people are "aware of someone" does not mean that 50 per cent of people are "doing something." If one student attempts suicide, for example, it is conceivable that an entire school could be aware of it. Moreover, information presumably travels faster and more efficiently in smaller communities.

What is clear from these survey findings is that the media attention given to child abuse, drug abuse, and suicide has heightened sensitivity in all three areas. But the fact that such large numbers of teenagers are personally aware of individuals who have been directly involved in each suggests that these issues are, in fact, serious problems for many Canadian young people.

DISCRIMINATION, VIOLENCE, ECONOMY

In a second category, seen as "very serious" by 50 to 60 per cent of teenagers, are racial discrimination, violence against women, and the economy — three fairly explicit "staying alive, living well" issues. Regional differences are noteworthy only in the case of the economy; as would be expected given current conditions, concern is higher in Ontario, Quebec, and the Atlantic provinces than in the West. There are racial differences in concern about discrimination: 66 per cent of members of visible minorities view it as a serious problem, compared to 57 per cent of whites. Considerably more females than males are concerned about discrimination and violence against women, but there is no gender difference in the case of the economy.

Once more, what is particularly striking are the sharp increases since 1984 in the proportion of young people who see discrimination, as well as violence against women, as "very serious" problems. The figures are far above those for adults.

For those who believe they are victims of **racism**, life is not easy. One 16-year-old native from Winnipeg comments:

No one cares about young native students. They are alone in this world. Their families are sometimes their only support.

Another native from Saskatoon expresses the view that people she knows "are discriminated against — so they turn to drugs and drinking." A black 16-year-old from Scarborough, Ontario, says that "the country's most serious problem is the police killing of our black-Afro youths." She maintains that the slayings have involved "innocent people" for "no reason." Another black female, 15, from the Toronto area maintains that racial discrimination is a very serious problem. "Before unity can take place in Canada," she says, "there first has to be unity between races."

The complexity of finding solutions to racial inequality is seen in the opposition to affirmative-action-type programs by this 17-year-old Manitoban who was born in India and has lived in Canada most of her life:

I don't feel that the power people have should have anything to do with what race they are. It should have to do with how well they can do the job. If they can do the job better than a white person, then they should get the job. Power is not a racial issue. It's an issue of competence.

Violence against women is also regarded as a "very serious" problem by about 60 per cent of teenagers. A distressing finding, however, is that the issue is viewed as a severe problem by 70 per cent of young females and only 44 per cent of young males. Men may be dramatically underestimating the problem. Women may be overestimating it.

Regardless, given their vastly different views of reality, the quality of life for women is being seriously eroded, while the inclination of men to empathize and respond may be far less than it needs to be. Such differences in perception point to an urgent need for teenage males and females to better understand what in fact is happening "out there," and respond to it, so that life can be improved for large numbers of women for whom anxiety and fear are real. We will return to this issue in chapter three.

More than one in two teens see the **economy** as a severe problem. Little wonder. The tough economic times in the early 90s are being experienced directly by teens across the country, as many parents face layoffs, business closures, and personal and corporate bankruptcies.

In 1991 alone, for example, bankruptcies rose 40 per cent over the previous year, totalling almost 76,000. The consumer count was greater than 62,000, the business tally almost 14,000.[22] Unemployment hit 15 per cent among blue-collar workers in 1991, and 7.5 per cent among their white-collar counterparts.[23] Many young people are among the human casualties of those impersonal numbers.

With the economy in trouble, the government is a particular target for frustration. Roughly 50 per cent of teens say that "government incompetence" is an extremely serious problem — virtually the same level as that of adults (53 per cent). Only 27 per cent of young people indicate they have "a great deal" or "quite a bit" of confidence in the federal government, with the figure only slightly higher, at 32 per cent, for provincial governments. The adult confidence levels are even lower at 13 per cent and 30 per cent respectively.

Teenagers levelled innumerable criticisms at government in general, the federal government more specifically and Prime Minister Brian Mulroney in particular. A 17-year-old from Toronto whose ancestry is Asian was among many who told us that the country's number-one problem is "Brian Mulroney!!" In elaborating on her lack of confidence in government, she had this to say:

Teens do not have respect for anything that has to do with the government, because the government has ignored us too much in the past. Most politicians are not only greedy but sneaky as well.

MODERATE SOCIAL CONCERNS				
% Indicating "Very Serious"				
	TEENS		ADULTS	
	1984	1992	1985	1990
Racial Discrimination	22	58	12	16
Violence against Women*	46	58	43	38
The Economy	37	57	57	58
Government Incompetence	–	51	–	53

*In all but the 1992 survey, the term "sexual assault" was used.

The remarks of this Sudbury male of the same age stood out precisely because they were so rare: "I think our federal government is doing a great job and the opposition should lay off." What especially seems to bother young people is their sense of having no power on the one hand, and their sense of government incompetence on the other. In the words of a 17-year-old woman from London, "The current government must be eliminated because nothing is improving. There still is racism, poverty, unemployment." While some offered detailed critiques and others decried their lack of input, this simple observation of a Deux-Montagnes, Quebec, teen captures something of their frustration:

> *Canada is dying and the government isn't smart enough to save it. I, a little 16-year-old, could do a better job.*

Veteran Canadian journalist Bruce Hutchinson is among those who would caution us to take seriously the frustration young people have about what adults are doing to their country and world. "The young alone," says Hutchinson, "have the right to remake the world they never made."[24]

OTHER ISSUES AND NON-ISSUES

There are a number of additional concerns viewed by around 40 per cent or less as "very serious" problems. Significantly, they include a number of high-profile national issues — the lack of unity, women, native people, and French-English relations. They also include the highly publicized issues of youth gangs and violence in schools. What again stands out are the large increases since 1984 — 15 to 25 percentage points — in the proportion of teenagers who regard comparable issues as representing "very serious" problems.

The tremendous attention being given to **unity and constitutional issues** has failed to capture the interest of the majority of Canadian young people. To begin with, less than 40 per cent view unity as a severe problem — virtually the same proportion as that for adults. Apathy is greatest in Quebec, where only 20 per cent regard unity as "very serious." Clearly, young people there believe they have options. There are no noteworthy differences by gender or race.

In a related finding, just 34 per cent of teenagers think that the government should be giving high priority to constitutional matters. What more, as we've discussed, $26-million later, 58 per cent of 15- to 19-year-olds say they have never heard of the Spicer Commission! They are not alone. A Gallup poll completed in July 1991 found that

43 per cent of adults were equally oblivious to that rather expensive travelling caravan.[25]

And while we're talking about adults, we also need to point out that polls by Gallup and others have found that the unity issue is not as pressing as politicians and the media would have us believe. As of April 1992, only 20 per cent of Canadians 18 and older believe our differences are so great they won't be solved. Even in Quebec, the figure, which had been about 50 per cent in the post-Meech summer of 1990, had fallen to 35 per cent. The alarm level was the lowest it had been since 1984, when it stood at only 13 per cent. Gallup points out that for all the talk about Confederation breaking up, at no time since 1945 have as many as three in 10 Canadians held such a view. The record high was just 27 per cent, in 1982.[26]

Compared to the environmental and economic issues, unity and French-English relations simply aren't that important to most adults and teenagers. Only about three in 10 young people think the problems of French and English Canada specifically deserve a "very serious" rating, with the figure highest in Quebec at 44 per cent, almost double the 20 per cent level of 1984, but still representing a minority of young people in that province.

Teenagers, like the rest of us, cannot be expected to stay excited forever about a crisis they have known about since they abandoned diapers. Social problems, like their beloved songs, can only stay at the top of the charts for so long. Unity is one such song. When we hear someone of no less stature than the prime minister proclaiming the following on an early 1992 swing through small-town Ontario, we know that the time has come to move on:

> *We've had enough of this. It must be done. It's got to be completed. Let's get together, finish the documentation, recognize it, celebrate our differences, put it in a Constitution, put the Constitution away. We'll only take it out when Uncle Harry comes to visit and only then. Meanwhile we'll get back to building a prosperous Canada.*[27]

That would please many young people, including this 16-year-old Montrealer:

> *Please be aware that teens are uninterested in constitutional issues, and would just like to get on to more important things.*

The view that **gender inequality** is a "very serious" problem is held by four in 10 young people, up markedly from 15 per cent in 1984, and well above the current 21 per cent level for adults. Such perception, however, differs fairly dramatically by gender, being almost twice as high for females (51 per cent) as males (28 per cent).

Further, while 44 per cent of teens disagree that "women in this country now encounter very little discrimination," the dissenting figure for females is 55 per cent, for males 32 per cent. When asked about power in our nation's affairs, 69 per cent of females say women have too little compared to only 36 per cent of males.

The disparity in the perception of the sexes can be seen in the comments of two Ontario teens. A 16-year-old female from Lake Rosseau says, "I'm worried that I will never be as equal as men in the workplace. I want sexism to stop." Yet, a 15-year-old male from a small western Ontario town has quite a different view of things: "I think that women's rights are being blown way out of proportion. They always want more power and are wondering why there are not more women politicians when there are more in Canada than anywhere else."

Differences in views of the status of women by region and race tend to be small, except for Asians, who are somewhat less inclined than others to view gender equality as a problem.

In the case of **native-white relations**, despite the fact that these are times of tough negotiations on the constitutional front, it seems that about six in 10 teens have the perception that things are proceeding reasonably well. As of early 1992, at least, a majority believe there is no reason for excessive alarm. On the other hand, some four in 10 are more than a little nervous. Variations by gender and race are slight. However, Quebec youth are less sympathetic to native concerns

---

OTHER SOCIAL CONCERNS

% Indicating "Very Serious"

	TEENS		ADULTS	
	1984	1992	1985	1990
Unequal Treatment of Women	15	40	19	21
Youth Gangs	–	40	–	–
Native-White Relations	–	39	–	24
Lack of Canadian Unity	13	39	18	38
Violence in Schools	–	36	–	–
French-English Relations	13	31	13	29

than teenagers elsewhere. We will return to this difference in chapter three.

GANGS AND SCHOOL VIOLENCE

Much attention has been given to youth gangs and the sometimes related phenomenon of rising levels of violence in schools. Gangs are said to be common in Toronto, Montreal, and Vancouver. School violence involving students as well as teachers is viewed by many as being on the rise. The fatal stabbing of a Calgary junior high student on a school soccer field in May 1992, for example, aroused fears that school violence is now commonplace across the country, and that students are increasingly arming themselves in order to survive.

Approximately 40 per cent of teenagers say the two problems of gangs and school violence have now reached a "very serious" stage. About one in three report they personally know someone who has been a victim of gang violence. That number increases to one in two when teens are asked about familiarity with people who have been "physically attacked at school."

While there is hardly a perfect fit between the perception that **youth gangs** constitute a serious problem and the actual incidence of violence, the survey has found that gangs are viewed as a particular problem in B.C. and Ontario, and in the country's larger cities. More males than females cite familiarity with actual violent incidents, but are less likely than females to regard gang violence as a serious problem. Racially, concern is greatest among east Indians and Pakistanis, and blacks, with blacks being more inclined than other young people to report awareness of victims of gang violence.

One 17-year-old from Niagara Falls, who says teenage gangs in his area represent a severe problem, nonetheless offers this corrective to the assumption that gang membership is synonymous with racism:

> I am involved in a teenage gang. At the same time, I am strongly against racism. I follow the gang not because I am a "hotshot," but because I find it gives me a sense of purpose — something to take a stand on.

As for **school violence**, there is little regional variation in both the perception that the issue is a serious problem and familiarity with actual incidents. However, as with gangs, school violence is viewed as somewhat more prevalent in larger cities and is more commonly encountered by males, even though females are more inclined to see it as a problem. Here again, blacks, and east Indians and Pakistanis are more likely than other teens to see school violence as a serious problem. When it comes down to actual knowledge of victims, these two groups are joined by natives in showing somewhat greater familiarity than others.

We remind readers that, once again, care needs to be used in interpreting these data on the prevalence of violence. The finding that one in three teens know of a victim of gang violence, or that one in two students know someone who has been beaten up at school, does not mean that 33 to 50 per cent of all teens are victims. It means rather that one-third to one-half of the students *know* a victim. In some community instances, the entire school body may know the same victim.

In addition to this "one victim, multiple awareness" issue, we need to remember that attacks at school take many forms. Probably all of us can readily recall school fights and skirmishes that might have led

	GANGS		SCHOOL VIOLENCE	
	Very Serious	Know of a Victim*	Very Serious	Know of a Victim
NATIONALLY	40	35	36	45
B.C.	53	42	36	47
Prairies	39	30	32	47
Ontario	48	35	38	47
Quebec	27	40	38	39
Atlantic	32	24	29	46
100,000-plus	43	42	37	47
99,000-10,000	35	34	33	47
under 10,000	38	25	36	41
Female	46	31	43	39
Male	34	40	29	52
E. Ind-Pak	61	38	51	52
Black	52	44	53	56
Native	46	31	35	57
Oriental	41	35	34	41
White	39	35	35	44

GANGS AND SCHOOL VIOLENCE

% "Yes"

*The item read, "APART FROM what you read in the papers and see on TV, do you yourself know anyone who... " Questions included, "Has been a victim of gang violence?" and "Has been physically attacked at school?"

us to say yes when asked if we knew of someone who had been "physically attacked at school."

These qualifications understood, it is clear that violence at school, whether witnessed or experienced personally, is a fairly common occurrence. The same is true of gang violence. In some instances the violence is severe, even fatal.

An Important Footnote The disparity between one's perception that gang and school violence are problems, and one's familiarity with actual incidents provides important information that should not go unnoticed. The gap between the two serves to remind us that the perception that something is a problem or a crisis is based on far more than personal experience or cold facts.

Equally important to what we see in formulating our perception is what we hear. We may not have caught a glimpse of the wolf, but if people we have confidence in say that one is roaming around, we assume it's true. In addition, what is extremely important to problem perception is *how we interpret* what we see and hear, not only using our rational equipment, but also our values and dispositions. The wolf and a few colleagues might be in our neck of the woods, but if we are prepared, all is well. We also might be fond of wolves and, frankly, quite protective lest some trigger-happy type callously guns them down.

To see a newspaper proclaim, "Violent Crime Soaring!" may result in some people staying off the streets. But others might head to the safety of the streets when they actually read the article and learn that two in three homicides are committed by people who know their victims well, including family members. Still others may take the position that "things may be bad, but not as bad as where I come from." Headlines don't necessarily scare reflective people.

To find that today's teenagers are "deeply concerned about everything" is not particularly good news. It suggests that young people have been fairly uncritically believing in numerous cries of wolf, with the result that they are high on anxiety and low on problem-solving. Such accelerated anxiety can be seen in their personal lives.

PERSONAL CONCERNS

As with social problems, Canadian teenagers in the 90s are concerned about essentially the same personal issues as their predecessors of the 80s. What is different is that far more members of this "crisis generation" say these issues are troubling them.

SCHOOL, TIME, MONEY, FUTURE

On an immediate personal level, Canadian young people have four dominant concerns: the pressure to do well at school, the feeling of never having enough time, lack of money, and wondering what they will do when they graduate. Some 70 to 75 per cent say these are issues they worry about either "a great deal" or "quite a bit." Post-graduation anxiety was high in 1984, and remains high. In the case of school, time, and money, the proportion expressing concern is up about 15 to 20 per cent from a decade earlier.

Variations Quebec teens are somewhat more inclined than others to express concern about life after graduation (80 per cent versus about 70 per cent elsewhere). Females are slightly more likely than males to indicate they have time problems. Greater numbers of visible-minority teens than whites report pressure to do well at school. Concern about money is marginally greater among blacks and natives, while worries about life after finishing school are a bit more common for natives and Asian Canadian teens than for other young people.

DOMINANT PERSONAL CONCERNS BY GENDER AND RACE			
% Indicating Bothered "A Great Deal" or "Quite A Bit"			
PRESSURE DO WELL AT SCHOOL	NEVER SEEM HAVE ENOUGH TIME	LACK OF MONEY	WHAT WILL DO WHEN FINISH SCHOOL
NATIONALLY	76	74	71	72
Male	73	68	71	70
Female	78	78	71	74
E. Ind-Pak	90	73	71	82
Native	86	84	77	78
Oriental	87	81	71	80
Black	84	73	84	70
White	74	73	71	72

School pressure is both self-imposed and brought on by others, notably parents. School is what teenagers do for a living, and, enjoy it or not, most want at least to pass their courses, earn their credits, and "get out alive." Their self-set goals, however, are typically exceeded by the expectations of their parents and some of their teachers. It all adds up to strain.

Asked to complete the sentence, "What I worry about the most is . . .", 35 per cent cited school. One young woman in grade 12, who lives in a small Manitoba community, sums up things this way:

> *I think teens have too much pressure put on them from school and from their parents. At school it's "You need high marks to go to university. You can't go anywhere without university." At home it's the same and more. "Those marks aren't high enough." It just all adds up after a while.*

A 15-year-old Toronto female offers these brief but sobering thoughts:

> *School is very stressful and worrisome. School should be fun, not a pain. And school is very important to me, because that's all I have left for me. My life has been a rough one.*

From the small Ontario community of Alliston comes this 15-year-old's expression of concern about the calibre of education:

> *We need to upgrade our educational system. I'm concerned that when I grow up, students from Japan, for example, will be much more advanced than North Americans, and we will have to settle for a second-rate job.*

Before graduation day, about one in three students across the country will drop out of high school. The good news is, despite the cries of alarm, many will come back. A 1991 Statistics Canada survey of some 10,000 students found that almost one in four had dropped out at some point during their school career. Significantly, most were good students: more than 30 per cent had at least a B average while only 10 per cent were pulling D's or less. About three in 10 left primarily because of two main factors: the desire to work and boredom.[28] Our 1988 national youth survey involving 15- to 24-year-olds isolated the same two key factors among high school dropouts — desire to work (47 per cent) and boredom (32 per cent). Money problems were a distant third (eight per cent).

The Project Canada national surveys through 1990 have consistently found that, on a personal level, Canadians say they have two primary concerns: not enough money and never enough time. Young people are no different.

Allowances average about $10 a week and jobs average 15 hours at $7 per. With some variations, we have the following picture:

- About 15 per cent have a job and receive an allowance = $115 per week.
- Some 35 per cent have a job, but are not given an allowance = $105 per week.
- A further 30 per cent have no job, but receive an allowance = $10 a week.
- The remaining 20 per cent have neither a job, nor a regular allowance = handouts.

The net result is similar to what many adults find: the money doesn't go far enough. For some, such as this 16-year-old female from a small Ontario community, the anxiety is acute:

Students have more and more expenses. I feel that I'm always worrying about money and I never have enough to get by. I owe people money and I'm always depressed. My schoolwork is getting behind, even though I want to go to university some day. I do have goals, but I can't reach them without funds.

As for time, young people have to tolerate the stereotypical belief that they have endless amounts of time on their hands. The fact is that the typical Canadian teen goes to school for about six hours a day, and then goes to work for another two. In between, they do about two hours of homework and, usually while eating or glancing at the paper, watch about three hours of television. In case you haven't been adding, that works out to 13 hours. If you throw in three hours for meals and eight hours of sleep, you've run out of hours — and you haven't counted travelling time and other necessary incidentals.

One 17-year-old Montrealer with east Indian roots is one such teen who finds himself without an abundance of time. He attends school full-time, and works five to 10 hours a week. Homework on weekends, he suggests, is asking too much:

Students commit five out of seven days of their life to education. Sometimes they have to go out of town with their parents, or have made plans for the weekend. And if they have homework, they may have to put off these plans. Homework also gets in the way of your weekend job. Hey, I'll do homework from Monday to Friday, but I need freedom on the weekends!

YORK UNIVERSITY BOOKSTORES

30 CASH-1   1836 0001 006

BIBBY   MDS 16   17.95
61673
            SUBTOTAL   17.95
7% GST R119306736   1.26
               TOTAL   19.21

CASH TENDER   20.25
              CHANGE   1.04
COURSEBOOK REFUNDS WITHIN 10 DAYS
         THANK YOU/MERCI

                    7/07/93 12:18

Concern about the **future** — life after graduation — is understandable. The days at home are running out. One soon will have to fend for oneself, if not doing so already. For some, the occupational choices are overwhelming. For others, the choices are underwhelming. University or technical school might provide a temporary reprieve from making a firm career choice. Then again, for many, dollars are a problem. One Glace Bay, Nova Scotia, graduating student sums up his predicament this way: "There are no jobs and there is no money for college." It used to be great to be young; but suddenly the clock is ticking a bit too loudly.

PERSONAL CONCERNS				
% Indicating Bothered by *"A Great Deal" or "Quite a Bit"*				
	TEENS		ADULTS	
	1984	1992	1985	1990
Pressure to do well at school	50[*]	76	–	–
Job	–	–	26	29
Never have enough time	48	74	47	38
What to do when finish school	68	72	–	–
Lack of money	54	71	48	50
Not understood by parents	–	58	–	–
Losing friends	–	57	–	–
Weight[*]	44	40	23	24
No girlfriend/boyfriend	–	39	44[**]	48[**]
Sex	28	30	22	22
Height	–	22	–	–

[*]In 1984, 1985, and 1990, the item used was "looks."
[**]In adult surveys, % based on singles.

FRIENDS AND PARENTS

For about 55 per cent of young people, two relational matters are important — losing friends, including romantic partners, and not being understood by parents.

The relatively fast turnover of friends is one of the anomalies of youth. It seems to particularly affect young women, and is a concern for 64 per cent of females versus 49 per cent of males. Further, given the value teens place on friendship and the inexperience they have with romance, the inability to sustain valued relationships is frequently painful. Therefore it's not surprising to find that 40 per cent of 15- to 19-year-olds acknowledge they are troubled "a great deal" or "quite a bit" by the fact that they currently don't have a girlfriend or boyfriend. For some it's a first-time, pre-relationship concern; for many it already reflects the struggle to adjust to the emptiness of having broken up. A good number of teenagers find that romance carries with it both pleasure and pain. One 15-year-old male from Valcourt, Quebec, sums up the sentiments of many in noting that what he enjoys most is "the time I spend with my girlfriend," while what he worries about most is the possibility that "my girlfriend and I will break up."

With regard to teens' feeling misunderstood by parents, our 1988 survey found, for example, that many frequently had disagreements with parents over such issues as jobs around the house (42 per cent), opinions (33 per cent), how they spent their time (27 per cent), school (26 per cent), appearance (20 per cent), and choice of friends (18 per cent). Little wonder teenagers feel misunderstood — and consequently don't enjoy their fathers and mothers all that much.

Feelings of not being understood by parents are somewhat more common among females than males, and among all racial minorities, especially east Indian and Pakistani teens. In the latter case, clashes between western and eastern cultures may well be part of the difficulty. Suggestive of conflict between first- and second-generation immigrants, 63 per cent of visible-minority young people born outside Canada regard not being understood by parents as a serious concern, compared to 72 per cent born in Canada.

LOOKS

Reflecting a culture where a lot of emphasis is put on appearance and fitness, 52 per cent of teenagers acknowledge that their looks are "very important" to them. One 17-year-old woman from Niagara Falls sums up things this way:

> If you look good, you feel good. People will want to talk to you. You make a good impression on yourself.

The degree of concern about height is about the same for females and males. Only about one in five say it troubles them. Where there *is* a significant gender difference, however, is in concern about weight. Some 40 per cent of teenagers say their weight bothers them "a great deal" or "quite a bit," with this overall figure including 26 per cent of males and no less than 53 per cent of females. It's not just being overweight that troubles young women. One Toronto 15-year-old, in acknowledging concern about her weight, comments, "I'm very skinny." A 17-year-old from a small Manitoba town has the same concern: "I'm too thin; I can't gain weight."

The message here seems clear: looks are *equally valued* by young men and women. But females are more likely than males to *worry* about them. And we as adults have to take most of the responsibility. We will look at this topic more closely in chapter three.

Physical appearance also tends to be somewhat more of an issue for teens from visible minorities than for other young people. Height and weight are of particular concern to many Oriental teens, weight something that troubles many natives. Visible minorities, like women, appear to feel definite pressure to meet the dominant cultural expectations of what constitutes attractiveness.

CONCERNS ABOUT PARENTS AND LOOKS BY GENDER AND RACE

In %'s

	NOT UNDERSTOOD BY PARENTS	LOOKS: VERY IMPORTANT	WEIGHT: CONCERNED ABOUT	HEIGHT: CONCERNED ABOUT
NATIONALLY	58	52	40	22
Male	52	53	26	21
Female	64	51	53	22
E. Ind-Pak	78	64	35	28
Native	73	54	62	36
Black	67	63	46	36
Oriental	61	48	48	43
White	57	52	39	19

* Parents, weight, height: % bothered *"A Great Deal"* or *"Quite A Bit"*.

SEX

Sex is obviously of considerable interest to teenagers. About 40 per cent confess they think about sex "very often" and another 45 per cent sometimes; just two in 100 say they "never" give it a thought. Yet, only 30 per cent say it troubles them, with only marginal differences by either gender or race. As one grade-12 student from Halifax, who acknowledges that she is sexually involved, bluntly puts it, "Sex doesn't seem to be a problem."

Among the concerned is this 15-year-old Montrealer who says that what he worries about most are "sexual relations that turn into disasters." A 15-year-old female from a small B.C. town, hoping to awaken some parents, offers this sobering information:

> *I know three 16-year-olds in my school who are all over three months' pregnant. Parents aren't usually aware that their children (or children's friends) are sexually active. If they did know, then maybe it would be easier for them to talk to their children about it.*

Some 85 per cent of teens tell us they have taken sex-education courses, with approximately the same proportion indicating they feel fairly well informed about birth control. When it comes right down to needing advice concerning sex, close to 60 per cent say they turn to their friends, and only eight per cent speak with their parents. Almost 30 per cent say they turn to no one.

HOW TOUGH IS IT TO BE A TEEN TODAY?

These findings on social and personal problems indicate that teens in the 90s are far more inclined that those of a decade ago to see problems everywhere. Does this mean that the old lament is true today — that "it's never been harder to be a teenager?"

Maybe, maybe not. True, they see problems in all places. True, they have much to worry about. Still, the irony in all of this is that the very people who have been working so hard to convince Canadians that there *are* crises and that their causes warrant attention are the very people who also claim to have solutions.

And so it is that the politicians who tell us that the Canadian sky will soon fall are working behind the scenes to ensure it won't. People who have a stake in the national scene — First Nations, women's groups, labour, business and professional organizations — all maintain we will have a unified Canada if they in fact are given their rightful voices. Organizations expending large amounts of energy to convince us we have an expanding range of social problems are also the very groups calling for ameliorative responses. In the course, then, of selling Canadians on the importance of their causes — and scaring the whatever out of teenagers and not a few adults — these social-problem entrepreneurs are also coming with game plans.

As a result, the current emerging generation might be a frightened generation. But it's also moving toward adulthood at a time when there's never been a better opportunity to deal with the problems. True, teens have anxiety about AIDS. The reality, however, is that previous generations had health concerns, too, and were far less prepared medically to deal with them. Today's young people are troubled about their physical and economic environments, but again, they are growing up in a society with both the technical knowledge and human expertise to address such problems. Drugs are available, but most teens are showing the good sense to ignore them, and if they falter, considerable resources are available to help them. Child abuse has become a major concern, but in large part seems to reflect heightened sensitivity toward a long-standing problem, one that is now finally being faced. Similarly, racial discrimination, violence against women, and violence generally are increasingly being recognized as existing, yet are increasingly being viewed as unacceptable.

Granted, it's disturbing to see an increase in the concern young people have about such personal issues as school, money, time, parents, friends, appearance, and the future. But, the number of experts available to provide guidance and counsel in every one of these areas has grown exponentially in recent decades. What's more, collectively we have greater financial resources than previous generations to help our young people deal with such issues.

The bottom line is that, yes, these are tough times to be a teenager. We are shaking them up well. But to an extent relatively few young people seem to be aware of, we have been crying wolf when we know full well that it's largely a ploy to get their attention. We can dance with the wolves if we so choose.

3. YOUNG PEOPLE HAVE NEVER HAD MORE CHOICES

In virtually every sphere of their lives, Canadian teenagers are surrounded by options. As they reflect on what they want to buy and how they want to look, where they want to go and how they want to spend their time, the name of the game is choice.

NICHE MARKETING

Newsweek correspondent Stephen Waldman observes that a typical North American supermarket had 9000 products in 1976; today it has more than 30,000. Specialty stores offer what seem like unlimited choices, whether one is in the market for videos or ice cream, socks or stuffed potatoes. Some cosmetic stores carry more than 1000 types and sizes of hair-care products. The number of TV channels has jumped from about six to 30-plus in less than 20 years. FM radio stations have doubled.[29] Further, in most parts of the country, young people find themselves wooed by endless restaurants, stores, radio and TV stations, theatres, individuals, and other companies and organizations.

Yet, at the same time, young people have never been fussier customers. We've already seen that their foremost personal concerns include not having enough money or enough time. Unlimited choices are being met with limited resources. The net result? Selective consumption.

Companies and consultants have been tuning in to the reality. Social and economic analyst Faith Popcorn uses the term "egonomics" to describe the phenomenon of individualized production and consumption. "Egonomics," she explains, "means simply this: there is profit to be reaped in providing for the consumer's need for personalization — whether it be in product concept, product design, 'customability,' or personal service." In egonomics, Popcorn says, the "I" takes centre stage: "Egonomics is niche marketing in the extreme . . . The marketer who enables each customer to feel unique will succeed." She points out that the trend can be seen everywhere — specialty magazines, cable television, customized fashion and furniture, specialized interest groups, and entertainment represent just a few examples.[30]

Marketing and communications consultant David Cravit points out that such individual-driven marketing is now common in Canada:

> *Every day, the consumer meets companies trying to respond, in ever more tightly focused ways, to highly individualized needs . . . There's a product that's just right for them. A magazine that's precisely tailored to their income, age, profession, hobby, phobia, you name it. . . . The marketplace screams at them: Focus. Specialize. Zero in.*[31]

Trends analysts John Naisbitt and Patricia Aburdene sum up the situation this way: "When the focus was on the institution, individuals got what suited the institution; everyone got the same thing. No more. With the rise of the individual," they maintain, "has come the primacy of the customer. It has been *said* for many years: The customer is king. Now it is true."[32]

Things are not about to ease up. As global economic competition intensifies over the next few decades, the choices will only accelerate. This in turn will heighten the selective-consumption mentality. The winners will be the products and activities young people define as the best.

For example, if the number of television offerings have been exploding in response to individual consumer tastes, newspapers can be expected to follow suit. The annual meeting of the Canadian Daily Newspapers Association in Toronto in the spring of 1992 heard the results of a major study carried out for Southam Inc. Consultant Len Kubas told the gathering:

> *Putting customers first is essential to our future. Give customers more of what they say they want and less of what you think they need. What's missing is whatever the people of a particular community think is missing.*[33]

The implications of such catering to consumer demand are intriguing, to say the least. We might end up with news that's more representative of what's happening across the country. We might also end up with the kinds of newspapers so popular in Britain, where staid offerings like *The Times* have been supplemented by a variety of tabloids, complete with the latest word on the local vicar and the two-headed dog. One thing is certain: we will have increasing choices.

A qualifier: in isolated rural areas of Canada, choice may still be largely a thing of the future. A 15-year-old girl from Inuvik, for example, reminds us, "In the NWT, we teenagers need more places to go and a whole lot more things to do." A classmate adds, "Teens party, do drugs, and have sex." A teen from Cranbrook, B.C., a community of about 10,000, comments:

> *We don't have anywhere to just hang out. Each town should have a cool place to hang out — a restaurant, dance club, a recreation centre, anything — where the cops aren't there if there are more than 10 people present.*

A 17-year-old from a small New Brunswick town says, "Many people here who are under age drink and use drugs (hashish and acid) on a regular basis. In most small communities there is nothing else to do — no hangout spots, arcades, etc."

Yet even in such geographical instances, the cultural mosaic is experienced in further ways.

MOSAIC MARKETING

Choices are hardly limited to the consumption of goods and services. As a direct result of our emphasizing the virtue of diversity in Canadian life, we have given legitimacy to what seems like an endless number of possibilities in virtually all areas of life.

We've already previewed some of them in talking about marriage and sex, along with religion and morality. Such flexibility of thought and life-style has been guaranteed in Canada's Charter of Rights and Freedoms. The multiple mosaics are not longer merely an ideal; they have been enshrined in law. Diversity of viewpoint and life-style has become the Canadian way. Ideally it should be appreciated; at minimum, tolerated.

So it is that today's 15- to 19-year-olds — 65 per cent strong — have come to accept the idea that what's right or wrong is a matter of personal opinion. In doing so, they are outdistancing Canadian adults, particularly older ones. The 1990 Project Canada national survey found that only 51 per cent of adults endorsed the same statement. These included 47 per cent of those older than 54, compared to 57 per cent of those younger than 35.

What's more, Canadian young people are outspoken about the appropriateness of many options. An 18-year-old woman from Halifax says that outside of such instances as murder, "decisions should be your own." A grade-10 student from the small community of Duncan, B.C., endorses the idea of all faiths getting equal merit. He adds, "I myself am not religious, but I won't judge other religions." A 15-year-old from Calgary, seemingly defying her Roman Catholic upbringing, argues that young people should have the right to choose, regardless of the outcomes of their choices:

> People who choose to use drugs, smoke, or drink shouldn't be hassled, because it's only themselves they are hurting.

Regarding censorship, a 17-year-old male from the small town of Seaforth, Ontario, says:

> Censorship is a law we don't need. Anyone should have the choice to watch what they want or listen to what they want.

With respect to sex, a 16-year-old girl from Victoria offers an interesting point of view.

I believe I have fairly old-fashioned values. However, I support my friends in their own moral decisions, which are usually well thought out. For example, I supported my friend's decision to go on the pill in case her boyfriend and her "got carried away."

Speaking about sex on the first date, a 17-year-old female from Bonaventure, Quebec, has this to say:

I don't believe it's my place to say whether someone should have sex on their first date — it's their decision. Even if it was myself, I still cannot answer this question because it depends on the other person and the situation.

And a 16-year-old female from Vancouver, commenting about sex before marriage, says:

People should be able to do what they want, if they can handle the responsibility or possible results. Whatever suits your fancy.

If some young people lack choices because of geographical isolation, others, it might be argued, lack choices because of the strong moral positions of their contexts. For example, one 16-year-old female who attends a Catholic school in a small Ontario town, has this to say:

I feel that schools should have condom machines. At least this way those who are sexually active will at least have the choice of using them and cutting down the risk of AIDS and other diseases. Also, sex education should be taught in Catholic and non-Catholic high schools. I know four people who got pregnant before they were sixteen. Isn't that telling you something?

A 15-year-old Muslim from a small community in southern Ontario, who says that having choices is very important to her, informs us she doesn't date because "my religion doesn't allow it." A 17-year-old from Halifax says, "I'm first-generation Lebanese and my parents don't let me date." She continues, "However, I would if I ever wanted to. I don't have a close relationship with my parents."

Certainly many groups and individuals in Canada are taking strong moral positions in a variety of areas. But beyond their specific contexts, the dominant cultural emphasis — sanctioned by the Charter of Rights, for example — is one of choice. One group's viewpoint must compete with an array of other viewpoints. A single priest's voice, a single mother's voice, a single interest group's voice, are all solo cries in a wilderness shared with the voices of television, friends, school, newspapers, movies, videos, and the like. Those who don't want condom machines, for example, find themselves in conflict with dominant cultural opinion. The results of a Gallup poll released in January 1991 found that 68 per cent of Canadians favour having condom-dispensing machines placed in high schools across the country. Roman Catholics (66 per cent) were just as likely as Protestants (65 per cent) to give their assent.[34]

We increase our freedom by widening our circles. If we don't like what one group says, we move on to another. We can do the same with individuals. The student in search of a condom need only move from the washroom of the school to the washroom of the nearby restaurant if he wants to experience choice.

MADE IN CANADA

Our post-industrial society has provided ever-increasing numbers of options as to how we can spend our money and time. But we're also members of a society that explicitly champions the free expression of viewpoint and behaviour. The early 1970s' declaration that Canada is a multicultural society has, over time, had a profound impact on Canadian life. Beyond sensitizing us to our variety of national backgrounds, the proclamation has helped to legitimize diverse ideas and life-styles. Multi*cultural*ism has evolved into multi*everything*ism.

Some time ago, the mosaic theme left its cultural group cradle. We now have not only a cultural mosaic but also a moral mosaic, a meaning-system mosaic, a family-structure mosaic, and a sexual mosaic, to mention just a few. Pluralism has come to pervade Canadian minds and Canadian institutions.[35] We have made diversity a national cause for celebration. A job-recruitment headline used a few years ago by IBM seems to summarize the citizen-recruitment guideline for Canada: "We're looking for great minds that don't think alike."[36]

The end result of all this is that today's teenagers, along with the rest of us, find themselves with unlimited choices in every sphere of their lives. When it comes to choices, no generation in Canadian history has ever had it so good.

Teenagers seem to like it that way. Almost eight in 10 place a high value on having choices, in sharp contrast to fewer than four in 10 who indicate truth is more than a personal matter. There are only minor variations in the valuing of choices as one travels from British Columbia to Newfoundland, visits communities of different sizes, or speaks to males and females, and whites and members of visible minorities.

But the differences are relative. *Choice* is the choice of most teenagers everywhere.

IMPORTANCE OF CHOICES AND MERIT OF PERSONAL OPINION		
In %s	
HAVING CHOICES	RIGHT-WRONG MATTER OF PERSONAL OPINION
"Very NB"	"Agree"
NATIONALLY	78	65
B.C.	82	68
Prairies	78	65
Ontario	78	67
Quebec	81	61
Atlantic	78	63
100,000-plus	79	64
99,000-10,000	84	63
under 10,000	77	67
Male	77	65
Female	82	65
White	80	64
Orientals	75	72
East Ind-Pak	73	67
Black	72	62
Native	71	78

4. YOUNG PEOPLE ARE EMBRACING THE JUST SOCIETY

Today's adolescents subscribe to the basic tenets of the "just society," which have been officially promoted by our major institutions since the 1960s. They have little patience with the overt racism, sexism, bigotry, and inequality that were once widespread.

Most 15- to 19-year-olds began school around 1980. They have grown up with the ideals of bilingualism, multiculturalism, and the equality of all Canadians. As the first "Charter Generation," they have been aware that the 1982 Constitution guarantees the rights of all people, regardless of their gender, race, ethnicity, religion, physical characteristics, or sexual orientation. They have watched native people gain increasing recognition in their efforts to achieve self-government and join the discussions about a new Constitution and a new Canada. Today's teens also have grown up at a time of unprecedented concern with the environment. They have been taught that a just and fair society is one that not only shows concern for all people now, but for generations to come.

In the language of Faith Popcorn, our youths are into S.O.S. — Save Our Society. She maintains that the "question of the survival of the world is *the* issue for this soon-to-take-over generation. It unites them. It politicizes them. It scares them to death." The trend, she says, represents the "effort that contributes to making the 90s our first truly responsible decade: the Decency Decade." Its emphases include ethics and the environment.[37]

NO SHORTAGE OF ISSUES

The wide range of just-society issues regarded as important by young people can be seen in comments such as these from a Port Hardy, B.C., 15-year-old, who signs her remarks, "A Concerned Student":

> *The government must pay off the national debt in order to concentrate on important federal spending (i.e., health care, education, recycling programs). The government must also come to agreement with the natives over land claims and not sell off parts of the country to foreign investors. The government must also heed the people's warnings on environmental disasters.*

The just-society emphases are apparent in the attitudes of today's young people in relationship both to adults and to their teenage counterparts in the early 80s.

BILINGUALISM AND MULTICULTURALISM

At a time when official bilingualism is being seriously questioned in English-speaking Canada and is being viewed as increasingly irrelevant in Quebec, almost 65 per cent of teenagers continue to support the policy. While the level of support has slipped from the time of the 1984 survey, it still exceeds the current 53 per cent level of adults. A Gallup poll released in March of 1992, found that 64 per cent of Canadian adults believe the bilingualism program has been a failure, including 61 per cent of Quebecers, 74 per cent of the people in B.C., 68 per cent in Ontario, 63 per cent in the Prairies, and 42 per cent of residents in the Atlantic region.[38]

Endorsement of the mosaic model for dealing with Canadian cultural-group diversity, as opposed to the melting-pot or assimilation-ist model, is also slipping, according to survey data and extensive information generated by the Spicer Commission. One 16-year-old Winnipeg student has this to say:

> *We should become a melting-pot society. We should first be Canadians, not Ukrainians or whatever. Quebec, then, will also learn that being a Cana-dian is a first priority, rather than being French Canadian. We should work on pulling our country together, not apart.*

A Halifax 17-year-old, who feels that groups such as black and natives do not have enough power in Canadian affairs, nonetheless complains that "the reason we have all the problems we do is because our government doesn't have the guts to *trash* multiculturalism."

Still, support for the mosaic ideal is slightly greater among young people (59 per cent) than adults (54 per cent). A grade-12 Jewish student, also from Nova Scotia, comments, "People who want to keep their heritage should. They should not have to give up their culture."

A reflective grade-11 student from Calgary is among those who feels multiculturalism is a plus for Canada:

> *I go to a very "white" school where multiculturalism isn't really played up, which is really disappointing. I think that one way to slow down prejudice is to learn the differences between cultures. But in order to do this, you need an environment that includes many nationalities. My mom teaches at a school which is very multicultural, and opens doors for a lot of new learning about self, others, and country. Global awareness is a good thing. We are all part of one world, instead of a country, province, city, or district.*

Variations Among teenagers, support for two official languages re-mains highest in Quebec at 77 per cent but in light of the province's ambivalent relationship to Canada, has dropped significantly from 86 per cent in 1980. Elsewhere, endorsement of bilingualism stands at about 60 per cent, down from about 65 per cent a decade ago. Conversely, support for the mosaic model is lowest in Quebec at about 50 per cent, compared to 60 per cent in each of the other four regions.

Understandably, teens from visible minorities (70 per cent) are considerably more likely than whites (58 per cent) to endorse the mosaic idea. More females than males tend to support both policies.

ATTITUDES TOWARD BILINGUALISM, THE MOSAIC, WOMEN, AND MINORITIES		
In %'s		
	TEENS	ADULTS
	1984	1992	1990
FAVOUR			
Bilingualism	71	66	53
Mosaic model	74	59	54
TOO LITTLE POWER			
Natives	53	52	50
Women	48	53	55
Blacks	42	54	43
VERY SERIOUS			
Racial discrimination	22	59	16
Unequal treatment of women	15	41	21

WOMEN AND MINORITIES

Beyond the controversial bilingualism and multiculturalism issues, teenagers solidly support the ideals of fairness and equality in greater numbers than they did in 1984, and on a level equal to or superior to that of adults.

More than one in two teenagers maintain that women, natives, and blacks do not have enough power in the nation's affairs. Roughly the same proportion say that women continue to experience discrimination and that the elimination of racism needs to be a top priority of the government. One in three young people also indicate that the resolution of native land claims should be given high priority. Among them is a 17-year-old male native from Inuvik who says, "We have to recognize native people in the country. Give us our deserved respect. Now!"

An 18-year-old female from Windsor illustrates the disdain that many young people have for discrimination:

> *I feel that grade-school children should be taught more about discrimination and the fact that we all are equal as human beings — regardless of what we do or what we become.*

A 17-year-old male from Pitt Meadows, British Columbia, comments, "As I see it, everyone is equal, regardless of their colour, culture, language, or religion." In the words of one 17-year-old New Brunswick female, "We have more to be worried about than the colour of people's skin." A grade-10 student from Calgary points out, "If we can't treat everyone with equality and respect, then how are we going to solve our other problems?"

A woman of the same age, who emigrated from Finland when she was a child, agrees: "The native people have been treated disrespectfully, and since Canada is really their country, we have to help them obtain the life they want."

And a grade-12 Asian student from Burnaby, B.C., who regards racial discrimination as a very serious problem, comments, "I'm getting sick and tired of racial discrimination. Let's get rid of it."

This is hardly to suggest that bigotry is a thing of the past among Canada's youth. The following comments of adolescents from Victoria to St. John's speak for themselves:

- It isn't fair that some of the taxpayers' dollars go to the natives. It was over a hundred years ago that we took the land from them. Natives should get off their asses and get a job.
- I'm not racist, but I think that if people move here they should change to our ways. Like no turbans on police officers, etc. If they want to do that, then they can stay in Pakistan.
- I'd like to say that blacks should be put on a boat and sent back to Africa. They have more rights than whites. Every time something happens they scream racism. Niggers shouldn't have special privileges.
- I don't think Canada should allow so many people to immigrate here every year. They take over *our* jobs and will probably eventually take over.

The just society is still in the making.

Variations Young people's concern for women tends to be somewhat greater in B.C. than elsewhere. The sense that natives and blacks have insufficient power is lowest in Quebec, yet there is little difference by region in the assertion that racial discrimination is a serious problem that requires government attention. Although teens from visible minorities are more inclined than whites to express concern about discrimination, they are generally not inclined to be any more supportive of women than whites are. In fact, Asians are noticeably less supportive.

The category that stands out as consistently different? Young women. Regardless of region, gender, or racial origin, they're more likely than males to express concern not only about women, but about all cultural minorities. Further, they are far more inclined than males to call for government responses. We regard this as an important pattern, and will examine it in detail in chapter three.

	BLACKS	WOMEN	NAT- IVES	ORIEN- TALS	E. IND- PAK	JEWS	AVG
PERCEPTION OF INADEQUATE POWER							
% Indicating Have "Too Little Power" in Nation's Affairs							
NATIONALLY	54	53	52	33	30	26	41
Female	60	69	56	37	32	30	47
Male	48	36	49	30	27	22	35
Blacks	83	58	73	49	52	40	59
Natives	68	53	73	52	46	42	56
E. Ind-Pak	54	47	72	42	60	32	51
Orientals	44	45	54	57	34	25	43
Whites	54	53	51	31	27	26	40

ABUSE AND VIOLENCE

Canada's teenagers, led by females, also express concern about a variety of other justice issues, including child abuse and violence against women. In the past decade, the proportion of young people who have regarded such areas as serious problems has jumped significantly, easily surpassing current adult levels. Young people are increasingly accepting the idea that a just Canada is a country where everyone is safe from violence and exploitation. In the succinct words of one 16-year-old from rural Quebec, "Violence shouldn't exist. What's the point?" Such an ideal means that blatant and widespread abuses, most frequently involving children and women, must be eradicated.

One 17-year-old woman from southern Ontario expresses things this way:

I think the government or the police or whoever has to do something about sexual assault, because many girls and women have gotten to the point where they feel no man can be trusted. It's scary to walk down the street.

Variations Concern about violence against women, along with child abuse, differs little by region or race. Both issues, however, are disproportionately a concern of young females rather than males. It's not clear why this should continue to be the case among justice-minded teenagers in the 1990s. We will return to the issue shortly.

CONCERN ABOUT CHILD ABUSE AND VIOLENCE AGAINST WOMEN			
% Viewing as "Very Serious"			
	TEENS		ADULTS
	1984	1992	1990
CHILD ABUSE	50	64	50
Females	58	74	62
Males	43	53	39
VIOLENCE AGAINST WOMEN	46	58	38
Females	55	70	48
Males	36	44	28

THE ENVIRONMENT

Today's teenagers also have a heightened awareness of environmental responsibility, personally, nationally, and globally. Concern has jumped markedly since 1984 and, at close to 70 per cent, well exceeds the 53 per cent of adults.

A 17-year-old from Belle River, Ontario, sums up the hopes and even expectations of many: "I want my children to live in a clean, pollution-free environment." A 15-year-old female from Newcastle, New Brunswick, sees the environmental crisis as extremely immediate: "Our grandchildren may never see trees." A 17-year-old from Lawn, Newfoundland, offers these thoughts about animals:

Although I live in Newfoundland and live off the sea, I feel very concerned when I see animals being caught and killed in their nets — or when I see an animal abused or mistreated in any way. I hope in some way to help the animals of the world because it is not our world. It belongs to the animals too. If animals are destroyed, then the world will be destroyed.

One 16-year-old female, a grade-11 student living in Cranbrook, B.C., illustrates the extent to which some students are concerned about environmental issues:

I would like, in my lifetime, to see: the Halbran Valley preserved as a national park, world peace, the Arab countries settling their disputes, disarmament of all nations, the Bornea, Sarawak, rainforest saved, and the Penan people restored to their rightful place in the Sarawak forests, rainforests given more protection, laws made to prevent oil spills and such disasters, acceptance of all different races in the world, and harmony between the races, an end to all our endless pollution problems, protection made for all species of dolphins, and people striving to gain a greater understanding of these wonderful creatures, world practices improved so that my children will inherit a healthy, beautiful planet.

Variations As with many other issues, concern about the environment varies little by region or race. However, once again, more females than males express both interest and alarm.

TRANSMITTING THE JUSTICE THEME

Since the 1960s, we have greatly increased our attempts to create a more just and fair society. The efforts of the federal government in the form of policies and programs associated with bilingualism, multiculturalism, and the Charter of Rights and Freedoms, have played a central role. We also have shared in a global culture where, in the words of trends analysts John Naisbitt and Patricia Aburdene, "The world's preoccupation with defence and the Cold War . . . is being replaced by concern about the destruction of our natural environment, now our most important common problem."[39]

Such emphases have been felt throughout Canadian society, reinforced by all our major institutions, notably the school, the media, and religion. Consequently, we have reared a generation of teenagers for whom the "just society" is something of a given. There is almost an impatience with things that seem to be unfair and unhealthy, personally and socially. As one 16-year-old female from Thompson, Manitoba, puts it, "The Canadian government needs to take care of the environment, and clean up native relations and relations with Quebec." This is not for a moment to suggest that racism, sexism, and bigotry belong to history. But it is to say that, increasingly, such attitudes and behaviour officially have no place in Canada. As one 18-year-old female from Granby, Quebec, says, "I believe that our generation will pay more attention to nature and people than you have."

5. YOUNG PEOPLE HAVE NEVER HAD GREATER EXPECTATIONS

Today's teenagers, along with their 80s' counterparts, have been able to experience a quality of life probably unmatched in Canadian history. As a result, they expect their good fortunes to continue; if anything, most expect to improve on the experiences of the parents. Those who have not shared in those fortunes aspire to do so.

DREAMING BIG

According to the 1992 national survey:

- More than 60 per cent expect to graduate from university, although only about 10 per cent of their parents were graduates.
- Close to 85 per cent expect to get the job they want after they graduate.
- Some 75 per cent expect to be more financially comfortable than their parents.
- More than 95 per cent expect to own their own homes.
- Almost 75 per cent expect to travel extensively outside Canada.
- Just 41 per cent expect to have to work overtime to get ahead.
- About 85 per cent expect to stay with the same person for life.

Such expectations are the result of young people sharing in the significant intergenerational gains of their parents, gains that have been particularly visible in the past two decades.

It worked this way. The parents of teens in the 80s were born during the 40s and 50s, your two authors among them. They themselves experienced their teen years in the late 50s and early 60s — in the so-called "happy days." It was a time when Canada experienced significant economic growth. Universities expanded dramatically; enrolments skyrocketed.

Like many others back then, in the light of our parents' relatively low incomes and educations, we ourselves had fairly modest aspirations. But with minimal effort, we also had the possibility of experiencing substantial intergenerational gains. In the words of University of Toronto economist-futurist David Foot, our age cohort has had "a fairly charmed life." Many were rapidly promoted and laid claim to real estate when it was cheap.[40]

And so we, like many others our age, quite easily exceeded our parents' educational levels, as well as their incomes. For our offspring, the teens of the 80s, those gains translated into solid middle class life-styles. They knew nothing less.

The teenagers of the 90s for the most part were children of parents who were born a decade later, in the 50s. Many have become at least as affluent and well educated as those of us who were born a decade earlier. The life-style result is that their teenage offspring are likewise experiencing a comfortable existence, where higher education is both appreciated and anticipated.

People who comment that these are tough times to be a teenager tend to lose sight of the fact that collectively, from a material point of view, teenagers probably have never had it better. The standard of living has been high. Education has been valued. Travel has been common. Good and lasting relationships have been viewed as possible. What our grandparents felt they needed and we felt we wanted, our offspring feel they deserve.

It all adds up to extremely high expectations.

EXPECTATIONS OF TEENAGERS BY REGION AND GENDER

"Do you expect to . . ."

% Yes

	NAT	BC	PR	ON	QUE	ATL	M	F
Get the job you want when you graduate	83	75	76	83	92	77	84	82
Own your own home	96	95	96	96	96	77	96	95
Be more financially secure than parents	77	77	78	80	73	77	81	74
Have to work overtime to get ahead	41	49	40	41	37	71	43	39
Travel extensively outside of Canada	73	77	70	70	78	71	69	75
Stay with the same partner for life	86	81	87	87	88	85	84	89

BUT WHAT ABOUT CULTURAL MINORITIES?

The Canadian dream is highly pervasive, shared by whites and members of visible minorities alike. Young people who haven't yet adequately shared in economic prosperity, higher education, and good jobs nonetheless are well aware of what they are missing. One cannot live in our society without fairly quickly becoming aware of one's relative success or relative deprivation.

On the heels of the May 1992 Toronto Yonge Street riots, much was said about the fact that blacks and other disprivileged groups, including poor whites, increasingly are constituting an "underclass" that has lost all hope of sharing in the good things Canadian society has to offer. Frustration and hostility, said many observers, are rampant among Canadian youth. Such ideas were being liberally tossed about, as evidenced by Toronto papers and Canadian Press releases in the week following the riot. Even a program like CBC's *Morningside* could not resist the temptation of such an interpretation.[41]

Our findings show little support for such widespread despair. Rather than dreaming less, young blacks — beyond those who went on the rampage in Toronto — proportionately have some of the highest expectations in the country. Hopes are also very high among teens of east Indian and Pakistani backgrounds, as well as those from other Asian countries. While young native people are somewhat less inclined to express high expectations, some three in four nonetheless expect both to get the job they want when they graduate and eventually be more financially comfortable than their parents.

The idealistic words of this 16-year-old male from Richmond, B.C., seem to express what many Canadian young people believe: "In this country, I feel that anyone of any race, sex, or sexuality can achieve power if they can do the job."

EXPECTATIONS BY RACE		
"Do you expect to . . ."		
% Indicating "Yes"		
	Get the Job You Want when You Graduate	Be More Financially Comfortable than Your Parents
NATIONALLY	83	77
Blacks	86	90
E. Ind./Pakistanis	83	78
Whites	83	76
Orientals	81	89
Natives	80	79

BUT HASN'T REALITY DIMINISHED THE DREAMS?

Surely, one would think, the recognition of their parents' fairly high achievements is intimidating to many young people. They know it will be tough to outdo dad and mom. As if that weren't enough, the current realities of tough economic times, university enrolment limits, high housing prices, and the rate of divorce are bringing teenagers down to earth.

There is little sign that such grounding is taking place. Yes, there are some young people who are anxious. One grade-11 student from a small central Alberta community comments:

> *I think the government is not aware of what teens are going through. It is so hard for us now, because we all have to get jobs in order to get money so we can go to college or university. Also, the college/university marks are so high that it is hard to get in, and once you get in, the cost of living is so high that many of us teens drop out, and then cannot find a job.*

She appears, however, to be in the minority. In the face of current economic turbulence in much of Canada, young people cling to the idea that they can be the exceptions to any bad-news rule:

- No less than 75 per cent agree with the statement, "Anyone who works hard will rise to the top" — in sharp contrast to only 48 per cent of adults.
- They don't just hope to find work; they're demanding. Says one 16-year-old from Winnipeg, "You tell Mulroney to get this country in order, 'cause I want a job when I get out of school."
- Some 90 per cent say that they have a *right* to the kind of work for which their education has prepared them.
- Even 43 per cent think that the national debt will be paid off in their lifetimes!

As we have seen, idealism is also found in the case of marriage. The 86 per cent of teens who say they expect to stay with the same person for life includes 78 per cent of young people from homes where parents have divorced or separated. The pain and strain associated with her parents' marriage are readily evident in the words of this 16-year-old girl from Wolfville, Nova Scotia:

> *Some people do not know what it feels like to go through a divorce, especially when you are only 10 years old. Maybe you guys should do a survey on all those who have a divorced family and what it feels like. This would allow the government and others to understand the pain, the anguish, the hurt, the hate, and the confusion created by divorce.*

The impact of such an experience on her dreams? She expects to stay with the same partner for life.

Not even the fact that Canada's future is in question dulls the hopes and dreams of young Canadians. True, it's a factor that has to be taken into consideration as they look ahead. But it isn't doing very much to alter their dreams and expectations. Although four in five acknowledge that the country's uncertain future makes it hard for them to plan ahead, their expectations have not exactly been cut back. Canada's future might be in question. But theirs is not. A 16-year-old male from Chipman, New Brunswick, is explicit. Asked to use one word to describe the future, he responded, "Canada's — shaky; mine — confident." He appears to be the rule rather than the exception.

Undaunted by their parents' achievements, current realities, and even the ambiguous future of the country, today's young people intend to fare at least as well as their parents, and hopefully better.

DREAM ALONG WITH US . . .

In view of the relative success many of us have known, we have tended to assume that our sons and daughters will emulate us. It's more than a hope; it's an expectation of the variety, "If we did it, they should be able to do it, too. If anything, there's no reason they can't do even better."

Educationally, many of us who are university graduates expect the same of our children. Anything less is almost an embarrassment. The prospect that our offspring won't also have solid incomes is simply not acceptable to us.

We as parents, educators, politicians, members of the media, and others in contact with youth, have tended to cultivate the idea that hard work will pay off, that good relationships are attainable, that there are no limits to what can be achieved.

We've done our work well. Lo and behold, today's young people have lofty expectations. They believe they will at least match our socio-economic achievements. They plan to improve on many of our relational experiences. They are dreaming and dreaming big.

These findings should send an important message to Canadian adults. There is much to the old adage that "Where there's hope, there's life." Many a proverb has carried the message of the import-ance of having dreams and goals toward which we can direct our energies. The very essence of mental health includes the idea that people who cope well with life are able to set goals, establish means, and get on with putting the two together.

Dreams are important. They can motivate, stimulate, inspire. They may well provide an index of a nation's health and an individual's possibilities. These days, it's easier for an American than an Iraqi to hold a dream, easier for a Canadian than a Russian.

But if dreams are unattainable, they can have the effect of demoralizing individuals and creating national unrest, precisely because what people hope for is beyond their grasp. Hitching wagons to stars that don't exist has the inglorious effect of immobilizing wagons and upsetting the passengers. There's a sobering possibility that this may well be the first generation in Canadian history that will have to settle for less than their parents.

In retrospect, we probably shouldn't have done such a thorough job of raising expectations. The truth is we ourselves have become a bit intimidated by the future, because we aren't exactly sure what it holds for us anymore. There are lots of uncertainties and doubts that have dampened much of our own uninhibited youthful enthusiasm. But it's too late to recant. Having helped to instil the hopes, we now have the responsibility of helping teenagers to realize them. This is not a time for debilitating cynicism, uninspiring negativism, or excessive realism. Before asking young people to relinquish their dreams, we need to do everything in our power to make them come true.

3

TWO DISTINCT DEPARTURES

Two major goals of the Trudeau years and beyond have been to bring Quebec and the rest of the country together, and to achieve equality for women. The survey findings indicate, however, that neither goal has yet been reached.

The observation of a grade-12 student from Burnaby, B.C., that "Quebec shouldn't be granted distinct society status because the only difference is that they speak French" simply is not true. Quebec remains both distinct and detached. Likewise, some significant and troubling differences by gender are persisting into the 90s, suggesting that equality is still a good distance away.

QUEBEC

The origins of Quebec's ongoing cultural distinctiveness are hardly mysterious. Young people growing up in the province find that close to 95 per cent of the people are either bilingual (59 per cent) or speak only French (35 per cent). Under six per cent speak English only, *down* from 12 per cent thirty years ago. Some 70 per cent of the residents of Montreal cite French as their mother tongue; elsewhere the figure is over 95 per cent.

Language transmits culture, and for most Quebecers, the French language has been passing on a culture that is decidedly Québécois — a French-rooted culture that has been reworked on this side of the Atlantic for close to 400 years.

Quebec's emergence in the 1960s from a past dominated by the Roman Catholic Church brought with it renewed concern for the protection of its culture. Such anxiety, along with the more general concern about control over its own affairs, was reflected in the election of the separatist Parti Québécois in 1976, the subsequent 1980 referendum on separation, and the resurgence of the Parti Québécois in recent years. The desire for cultural autonomy and appropriate political power has resulted in accelerated tension between Quebec and Ottawa, as well as between Quebec and the other nine provinces.

A DISTINCT SOCIETY

Beyond political rhetoric, Quebec's uniqueness can readily be seen in the province's young people of the 90s — their flexible approach to life, their sense of community, and their intense nationalism.

A DISTINCT LIFE-STYLE

When it comes to the living out of life, the Quebec outlook seems to be one of "Do what you're comfortable with." Such a posture can be seen in young people's attitudes toward sexuality and family life, as well as their view of the place of religion.

Quebec teens, be they francophones or anglophones,[1] are far more open than teens elsewhere in the country to premarital sex and homosexuality. A slightly higher proportion further maintain that women should have the option of a legal abortion in situations where rape, for example, is involved.

While family life is valued as highly as anywhere else, and relationships with family members are perhaps enjoyed even more highly, marriage as such is increasingly seen as optional, even when a couple want to have children. As we saw earlier, in Quebec, 79 per cent of teens plan to marry, slightly below the national average. Yet a slightly higher proportion, 87 per cent, plan to have children. A nation-leading 87 per cent of Quebec teens — versus 64 per cent elsewhere — approve of couples having children without being married. Here francophones (88 per cent) break with the province's anglophones, who in turn have an endorsement level (about 70 per cent) that mirrors "English Canada."

In expressing such thoughts, young Quebecers are simply following in the footsteps of adults now in their 20s and 30s. In 1990, Quebec's percentage of common-law unions among adults was the highest in the country (13 per cent), well above the next-closest provinces.[2] And in the same year, the parents of almost one in two first-borns in Quebec were unmarried.[3]

This is not to say that Quebec flexibility lacks for breaking points. Extramarital sex, for example, is considered inappropriate by about 90 per cent — the same as elsewhere. Abortion on demand is rejected by a majority of close to 60 per cent — also the same as elsewhere.

But overall, there seems to be a life-style flexibility in Quebec greater than that found in the other provinces, including, the analyses have found, much-heralded "live life as you please" British Columbia. What's more, comparisons with 1984 indicate that, if anything, the "life-style laissez-faire" outlook is increasing rather than diminishing.

Given their flexible views on sex and family life, it should not be surprising to learn that Quebecers, young and old, tend to allow the Roman Catholic Church — or any other religious group — to play only a highly specialized role in their lives. They provide a classic example of Canadians who, to use a phrase from *Fragmented Gods*, are into *religion à la carte*.[4] While the pattern characterizes the entire country, it is particularly pronounced in Quebec.

Teenagers there don't tend to cut their ties completely with organized religion. Some 81 per cent continue to identify with Roman Catholicism, Protestantism, and other faiths. These include 84 per cent of Quebec teens who've come out of Roman Catholic homes. Further, the 1988 survey found that some 85 to 90 per cent say they plan to turn to religious groups for weddings, baptisms, and funerals. Both the identification and rites-of-passage levels are somewhat higher than those for young people in the rest of the country.

But while they don't totally discard organized religion, Quebec youth tend to want their ties to be very limited. A mere five per cent say religious group involvement is very important to them, compared to 12 per cent in the rest of Canada. Just 10 per cent are attending religious services on a weekly basis, as opposed to 21 per cent of teens elsewhere. Further, only 18 per cent say they are committed to a religion (Christianity, 16 per cent; other faiths, two per cent), somewhat less than the 25 per cent level of other regions. Quebec's anglophone teens exhibit slightly higher attendance (14 per cent) and commitment (21 per cent) levels than francophones.

Despite the well-known position of the Roman Catholic Church on premarital sex, homosexuality, abortion, and parenthood outside marriage, even active attendees defy the church to an extent unmatched in the rest of the country. Quebec culture appears to be overriding religion in contributing to a life-style that flies in the face of the church's teachings. A sampling of comments tells the story so characteristic of Quebec francophones:

- I go to mass but I'm not interested. — *a 15-year-old male from the small community of Saint-Martin, who attends weekly with his Roman Catholic parents, yet describes himself as having no religious preference*
- I believe in a universal God who I respect. But I don't do anything for him. — *a 17-year-old female from Quebec City, who attends Roman Catholic services once a year or less*
- I consider myself a Christian, but I don't practise. — *a 17-year-old Montreal male, who describes himself as a Roman Catholic and attends once a year or less*

These findings suggest that Quebec young people — as with Quebec adults — tend to have a very flexible, situational approach to life. The style, not exclusive to Quebec, appears far more common there than elsewhere.

VIEWS OF SEX AND FAMILY: FRANCOPHONES, ANGLOPHONES, ACTIVE RCs*					
% Approving					
	QUEBEC Franco	Anglo	REST CANADA	QUEBEC RCs	REST RCs
Premarital sex: love	94	91	85	83	80
Premarital sex: like	91	66	56	78	39
Homosexual rights	83	83	68	84	78
Homosexual relations	55	49	33	43	27
Extramarital sex	12	9	9	5	3
Abortion: rape involved	94	92	86	86	72
Abortion: for any reason	40	45	41	20	16
Unmarried couple living together	95	90	87	83	80
Children without being married	88	71	65	70	58

*Attend religious services 2-3 times a month or more.

A DISTINCT SENSE OF COMMUNITY

Quebec teens, particularly francophones, exhibit a pronounced tendency to value relationships. They also have what social scientists refer to as "a conscious of kind," summed up in this much-quoted observation of René Lévesque.

> We are Québécois. What that means first and foremost — and if need be, all that it means — is that we are attached to this one corner of the earth where we can be completely ourselves; this Quebec, the only place where we have the unmistakable feeling that "here we can be really at home." Being ourselves is essentially a matter of keeping and developing a personality that has survived for three and a half centuries.[5]

In larger numbers than in other regions, they report receiving high levels of enjoyment from family members — mothers, fathers, siblings, and grandparents. They are also less inclined to highly value being by themselves. Consistent with such patterns, young people in Quebec tend to place less importance than other teens on such individualistic traits as freedom, success, a comfortable life, and recognition. If anything, since 1984, Quebec teens have come to value relational traits even more highly than individual characteristics.

Differences are pronounced, not only between Quebec and the rest of the country, but between the province's francophones and anglophones — providing strong support for the distinctive emphasis on community that characterizes the Québécois.

Family life may have changed rather dramatically from what Quebec knew in the pre-1960s. That era of early marriages, large families, and few divorces belongs to history. But the legacy of the centrality of the family specifically, and the importance of social ties generally, clearly lives on.

As well, Quebec young people are much more positive than other teenagers about the immediate society in which they live. They are considerably less critical, for example, of their major institutions. They show much more confidence than their counterparts elsewhere in the school, the media, and the police, and are no more critical of government and religion than other young people. Consistent with our argument, confidence in institutions is considerably higher among the province's francophones than anglophones.

"Consciousness of kind" is further reflected in what Quebecers regard as their favourites and heroes. In sharp contrast to young people elsewhere, the heroes of Quebec teens tend to be primarily Canadian and, more precisely, *French* Canadian. Once more, the

IMPORTANCE OF GROUP LIFE					
In %'s					
	QUEBEC		REST CANADA		QUEBEC
	1992	1984	1992	1984	Franco Anglo[*]
HIGHLY ENJOY						
Your mother	78	83	64	76	80	69
Your father	70	75	57	69	71	64
Brother(s) or sister(s)	64	57	53	52	65	58
Grandparent(s)	52	58	47	55	55	41
Being by yourself	33	–	50	–	29	46
HIGHLY VALUE						
Freedom	81	81	87	86	79	88
Success in what you do	66	75	79	80	62	83
A comfortable life	62	68	72	82	59	74
HIGH LEVEL OF CONFIDENCE						
The Schools	75	74	64	65	80	58
The Police	71	72	69	78	77	47
Television	71	69	57	53	77	45
Religious Organizations	35	61	41	62	35	37
Your Provincial Government	33	41	32	37	37	18
The Federal Government	27	47	27	36	28	24

contrast between Quebec's francophone and anglophone teenagers is striking: Quebec anglophones tend to resemble their linguistic cousins in the rest of Canada, while Quebec francophones are distinct. It doesn't matter whether we are talking politicians or TV programs or athletes or movie stars.

Unlike teens in the other regions and anglophones in Quebec, the province's francophones do not take their lead from the Americans in determining what has real worth. They pretty much decide on their own terms if something is best or someone is a star. Therein lies another footnote for entrepreneurs — like the owners of the Canadian Football League — who want to succeed in Quebec: the Quécécois need to be given the opportunity to create their own winners and superstars, rather than having them parachuted in from English Canada or the United States.

Young francophone Quebecers act increasingly appreciative and supportive of their media, capable as the media are of relating to them in French. Confidence in the television industry, for example, has jumped about 10 per cent since 1984. When adults across Canada were asked by Gallup in early 1992 if they favoured or opposed implementing regulations that would increase the amount of Canadian content on Canadian radio stations, 53 per cent said yes. In Quebec, the figure was 64 per cent, second only to the Atlantic provinces (70 per cent), and well ahead of Ontario (56 per cent) and the West (52 per cent). In Montreal, 67 per cent approved, compared to 59 per cent in Toronto.[6]

Regarding television, journalist Peter Black writes that, because Quebec "is a relatively small and culturally independent society, television fiction and reality often intertwine." Noting that Quebecers are Canada's top TV fans, Black points out that "Quebec television productions strike chords of cultural identification to a degree seldom experienced in the rest of Canada — 'Anne of Green Gables' and 'The Beachcombers' notwithstanding." The link between Quebec life and television fiction, as seen in such programs as "Les Filles de Caleb" and, more recently, "Scoop," has been dubbed by *Le Devoir* journalist Nathalie Petrowski as "realfiction." She proclaims that "Quebec is on the way to becoming not a distinct society but a television show."[7]

	FAVOURITES			
	% Citing Canadian			
	QUEBEC	REST OF CANADA	QUEBEC FRANCO	QUEBEC ANGLO
TV Newsperson	85	65	93	65
Politician	82	69	88	68
Pro Sports Team	70	48	73	26
TV Program	62	10	74	10
Pro Athlete	52	38	57	38
Singer or Group	29	12	32	12
Movie Star	25	8	28	8
World Leader	12	4	14	4
Author	10	5	12	5

Sports also tell us much about culture. In Quebec, team loyalties in hockey say a great deal about sense of community. Outside Quebec, teens and adults are inclined to cite their own teams as their favourites — B.C. residents, the Canucks; people on the Prairies, the Oilers, Flames, and Jets; in Ontario, many like the Maple Leafs. But they also cite other teams in large numbers. Ontario teens, for example, growing up with Leaf teams that have been less than awesome, are even inclined to prefer the Canadiens over Toronto.

In Quebec, however, the tendency is to cite the Canadiens and, to a lesser extent, the Nordiques — or no team at all. The pattern in baseball is similar: it's either the Expos or nobody.

Such findings reflect more than simply favourite sports teams: they say much about the social integration or cohesiveness that characterizes regions of the country. The Montreal Canadiens are not popular in Quebec simply because they are a good hockey team. Their nickname, the Habs, tells the story of a roster that historically has been heavily French Canadian. More than just a legendary hockey club, the Canadiens represent Quebec to the rest of the world. Their latest coach, Jacques Demers, explaining to his anglophone wife why he would renege on both a newly signed four-year contract as a colour commentator — not to mention his vow to never coach again — is said to have exclaimed, "But honey, they're not just a hockey team, they're *Les Canadiens!*"[8]

HOCKEY FAVOURITES OF TEENS AND BASEBALL FAVOURITES OF ADULTS[*]									
Top Three in %'s									
QUEBEC		B.C.		PRAIRIES		ONTARIO		ATLANTIC	
Canadiens	78	Canucks	61	Oilers	28	Canadiens	30	Canadiens	47
Nordiques	12	Flames	9	Flames	24	Leafs	19	Bruins	12
Bruins	5	Canadiens	7	Kings	13	Kings	14	Oilers	11
Others	5	Others	23	Others	35	Others	37	Others	30
Expos	93	Jays	69	Jays	74	Jays	89	Jays	71
Tigers	1	Expos	10	Expos	8	Expos	5	Expos	24
Jays	<7	Indians	7	Reds	4	Red Sox	1	Pirates	2
Others	6	Others	14	Others	14	Others	5	Others	3

*Adult source: (Project Can90).

And so it is that the ambiguous future of the province has implications well beyond the obvious political and economic realms. One avid sports fan from Montreal envisions that separation will bring about better things for the province's puck stars:

I want Quebec to be independent so that hockey players from Quebec will have a better chance to play in the National Hockey League.

A 15-year-old male from a small community, however, isn't so sure:

I am worried about what will happen to me in the future, and what will happen to Quebec, to the environment, to the economy, and to the marvellous world of sports.

A DISTINCT NATIONALISM

It's a statement that could come from only one province. Few teens from B.C., Alberta, Ontario, or Nova Scotia would think to say that their country is anything but Canada. But the words of this 16-year-old male from Chicoutimi seem predictable: "My language is French and my country is Quebec."

Nationalism is hardly new to Quebec. Since at least Confederation, nationalism as an ideology has been popular in the province. Before and during the 1950s, however, it tended to be conservative, oriented toward preserving the past.[9] With the 1960s came a new emphasis on modernization, led by new provincial intervention in areas including education, health, and welfare. Around the same time, as sociologist Marcel Rioux of the University of Montreal observed, French Canadians in Quebec ceased to see themselves as an ethnic community, and began to view themselves as an industrial society.[10]

Young Quebec francophones are conscious of the fact that their beloved Québécois culture is an endangered species in an English-speaking world. That culture is no less threatened by the possible influx of allegedly neutral "allophones" — those newcomers whose mother tongue is neither English nor French. "If the government does not change its immigration policy," says one 15-year-old from Laval, "the country will be populated by immigrants only." As one 17-year-old female from St. Hubert pessimistically puts it, "We have no more culture, tradition, legend, or respect. What's more, our language and family life are in danger." Blatant signs of the repudiation of Québécois culture obviously receive a hostile reaction. The infamous flag-stomping that took place in Brockville in 1990 became a rallying point for nationalists. The memory is still fresh for this 18-year-old woman from St.-Jean-sur-Richelieu who says, "I hope that the English will acknowledge that we are different and never again trample on our flag."

There has been nothing subtle about the provincial government's attempts, since at least the mid-70s, to ensure that Québécois culture not only survives but flourishes in the face of a lower birthrate, immigration, and the influence of anglo-American culture. Provincial legislation has attempted to address the key issues of language and education. Examples include:

- Bill 22, enacted in 1974, stating that children of immigrants had to be enrolled in French schools
- the wide-sweeping French Language Charter Bill 101 of 1977, ruling that French alone was the province's official language, requiring that education be in French for people from out of province, renaming towns and geographical sites, "frenchising" businesses, and requiring that commercial signs be in French within four years.
- Bill 178, introduced in 1988, responding to the Supreme Court's striking down the "French only" portions of Bill 101's sign law. Premier Bourassa invoked the "notwithstanding clause" and proposed legislation requiring signs outside businesses be in French, but permitting signs inside to be bilingual — providing the French was predominant.

Sociologist Raymond Breton of the University of Toronto points out that the overall objective of such efforts has been "to create a society that would be predominantly if not exclusively French." The dream has been the creation of a Quebec that is "the homeland of the French in North America," where the French community would not be a minority in Canada, but a majority in its own territory.[11] Gregory Baum of McGill suggests that while multiculturalism is not acceptable to Quebec for cultural-preservation reasons, the ideal emerging in the province is one "cultural convergence." Quebec is the host culture that receives immigrants and "opens itself to the various immigrant cultures in a process of respect, dialogue (in French), and co-operation." Here, says Baum, both the host and immigrant cultures undergo changes, coming closer to one another while saving the immigrant heritage. "Cultural convergence," Baum maintains, thereby differs from both multiculturalism and assimilation.[12]

The nationally known and controversial effort to have the rest of Canada recognize Quebec as a distinct society, with increasing control over areas such as immigration, has been basic to Quebec's efforts to achieve a better deal with the other provinces. The failure of the Meech Lake accord in 1990 has seen renewed attempts by the federal government to gain national consensus on such a provision, with constitutional reform extremely high on Ottawa's 1991-92 agenda.

Outsiders frequently interpret this desire to protect their culture as racism. It is not merely a coincidence that, in the past few years, some observers have charged that heightened nationalism in Quebec has resulted in a significant increase in racism in the province. The fact of the matter is that it is difficult to favour one's own group without at the same time being, at minimum, less passionate about other people. Quebec is no exception.

Despite the ideals of cultural convergence, many teenage francophones in Quebec give evidence of seeing newcomers as a threat to the health of their culture. They are considerably more likely than both Quebec anglophones and their peers in the rest of the country to think that a number of cultural groups have too much power in the nation's affairs; Americans, Canadian anglophones, and natives are particularly singled out. They are inclined to think that francophones don't have enough power. Quebec's anglophones, on the other hand, again tend to resemble the rest of Canada in their perception of the power of various groups — except for their much greater tendency to believe that francophones have excessive power.

PERCEPTION OF POWER			
% *Indicating Have "Too Much"*			
	QUEBEC FRANCO	REST OF ANGLO	CANADA
English-speaking Canadians	60	15	18
Americans	52	49	52
Natives	47	10	13
Men	40	40	45
Blacks	17	2	6
East Indians or Pakistanis	17	9	12
Orientals	17	9	16
Jews	16	13	8
French-speaking Canadians	8	50	32
Women	3	3	8

The numerous and wide-ranging comments Quebec teens offered on intergroup relations indicates the issue is perceived by many as significant.

In the case of native peoples, the Oka experience appears to have increased anti-aboriginal sentiments. Among adults, Quebecers who think native peoples have "too much power" in the nation's affairs increased from three to 26 per cent between 1985 and the end of 1990. A mid-1991 Gallup poll asking Canadians how well they feel natives are being treated "by the governments of Canada" found 77 per cent of Quebecers maintaining natives have been treated well or fair — a view held by 63 per cent in B.C., 55 per cent in the Atlantic and Prairie regions, and only 33 per cent in Ontario.[13]

The belief that native peoples have too much power in the nation's affairs is held by 47 per cent of Quebec francophones, compared to just 13 per cent in the rest of the country. Emotions often run high, the comments revealed. One 16-year-old male from Verdun writes:

I am anxious to see the government settle the Indian problems. It cannot last; the Indians are taking too much. I don't like them, especially after Oka and Chateauguay.

Another 16-year-old, a young woman from a small Quebec community, states, "I am not racist, but I do not particularly like the Indians." Her sentiments are shared by a 15-year-old from Saint Agapit:

I don't think we should give the Canadian Indians all they want. It's not our fault if our ancestors took over their territory.

For their part, some native teens are not at all docile. One 15-year-old from Montreal, for example, says francophones and anglophones both have too much power, while natives do not have enough, and adds, "The damn Canadians invaded my territory."

Attitudes of Quebec teens toward anglophones are also frequently negative. Some six in 10 of the province's francophones maintain that English-speaking Canadians have too much power in national life, while just over three in 10 young people in the rest of Canada have the same view of francophones. One 16-year-old, a self-declared sovereignist from Montreal, says that Quebec anglophones represent the province's biggest problem, and describes both anglophones and Americans as "bastard races." A 17-year-old from La Pocatière, who favours sovereignty association, fills out some details:

Quebecers are not respected and understood by anglophones. Quebecers try to speak English outside Quebec; but anglophones don't even try to speak

French in Quebec. Even in Montreal, people would rather speak English than French. All of our signs should be in French. Let's boycott English in Quebec like other provinces boycott French. If anglophones don't like it, let them go.

Given the presence of these kind of sentiments, it's not surprising that Quebec's cultural minorities sometimes feel less than wanted. A 17-year-old bilingual woman from Bonaventure says:

We, the English-speaking residents of Quebec, are very concerned about our rights as a minority. We feel discriminated against. We are becoming fed up.

A 16-year-old from the Montreal suburb of Westmount comments, "I'd like Quebec to realize that while they're being 'distinct,' they're discriminating against anglophones." Asked where she would like to live, she says, "anywhere but Quebec." And a bilingual, 17-year-old Jewish woman with American parents says she is confronted constantly with racism in Trois Rivières:

I live out religious, cultural, and language racism everyday. I am Jewish, Canadian, American, French, and bilingual. People call me dirty Jew; I killed Jesus. I am told to return to my dirty country. They don't realize that I was born in Quebec.

But many Quebec young people abhor isolationist and racist tendencies. A 17-year-old male, also from Trois Rivières, says, "I am all for Quebec sovereignty. But I respect Canadian anglophones and others." Another male of the same age from Longueuil identifies himself as having French origins, and acknowledges he does not place much value on being a Canadian. Nonetheless, he stresses:

We need to stop isolating ourselves as cultures — Québécois, Canadians, natives. The greatest problems we face is the mentality that we all are unique. People need to stop thinking of themselves as separate nations. After all, when it comes to feelings, we are all the same.

These overall findings suggest that Quebec francophones are taking a strong collective position on culture and power, sometimes accompanied by negative attitudes toward outsiders. In the process, they demonstrate that, far from being isolated individuals, they have an intense "consciousness of kind." On a provincial basis, the level is unique to Canada.

A DETACHED SOCIETY

CULTURAL ISOLATION

Historically, geography and language have combined to isolate Quebecers from Canada and the rest of the world. The latest survey shows that Quebec's cultural isolation has not yet been relegated to the past. The province's young people continue to exhibit a higher level of isolation than teenagers in the other Canadian regions. Yes, they, too, have been experiencing increasing levels of education. They, too, have been touched by the three Ts of television, technology, and travel. But not as much.

While the popularity in Quebec of French-language television over U.S. stations has certainly not neutralized the impact of American TV, it seems to have significantly reduced it. The same can be said of the print media, notably newspapers and magazines.

One result is that, despite the fact they watch more television than young people in any other Canadian region, Quebec's francophone teenagers do not tend to have as much familiarity with national and international events as Quebec anglophones and young people from English Canada. For example, responding to sample news items, Quebec francophones understandably showed familiarity with the Oka crisis, which took place in their province. But they had somewhat less interest in and awareness of items such as the Gulf War, the Communist Bloc breakdown, and the serial murders in Milwaukee. Asked straight out, 27 per cent of Quebec teens say that "global awareness" is important to them, compared to 42 per cent of Quebec anglophones and 30 per cent of young people in the rest of the country.

In sports, things American do not seem to stir Quebec francophones to the same extent they do English-speaking Quebecers and teens in the rest of the country. This would seem in part to reflect exposure and in part a lack of involvement in those sports.

While approximately the same proportion of francophone young people in the province follow the NHL as elsewhere, they trail Quebec anglophones and every other region of the country in their interest

FAMILIARITY WITH SELECT NEWS EVENTS						
% "Very Interested" and "Never Heard of It"						
	QUEBEC				REST OF CANADA	
	Very Interested		Never Heard of It		Very Inter	Never Heard
	Franco	Anglo	Franco	Anglo		
The Oka crisis	43	49	2	1	21	14
The War in the Gulf	41	50	1	<1	51	1
The GST debate	30	31	4	2	33	4
The Communist Bloc breakdown	20	30	2	19	27	27
The mass slayings in Milwaukee	10	19	19	26	21	26

in the three premier American professional sports leagues — the National Football League, the National Basketball Association, and — despite the presence of the Expos — major league baseball. The Canadian Football League, with no entry from Quebec, has no region with a smaller proportional following than Quebec.

In view of the power of the Quebec media, led by television, to offset the ability of the outside media to influence perception and life itself, it seems that Quebec is succeeding where the rest of Canada is failing. The province that has been so concerned about the preservation of its culture shows signs of doing a good job of resisting the impact of "foreign media," precisely at a time when English Canada is being overwhelmed by the American media.

Further to the two other Ts, there is no reason to believe that Quebec young people have any less access to available technology, which allows entrance into the "information society" — although it could be argued that the inability of some to understand English cuts them off from considerable amounts of material that are available.

But if access to technology is not necessarily a barrier to greater information, limited travel is. The 1992 survey has found that no less than 21 per cent of Quebec's 15- to 19-year-old francophones have *never* been outside of their province. The figure is far above the two to eight per cent of Quebec anglophones and teens in the rest of Canada who have never crossed their respective provincial borders. Some four in 10 Quebec francophones have never been to another Canadian province, while the same proportion have never been to

INTEREST IN PROFESSIONAL SPORTS		
% Indicating Following "Very Closely" or "Fairly Closely"		
QUEBEC		REST OF
FRANCO	ANGLO	CANADA
The National Hockey League — 40	50	45
Major League Baseball — 19	21	38
The National Football League — 18	22	29
The National Basketball Association — 17	27	31
The Canadian Football League — 9	12	26

the U.S. — both nation-leading mobility lows. Fewer than three in 10 Quebec teens have been outside of North America, well below the levels for their peers in B.C. and Ontario, and on a par with young people from the Prairies and the Atlantic region.

There are some other strange and interesting findings about travel. For example, one in four teens from Ontario have never been to another Canadian province; yet only one in 10 have not been to "the States." When it comes to travel outside Canada, young people from the Atlantic region are nearly as inexperienced as their francophone counterparts in Quebec. In addition, reflecting in large measure both immigration to Canada and visits to homelands, the largest number of young people who have travelled outside of North America come from Ontario and British Columbia.

Still, variations aside, francophone young people living in Quebec have had very limited, first-hand exposure to other places, including the rest of Canada. That fact, when combined with their high dependence on the Quebec media — in whom they place considerable confidence — has extremely important implications for the way they construct reality.

Finally, cultural commonality and a sense of belonging appear to contribute to 61 per cent of Quebec teenagers saying if they could live in any province, they would opt to stay where they are. The figure includes 70 per cent of francophones and 37 per cent of anglophones. The stay-put average for the other nine provinces, interestingly, is also 37 per cent. Only in B.C. (86 per cent) is the percentage higher than for Quebec francophones, with quality of life and economic factors seemingly more salient than commonality of culture in the B.C. case. In the words of one 17-year-old male from Montreal, "For me, Quebec is my country. I was born here and I will die here." The 30 per cent

TRAVEL EXPERIENCES						
In %'s						
QUEBEC		BC	PR	ON	ATL	ALL
FRANCO	ANGLO					CDA
TO OTHER PROVINCES						
Several times year or more	12	30	18	31	21	27	21
Yearly or less	46	61	64	64	54	63	57
Never have	42	9	18	5	25	10	22
TO THE UNITED STATES						
Several times year or more	11	35	38	14	35	12	25
Yearly or less	47	55	51	66	52	55	54
Never have	42	10	11	20	13	33	21
OUTSIDE OF N. AMERICA						
Several times year or more	2	6	5	1	4	1	3
Yearly or less	24	37	53	26	44	19	35
Never have	74	57	42	73	52	80	62
NEVER OUTSIDE OWN PROVINCE	21	2	2	3	4	8	7

of francophone teens who *are* open to leaving, incidentally, are equally divided in their preferences for B.C. and Ontario.

Indicative of how young people outside Quebec view the province's cultural homogeneity, only two per cent of teens in English Canada — including two per cent in neighbouring Ontario — say that Quebec would be their number-one choice as a place to live. And about half of these aspirants are francophones.

In short, more than six in 10 Quebec teenagers want to stay in the province, while four in 10 — led by anglophones — are open to moving to English Canada if they had the opportunity. But the geographical mobility does not work both ways. Young people outside Quebec tend to be more likely to be on the move, but almost all expect to bypass Quebec. The cultural distinctiveness that functions to attract francophones has the opposite effect on most teens outside of Quebec.

Such findings are reflected in actual interprovincial movement of Canadians of all ages. In 1991, only 13,000 people moved to Quebec, while just 17,000 Quebecers left the province. The numbers in and out were far less than provinces such as Alberta and B.C. — which are less than half the size of Quebec — and considerably below the only larger province, Ontario. When movement in and out is computed as a percentage of total provincial population, Quebec has the lowest mobility level in the country.

INTERPROVINCIAL MOVEMENT: 1991			
In 1000's			
IN	OUT	TOTAL	TOTAL AS % OF POP
Ontario	33	35	68	.70
Alberta	27	24	51	2.08
British Columbia	30	17	47	1.51
QUEBEC	13	17	30	.45
Saskatchewan	7	12	19	1.90
Nova Scotia	9	9	18	2.02
Manitoba	7	11	18	1.66
New Brunswick	6	7	13	1.80
Newfoundland	4	5	9	1.57
Prince Edward Island	1	3	4	3.05
NWT	1	1	2	5.09
Yukon	<1	<1	1	5.20

Computed from *Statistics Canada, 1992.*

RELATIONSHIP TO CANADA

Culture, nationalism, and geography contribute to a net situation where Quebec youth do not particularly identify with Canada. Just 30 per cent say that "being a Canadian" is very important to them, compared to 50 per cent of teenagers in the other four regions.

The figure for Quebec's francophones is 26 per cent, for anglophones, 44 per cent. An 18-year-old from Quebec City reminds us, "Canadians and Québécois are very different." Another 18-year-old from a CEGEP in a small town comments, "I am a Québécois — I don't know what it is to be Canadian."

Here Quebec teens are again following the patterns of their parents. Asked by Gallup in the summer of 1991 whether their primary allegiance is to Canada, their province, or their local community, 59 per cent of Canadians said Canada and 25 per cent province. In Quebec, however, 32 per cent said Canada and 53 per cent indicated province.[14] Consistent with such views, while close to one in two teens in each of the four regions outside Quebec think Canada will gain influence by the year 2000, the figure for Quebec is only one in four with the province's anglophones no more hopeful than francophones.

But it's not just that many Quebec youth are lukewarm to Canada, compared to teens elsewhere in the country. As we have already seen, they are also more inclined to be supportive of their institutions, including their media, their teams, and even their politicians. Moreover, a majority aspire to stay in the province. For many, cultural preservation and enhancement calls for a change in Quebec's relationship to Canada. In the words of one 16-year-old male francophone from Laval, "Let's look after our language and traditional values. *Vive le Québec libre!*"

Nationalism is leading many Quebec teenagers to seriously consider the possibility of separation. The 1992 survey has found that some 60 per cent of Quebec francophone youth indicate they favour Quebec's either leaving Canada altogether or having sovereignty association with the other provinces. In sharp contrast, about 65 per cent of young people in English Canada say they would like to see Quebec continue to be part of the country.

So it is that the comments of two 16-year-old males from small communities in Quebec and New Brunswick respectively stand in such sharp contrast to one another. One writes that his prediction for 1992 is "an independent Quebec managed by the Bloc Québécois," while the other says, "I don't understand why Quebec wants independence; we don't have much money and the results will be disastrous for the Maritimes."

A well-spoken 18-year-old from St-Jean-sur-Richelieu has this to say:

> *I just about didn't bother to answer this survey, since I am not particularly concerned about youth in Canada. But if you want to know . . .*
>
> *I am a young Québécois ready to fight (with words, not arms) for my nation to achieve sovereignty — for Quebec to become a country. I would hope that this could be done with great respect for our Canadian partners. We need each other (economically), but also need to recognize the failure of federalism, and the fact that we probably will never understand each other. It is not a tragedy. What we need is to have our own countries, side by side. We can understand each other better as neighbours than as partners in our forced marriage.*

A solid majority — eight in 10 — of Quebec anglophone young people, however, want the province to remain in Canada. From Deux-Montagnes comes this view of a 15-year-old anglophone female:

> *Canada is my country, and separation from Canada would be heartbreak-*

ing. This country is full of promise and hope for the generations that are to come. If we work together, we will be able to carry on for centuries.

There are some, like this 15-year-old francophone from Quebec City, who are not convinced separation will result in greater emancipation: "I am proud to be a free Quebecer. But I do not believe that if we separate from Canada, we will have more freedom." A 16-year-old from a small city close to the Quebec capital expresses similar sentiments: "I consider myself more Québécois than Canadian. But I believe there are no advantages for us to separate from the rest of Canada."

Such teens, however, appear to be in the minority. A 16-year-old Québécois from Noranda maintains the only possibility for Quebec's staying in Canada would be "a radical alteration of the Constitution." A 15-year-old from Trois Rivières expresses her thoughts of what some see as an option: "I would like to see Quebec separate from Canada and join the United States." A male of the same age from Asbestos seems to speak for a great number when reflecting on our questionnaire booklet logo. He comments: "I hope that the next time you do a survey, the front cover will show a fleur de lys instead of a maple leaf."

	HOPES FOR QUEBEC'S FUTURE				
	% *"Would you like to see Quebec . . ."*				
	In %'s				
	SEPARATE FROM CANADA	STAY IN CAN- ADA	SOV ASSOCN WITH CANADA	OTHER	TOTALS
QUEBEC					
Francophones	40	36	20	4	100
Anglophones	7	82	4	7	100
REST OF CANADA	20	65	7	8	100

A FLAIR FOR THE FUTURE

This current generation of Quebec teenagers, born in the mid-70s, has never known a time when Quebec's relationship to Canada was not in question.

However, they are relatively upbeat about the future. It's true that the present uncertainty about Canada's future is making it hard for young people to plan for the future; some eight in 10 across the country acknowledge that fact. But if any region should be particularly in limbo, it's Quebec, and more specifically, Quebec young people, who are just now heading toward graduation.

Some are obviously anxious, and explicitly mention Quebec's ambiguous future. A grade-11 student at an anglophone school in Montreal comments, "I find it difficult to answer questions concerning my future because, as a Quebecer, my future is still very undecided by the elements that I myself cannot control." A 16-year-old from Laval says, "Not knowing what will happen to Quebec makes it difficult to plan for the future." For an 18-year-old CEGEP student from La Pocatière, current economic conditions add to anxiety about what lies ahead:

> I wonder what young people can hope for in life with the increasing cost of living and taxes which never stop climbing. Most of us are in debt over our heads, even before we start working.

Yet, overall, Quebec teenagers (78 per cent) are no more likely than teens in the rest of the country to indicate that the present situation makes planning for the future difficult. The figure is slightly higher for anglophones (82 per cent) than francophones (77 per cent).

Still, what's remarkable is that, *regardless* of the preference they have for Quebec's future — separating, staying, associating — Quebec young people, francophone and anglophone alike, are buoyant about their own personal futures. They are determined to prosper, and differ little in their expectations. Most expect to get the job they want when they graduate, to own their own homes, know a level of economic well-being that exceeds their parents', and to travel exten-

EXPECTATIONS OF QUEBEC TEENS					
In %'s					
	PREFERENCE FOR FUTURE			LANGUAGE	
	STAY IN CANADA	SOVER ASSOC	SEPAR- ATION	FRANCO	ANGLO
Get the job you want when graduate	92	94	90	93	86
Own your own home	96	94	96	96	96
Be more financially secure than parents	75	70	75	73	74
Travel extensively outside of Canada	76	78	82	78	76

sively outside of the country. They have their concerns. But there are few signs of despair.

What is apparent, however, is that Quebec youth are anxious to get on with life. Asked to use one word to describe her feelings about the future, an 18-year-old woman from Longueuil was among many who said, "Impatient." A 16-year-old male from Trois Rivières doesn't mince his words: "If Quebec is to separate from Canada, let's do it now and stop wasting our time." And from the small community of Grande-Vallée comes this summation from a 15-year-old, who adds a touch of humour:

> *I hope in the near future I will see Quebec become a free country managed by the honourable Mr. Jacques Parizeau. Yes, a free country separated from Canada with Brian Mulroney overthrown. Then we could talk about pleasant things, like Nintendo and Pepsi.*

WOMEN

A second distinct departure from both the survey patterns and our social dreams is found with women. The dream is that they will experience equality. The findings indicate that young women in the 90s are not equal to men. They receive treatment that is inferior, even though their behaviour tends to be superior.

Historically, Canadian women were treated as subordinates to men.[15] They were not allowed to vote until the 1920s, were not particularly encouraged to pursue higher education until the 60s, and were virtually excluded from many professional occupations through the 70s. The workplace found them tending to play support roles to men, and paid less even when they performed the same kinds of jobs. They also were judged to be more dispensable in tough economic times. Even within the home, women frequently experienced male domination. The division of labour commonly called for them to stay home, raise the children, and care for their husbands.

Beyond discrimination in the political, educational, economic, and even domestic arenas, women faced the more general problem of not being treated as equals to men. Interaction commonly told the story of depersonalization, where women were valued more for their looks than their minds, and commonly had to put up with comments, jokes, stares, whistles, gestures, and the like. Verbal and physical harassment was widespread; sexual assault seems also to have been all too common.

Fortunately, Canada has not stood still. With the 1960s came an increase in concern about such issues as equality, freedom, and dignity for all people. In 1970, Canada's Royal Commission on the Status of Women released its report, declaring that "the equality of opportunity for Canadian men and women is possible, desirable, and ethically necessary."[16] For more than two decades, reform has been in the making, watched carefully by such entities as the federally appointed Advisory Council on the Status of Women, and prodded constantly by such interest groups as the National Action Committee on the Status of Women.

The movement to gain equality for women seeks to demonstrate that virtually all differences between women and men are the result of different types of socialization, which in turn are the product of power relations.

Academics have given their support to such a view by arguing that the more our society rids itself of such sexist socialization tendencies, the more women and men will come to resemble each other. In the words of University of Toronto sociologist Metta Spencer, "It is no longer generally assumed that 'anatomy is destiny,' that any division of labour is 'naturally' based on the biological differences between the sexes." Indeed, says Spencer, the prevalent view today is that "distinctions between male and female roles mainly reflect the history of male domination."[17]

Perhaps it's indicative of the fact that "similar socialization" is still a long way off; perhaps it's indicative of the fact that factors besides socialization are at work. But the national survey findings point to significant ongoing differences between teenage females and males in the Canadian 90s.

No, it's not just in the stereotypical areas of looks and career aspirations that the differences persist. The variations are far more culturally pervasive than all of that — so much so as to raise important questions about the kind of women and men our society is creating.

SUPERIOR BEHAVIOUR

GREATER VALUING OF THE RELATIONAL
Females continue to be far more inclined than males both to place high value on relationships and link sexual involvement to significant ties.

It's not that many males don't place a high value on relationships; it's just that a greater proportion of females do. Such a pattern can be seen in the value placed on being loved, along with friendship. About nine in 10 females say they "highly value" both, compared to about eight in 10 males in the case of friendship and seven in 10 in the being-loved instance. As we observed earlier, there has been a modest devaluing of relationships among both females and males since 1984.

Some might suggest males have difficulty with a "gooey" phrase like "being loved," even though males may very well want to have such an experience. Perhaps. But even if that's the case, such a situation still points to a culture where males are not able to express their deepest feelings with the same ease as females. Either way, the gender difference persists.

Beyond what they value, females are somewhat more inclined than males to report they receive a high level of enjoyment from their friends, mothers, brothers and sisters, and even pets. They also are no less likely to say they receive enjoyment from their fathers.

Such findings are consistent with those of University of Calgary researchers Janelle Holmes and Eliane Silverman. In their previously mentioned spring 1990 national survey of students in grade eight to 10, they found that concern about relationships, including families, friends, and the opposite sex, was greater among females than males. They concluded, "Young women are more concerned about their connections than are young men." They "cherish intimacy . . . They desire connections with their families, with other adults and with friends, as well as with their schools."[18]

These gender differences persist across region and race. In Quebec, for example, francophones, as we have seen, tend to value relationships more than other Canadian young people. Yet female francophones are even more inclined than male francophones to place importance on relationships. The same is true of females who are white or members of visible minorities, versus males in either respective category.

Research involving adults has come up with similar results. Friendships, for example, are valued by the vast majority of both women and men. But the purpose of friendship often is not viewed the same way. Sociologist Marlene Mackie reports that women's friendships stress expressiveness while men's stress activity. Women tend to turn to each other for emotional support and intimate sharing. In contrast, men are inclined to look to each other to do things, often withholding their personal thoughts and feelings from even their closest friends.

Current research also suggests that concern about being perceived as having homosexual leanings, as well as age-old cultural pressure to "act like a man," inhibits many men from expressing emotions, including fear or sadness.[19]

Women such as this grade-11 native student from Thompson, Manitoba, do not exhibit such inhibition about the importance of people and feelings:

> *I love my family and friends, I care about the world and environment. I care about other people. I like school and would like to graduate and have a career. I would like a family.*

Words like those are not readily spoken by males.

Sex continues to have different meaning for females and males. In the movie *City Slickers*, Billy Crystal turns to his buddy and says, "Women need a reason to have sex; men just need a place." His observation seems applicable to Canadian teens.

RELATIONAL VALUES AND ENJOYMENT: FEMALES AND MALES				
In %'s				
	1992		1984	
	F	M	F	M
HIGHLY VALUE				
Friendship	89	79	94	88
Being loved	90	68	93	81
HIGHLY ENJOY				
Friendships	96	90	97	94
Brother(s) or sister(s)	58	51	55	52
Mother	70	63	80	76
Father	59	61	69	73
Pet(s)	45	52	–	–

We saw earlier that more than eight in 10 females and males approve of sex before marriage when the people involved *love* each other. However, in cases where the couple just *like* each other, the number of females who endorse such behaviour drops from 86 per cent to 51 per cent, while the male figure declines only slightly, from 88 per cent to 77 per cent. One 15-year-old female from Alberta puts it this way:

If I choose to have sex, it would be because I love the person extremely, and that I have accepted the possibility of maybe getting married. I'm not saving myself but I'm not going to abuse my body.

Says a 17-year-old from Niagara Falls:

People who engage in sex before marriage have to love each other, and be willing to be committed and take on responsibilities. They shouldn't do it just for thrills.

Another 17-year-old, also from southern Ontario, comments:

I strongly disagree with sex before marriage when people just like each other because I had this bad experience and believe we are not emotionally ready. I got hurt, and know of other girls who are getting hurt by getting involved with people who don't care. Something needs to be done.

Consistent with such gender differences, only two in 10 females compared to seven in 10 males, think sexual relations are appropriate after a few dates — where presumably the love tie has not yet been established. In fact, one in five males think that sex on the first date is not out of order, compared to only one in 20 females!

Further to our argument that the sexual revolution is over, there indeed has been an increase in the last decade in the inclination of both females and males to approve of premarital sex when love is involved. But their attitudes concerning appropriate behaviour on dates indicate that there has been very little change among both females and males in their views of casual sex.[20] About 60 per cent of females and 30 per cent of males continue to disapprove.

The gender difference persists among both whites and members of visible minorities. Regionally, even though Quebec francophone teens are much more inclined than other young people to approve of premarital sex in situations beyond those where love is involved, the inclination is still slightly less among females than males. For example, while 23 per cent of francophone males in Quebec approve of sexual relations on the first date, just nine per cent of francophone females feel the same way.

It's noteworthy that, during the past decade, when gender equality has been so strongly sought and increasingly realized, female and male attitudes about casual sex have changed very little. Differences persist.

SEXUAL ATTITUDES: FEMALES AND MALES					
% Agreeing					
	1992		1984		QUEBEC
	F	M	F	M	F	M

	1992 F	1992 M	1984 F	1984 M	QUEBEC F	QUEBEC M
Sex before marriage is alright when people LOVE each other	86	88	77	81	93	93
Sex before marriage is alright when people LIKE each other	51	77	–	–	81	91
Sexual relations are okay within a few dates	40	73	36	70	60	82
Sexual relations are okay on the first date if people like each other	5	20	3	19	9	23

GREATER COMPASSION

One of the striking findings of the surveys is the consistent tendency of young women to outdistance males in the positive attitudes they have toward others. Regardless of whether we are talking about interpersonal values, social concerns, or resolving problems, the findings remain the same. Young females are far more caring, sympathetic, and responsive toward people in general and the disprivileged in particular.

Earlier we noted that a major trend characterizing life for young people is the devaluing of interpersonal ideals, such as honesty and compassion. The drop in the past decade, however, has been greater among males than females. Take honesty, for example. In 1984, 80 per cent of males and 90 per cent of females said that it is "very important to them." Today, the figure for males has fallen to just 56 per cent, while the figure for females has slipped much more moder-

INTERPERSONAL VALUES: FEMALES AND MALES			
% Viewing as "Very Important"			
	1992		1984
	F	M	F	M

	1992 F	1992 M	1984 F	1984 M
Honesty	82	56	90	80
Concern for others	75	48	–	–
Forgiveness	71	45	72	62
Politeness	60	46	70	60
Generosity	48	32	–	–

ately, to 82 per cent. The importance accorded forgiveness by males has plummeted from 62 per cent to 45 per cent; among females there has been no significant change.

Young women in the 90s are also far more likely than males to place a very high value on other interpersonal traits, including being respected, concern for others, trustworthy leaders, and generosity.

The current low proportion, less than one in two, of young males who highly value such interpersonal traits is enough to make one wonder about the confidence people can have in their dealings with these emerging men. When honesty is being downplayed, along with concern and courtesy, the implications for social life are a bit scary.

Such is the grim prospect we face if these rather basic values are translated into behaviour. The good news in all this is the finding that perhaps as many as three in four females show signs of being a better bet for social interaction. Teenage males seem high-risk.

Young women — possibly reflecting continuing socialization whereby our society expected them to be care-givers — are also far more likely than young men to express concern about social issues that have a strong person-centred emphasis. For example, larger numbers of females than males are troubled about such Canadian

---

SOCIAL CONCERNS AND POWER: FEMALES AND MALES

% Viewing as "Very Serious"

	FEMALES	MALES
PERSON-CENTERED ISSUES		
Child Abuse	74	53
Drugs	69	57
Racial Discrimination	67	48
Human Rights Legislation	64	50
STRUCTURAL-CENTERED ISSUES		
The Economy	56	59
Government Incompetence	54	49
Lack of Canadian Unity	39	38
Conflict between Countries	32	27
INSUFFICIENT POWER		
Blacks	60	48
Natives	56	49
Orientals	37	30
East Indians or Pakistanis	32	27
Jews	34	22

problems as child abuse, suicide, drugs, racial discrimination, AIDS, violence in schools, alcoholism, poverty, and unemployment. Globally, they are more apt to express concern about the environment, illiteracy and human rights violations.

Interestingly, when more abstract, structurally related issues are raised, such as the economy, government incompetence, or international conflict, males match or exceed females in their expression of concern. But if a person is explicitly associated with an issue, the extent of female concern is typically higher.

Further, young women are much more inclined than young men to be sympathetic with Canada's cultural minorities' relative lack of power. The pattern holds regardless of the young woman's region or race. The concern that cultural minorities may have *too much* power is lower among Quebec francophone females than males, for example, and less common among Asian females than Asian males.

These varied findings on values, social concerns, and the call for responses add up to a picture of young Canadian females showing a greater tendency than males to be compassionate, both at home and abroad. Differences are not large, but they are very consistent, regardless of the specific value or issue involved.

The argument that a greater level of compassion characterizes women was made in 1982 by Carol Gilligan in her book, *In a Different Voice*.[21] Flying in the face of the arguments of developmental theorist Lawrence Kohlberg[22] that women are less morally advanced than men, Gilligan argued from data on children's play and perceptions of abortion that females are characterized by an *ethic of care*. Theirs, she said, tends to be a morality of "the web" that emphasizes the fulfillment of responsibilities of people who are connected to one another. In contrast, male morality, Gilligan maintained, tends to be analogous to "the ladder," where morality consists of a hierarchy of rights and freedoms, and results in an *ethic of justice*.

To be sure, Gilligan has had her critics.[23] Nonetheless, our national findings point to a compassion difference between young women and men. What is up for grabs is not whether or not a difference exists, but why it exists.

This is one instance of a gender gap that most of us would like to see closed, not by having women match men, but by having men match women — where the level of male concern for others is raised to that exhibited by females. We all can consequently benefit from identifying the sources of "the compassion gap."

GREATER SPIRITUALLY

Much has been written and said about female versus male inclinations to be spiritual. Even though, with a few exceptions, women frequently have not been allowed to hold leadership positions in religious organizations, they typically have been involved in greater numbers than men.[24]

Women have been seen by many as having a particular penchant for the spiritual, perhaps because of their disadvantaged status in many instances, and also because of their greater openness to the mysteries than transcend everyday life.

Journalist Leona Flim is among those who maintain that distinct differences between women and men affect how they understand and relate to spiritual issues. She suggests that feminine spirituality reflects such characteristics as caring and sensitivity, in contrast to the "heady, intellectual, approach to faith" that characterizes men. In the case of adult women, argues Flim, the experience of childbirth may also play a highly significant role. She cites one woman, for example, who says the unique female experience of childbirth is "a catalyst for the experience of unity between soul and body."[25]

Consistent with such thinking, young males in the national surveys frequently stressed an independent, rational style of thought. One 17-year-old from a small Manitoba community stated, "I believe in all religions. However, I refuse to let anything other than my own free will control my actions." Young women were typically far less guarded.

Innate? Learned? Experiential? Well, what's interesting is that receptivity to spiritual matters in Canada continues to characterize young females more than males. Survey research does not permit the in-depth probing of such an area we would like. Still, the findings provide something of an aerial photograph.

Here are some of the things we have learned:

- Females are more likely than males to place a high value on characteristics such as personal fulfillment, the quest for truth, harmony with nature, acceptance by God, and spirituality.
- Although the differences are small, females consistently score higher on religion measures, such as weekly attendance, enjoyment from religious groups, and the importance of living out faith in everyday life.
- Females are somewhat more likely than males to believe in God, give credibility to astrology, believe contact with the spirit world is possible, and feel they have experienced God's presence.

• A slightly larger number of females than males anticipate turning to religious groups for ceremonies relating to marriage, birth, and death. As some clergy have put it, beyond mere cultural habit, there is a sense — however poorly articulated — that "God needs to be brought in" on these passage occasions.

Our information is limited and the variations are not large. Still, differences persist. Perhaps they can be accounted for by identifying dissimilar socialization experiences of females and males. Perhaps they cannot.

SPIRITUALITY AND RELIGION: FEMALES AND MALES *In %'s*		
	FEMALES	MALES
HIGHLY VALUE		
Personal fulfillment	64	53
The quest for truth	56	36
Harmony with nature	39	34
Acceptance by God	32	26
Spirituality	27	21
ORGANIZED RELIGION		
Attend weekly	20	16
Highly enjoy involvement	16	14
Important to live out faith	19	15
BELIEVE		
In the existence of God	84	77
In astrology	61	46
In contact with the spirit world	46	43
Have experienced God's presence	37	31
WANT RELIGIOUS CEREMONIES RE:		
Marriage	90	85
Birth	82	70
Death	90	84

INFERIOR TREATMENT

The picture the data add up to is one where women, young and old, are more sensitive than their male counterparts to the relational and the problems of others, where they give greater value to integrity and courtesy, and are more receptive to the spiritual and the unknown.

One would think such people would be valued by a society and in turn would feel valued. If we were talking about a particular cultural group, we would presumably welcome them to Canada with open arms, and be happy to treat them well.

That's why the current situation is so puzzling and, frankly, upsetting. Rather than being given special treatment, Canada's young women are showing signs of not faring as well as young men. Many exhibit low self-esteem, are afraid for their safety, have to deal with unwanted attention, and are expected to play outdated roles.

CONCERN ABOUT APPEARANCE

The problem is well-known. Historically, our culture has been guilty of placing excessive emphasis on looks in the case of women. Not that men have been exempted. It's just that a woman's value has often rested primarily on her appearance.[26]

In the 1990s, for all the apparent virtues that young women are exhibiting, they still are more inclined than men to worry about their appearance. Approximately the same proportion of young women and men say both that their looks are very important to them (about 55 per cent) and that they consider themselves to be at least fairly good-looking (about 80 per cent). However:

- Some 53 per cent of females say their weight is a concern for them, roughly double the 26 per cent figure for males.
- Asked in an open-ended question to indicate "what worries them the most," the issues young women cited most were school (21 per cent), the future (17 per cent), and their looks (9 per cent).
- For males, the top three concerns listed were school (25 per cent), the future (13 per cent), and money (10 per cent); only two per cent mentioned their looks.

Anxiety about appearance is not limited to any region or racial group. Females in all parts of the country and from all racial categories are more inclined than their male counterparts to be concerned about their appearances.[27]

CONCERN ABOUT COMPETENCE

Social psychology tells us our sense of self emerges from our interaction with others. To sum up some complex theorizing in one sentence, we read ourselves through the feedback we receive from the people around us, and develop a subsequent sense of what we are like.

In Canada today, young females tend to continue to feel significantly inferior to young males when it comes to general competence. Asked how accurately the statement "I can do most things well" depicts them, 82 per cent indicated "very well" or "fairly well" — but still less than the 90 per cent level for teenage males. But, when also asked how accurately the statement "I have lots of confidence" describes them, the affirming response for females dropped to 61 per cent, compared to 81 per cent for males.

The gender imbalance once more remains constant across the regions of the country. In Quebec, for example, 78 per cent of young males express high levels of confidence, compared to 63 per cent of females; elsewhere, the breakdown is 81 per cent and 60 per cent. While approximately 80 per cent of males, whether white or members of visible minorities, indicate they have "lots of confidence," the comparable figure for white females is 62 per cent; for women from visible minorities, only 54 per cent.

Somehow, a disproportionate number of young Canadian females are getting the message that they are not up to scratch. The result is a collective level of self-esteem that continues to be well below that of young males. Leo Durocher's classic line seems to apply to Canada's 15- to 19-year-old females: "Nice guys [and non-guys] finish last."

Again, these findings are consistent with those of Holmes and Silverman for 13- to 16-year-olds. They found that young females were slightly less likely than males to say they feel good about themselves,

SELF-IMAGE: FEMALES AND MALES

% Indicating How Well Statements Describe Them

	Very Well	Fairly Well	Not Very/ Not At All	TOTALS
"I am well-liked"				
Females	34	62	4	100
Males	32	63	5	100
"I am good-looking"				
Females	10	69	21	100
Males	16	69	15	100
"I can do most things well"				
Females	16	66	18	100
Males	28	62	10	100
"I have lots of confidence"				
Females	18	43	39	100
Males	33	48	19	100

have a number of good qualities, and feel self-confident. Further, rather than things improving with age, they found that the gap increased by the time young people reached 16.[28]

CONCERN ABOUT SAFETY

When it comes to personal safety, significant differences exist between young females and males. Earlier we noted the major disparity in the perception females and males have about the seriousness of violence against women. Some 70 per cent of females say it is a "very serious" problem, compared to only 44 per cent of males.

Ongoing Project Canada and Gallup surveys have been asking women about their sense of safety, using the question "Is there any area within a mile (or kilometre) of your home where you would be afraid to walk at night?" The good news is that there has been no significant increase in anxiety since the mid-70s. The bad news is that there has been no significant decrease; women are not feeling any safer. The 1990 figure for women was 56 per cent and the figure for 1985, 1980, and 1975 was 60 per cent. The comparable figures for men in all of the surveys has been a steady 20 per cent.[29]

These findings tell us women are about three times as likely as men to express fear about walking close to home at night. The cry of women's groups to "take back the night" is justified.

Endless hours could be spent debating the meaning of these large differences in the perception of violence. Some might say the levels of females' fear is objectively warranted. Others might maintain they're subjectively exaggerated.

On the objective side, it's clear women have considerable cause for alarm:[30]

- As of mid-1991, one in five Canadian women said they or someone in their neighbourhood had been abused physically.
- Some 70 to 80 per cent of assaults involve men the women know.
- It is estimated that one woman in eight is physically abused by her partner.
- About 80 per cent of violence against mothers is witnessed by children.
- Women are beaten an average of 35 times before they report the abuse to the police.
- A woman is raped every 17 minutes in Canada.

- Most rapes involve not strangers, but friends, acquaintances, and spouses.

But whether or not the anxiety of women accurately reflects actual conditions is, in many ways, academic. The sheer fact that women perceive themselves to be physically endangered has very real consequences. Here again, social psychology is helpful. Many years ago, University of Chicago social psychologist W.I. Thomas introduced us to what has come to be known as the "Thomas theorem." It goes like this: If we define things as real, they are real in their consequences. What Thomas meant is that we respond on the basis of what *we think is real*. What in fact *is* real is largely irrelevant.[31] Remember the last time a noise in the basement made you realize you had nerve endings you never knew you had?

If women see themselves as physically endangered, their quality of life suffers dramatically. And in Canada, large numbers of women, young and old, believe they are not safe. So it is that one 16-year-old from Montreal tells us, "As time passes, we are increasingly afraid to go out because we may be attacked." A 15-year-old female living in the small B.C. community of Golden comments, "We are all supposed to be happy and the most important thing is to be safe. But with the way this world is, we can't be happy and safe."

For males of all ages — who don't give a second thought to walking out to a parking lot alone at night, or going to bed alone in their own house or apartment, or jogging around a park alone early in the morning, or working alone in their residence during the day — such persistent fear is often hard to grasp. But it's a reality that doesn't make for a life where women can feel like equals to men.

Dr. Peter Jaffe, a member of the Canadian Panel on Violence against Women, maintains that the problem of violence and fear is a reflection of a society that not only tolerates but promotes violence in sports, videos, on television, in the movies, and in song lyrics. "We are always talking about eliminating violence," he says, "but then we glorify it." The result is that our young people are receiving conflicting messages. Along with others, Jaffe is particularly concerned about the way in which our extensive exposure to violence in the media desensitizes us to its effects on victims. He maintains that "we have to get back to zero tolerance where we don't minimize or make excuses for violence.[32] Jaffe's thoughts are shared by a grade-12 student from

Leamington, Ontario: "This generation of teens is trying to be less racist and destructive, but it's hard when TV shows, movies, and other forms of mass media are practically promoting those things."

CONCERN ABOUT UNWANTED ATTENTION

Teenage women are clearly interested in young men. Most are dating. The majority say they have a boyfriend. Few exhibit any aversion to sex in what they define as proper contexts.

But given that more than eight in 10 highly value both freedom and being respected, young women do not want to find themselves in situations where men are showing them attention they do not want. To be treated as sex objects is a flagrant contradiction of the characteristics they value. At worst, unwanted attention takes the form of violence against women. At best, sexual harassment.

Sexual harassment, which flies in the face of one's freedom and respect, is just now coming to be better understood by both females and males. It's extremely common. A late 1991 Gallup poll found that 35 per cent of Canadian women 18 and older say that either they or someone they know personally have been sexually harassed.[33] Such behaviour is apparently found in all areas of life where women and men are together, involving not only superiors and subordinates,[34] but peers in every profession — including ones where the players should supposedly know better. In a recent survey of 2500 active members of the Law Society of Alberta, for example, 30 per cent of the women sampled said they had observed male lawyers making unwanted sexual advances toward female lawyers. Obviously there's a problem with differences in perception — only about five per cent of the male lawyers said they had seen such advances.[35]

THE PERSISTENCE OF OLD ROLES

Some 95 per cent of young women plan to have careers — the same number as men. About 85 to 90 per cent of females also want to marry, have children, and continue their careers — also approximately the same proportion as men. Further, two in three young women say they plan to combine career and parenthood.

The expectations are impressive. What is more than a shade disconcerting, however, is the widespread hope of most young women that they can put the two roles of parenthood and career together, and still end up winning occupationally, financially, maritally, and emotionally.

Journalists like to write stories about the new kind of dads who are bonding with children, sharing the housework, and even staying home in increasing numbers. An Associated Press story, for example, was circulated across Canada in June 1991, claiming that fathers are showing a greater inclination to share more family responsibilities with their working wives than their own fathers did:

> *He's slumped in an easy chair at daybreak with the baby finally asleep in his arms. He's watching the kids while his wife works late. He's changing diapers.*

The story noted that the number of stay-at-home dads in the U.S. increased from 61,000 to 257,000 between 1975 and 1990 — a proportional increase that, in reality, represented the mammoth jump from perhaps one to three per cent of American households.[36]

Such wire-service items make good copy. But they are largely figments of journalists' imaginations. The 1988 national youth survey found that, among 15- and 24-year-olds who were married or living together, a discouraging pattern was still in place. Asked about the arrangement "for doing things like cooking, cleaning, and laundry," 46 per cent of respondents said *she* does either "all of it" or "most of it." At best, in most of the remaining situations, *he* was sharing the work equally. In only four per cent of the cases was *he* doing most or all of such jobs.

Those kinds of findings have been turning up for the past couple of decades, despite the women's movement and changing social and economic climes.[37] Surely by now, we'd like to think, things are different. But the findings of the 1990 Project Canada adult survey indicate that change at home is gradual, to say the most. First, the patterns of division of labour were similar to the youth findings and earlier research. And second, as we enter the allegedly progressive 90s, when couples have children, the tendency for men to share the household workload with women is actually *less* than when no children are involved! In the no-children instance, 74 per cent of employed men and 61 per cent of employed women said they share the tasks at least equally. But when children were present, only 54 per cent of men and 31 per cent of women said the tasks were being shared equally.

Put simply, when kids are not around, Canadian career-minded couples are inclined to be egalitarian as they attend to jobs around the house or apartment. But when kids are on the scene, dad's contribution frequently is conspicuous by its absence.

As for the popular folk wisdom that today's fathers are different when it comes to sharing workload, the survey further found that fathers younger than 40 were no more inclined to be helpful than older fathers.

There's little doubt that multiple demands on working mothers contribute to considerable stress. The same survey found that "mothers who work for pay full-time" are somewhat more troubled about their children and marriages than either employed fathers or non-employed married mothers. Concern about children was particularly high for financially deprived single mothers — more than 50 per cent compared to about 30 per cent nationally.

These findings suggest that Meg Luxton's words of a decade ago are still appropriate:

> *Women working the double day carry an extraordinarily heavy load, and the price they pay is enormous. They work long hours and have virtually no leisure time for themselves. They are subject to high levels of stress . . .*[38]

It is to be hoped that the aspirations of young women concerning career and family will be met with the necessary assistance from their partners, which to date, has frequently been absent. However, given the tremendous disparity between men and women in their perception of what is taking place, it is difficult to be particularly optimistic.

THE ONGOING GENDER GAP

By most of our standards, women come across as sensitive and caring people — especially when compared to many in the male category, who come out woefully short on altruism, compassion, and appreciation for the mysterious.

Most people agree with our assessment. A mid-summer 1991 Gallup poll asked Canadian men and women how accurately certain characteristics describe both males and females. Presumably speaking from their life experiences, both men and women gave females a higher rating than males in areas such as kindness and thoughtfulness, concern for family and friends, and for working hard. Yet, for all the recognized virtues of women, 54 per cent of men and 64 per cent of women acknowledged that males are inclined to think they are superior to females; less than 30 per cent of either sex felt females have such an attitude of superiority.

The obvious question arises: where have we gone wrong, or where have we gone right? Immediately we are caught in the ideological cross-fire. Are we doing something good with young women that we are not doing with young men? Or are we doing something wrong with young women that we are doing right with young men?

There's another possibility. Maybe both males and females start out okay, but we do something to males that we don't do to females — such as toughen them up, make them more callous and uncaring. Something like turning naturally friendly puppies into wary and sometimes mean dogs.

Or — and here comes the ideological heresy — could it be we're not doing anything much at all? Is it possible the differences are purely biological or physiological? And so rings the bell on another round of the infamous "nature-nurture" brawl.

For whatever reasons, significant differences continue to exist between Canadian females and males. As long as that remains the case, *both* nurture and nature arguments are plausible. Regardless of the interpretation, what is apparent is that young women are excelling

HOW MEN AND WOMEN VIEW EACH OTHER		
In %'s		
	IS TRUE OF:	
	MALES	FEMALES
Kind, thoughtful, caring		
Men's view	67	85
Women's view	63	84
Care more about family and friends than about their job		
Men's view	50	69
Women's view	29	71
Are hard-working		
Men's view	65	83
Women's view	73	90
Believe they are superior to other sex		
Men's view	54	28
Women's view	64	16

SOURCE: Computed from *Gallup Report, July 22, 1991.*

in some areas we all value. Paradoxically, they are frequently being treated very differently from men, with significant consequences for their quality of life. That needs to change.

We believe that enhanced living for both women and men will come about not through polarization but through the sexes working very hard together to raise awareness of the problems and to pursue appropriate solutions. As Toronto writer Emil Sher reminds us, "Any hope of long-term change is going to have to begin with those who are in diapers today." Yet, Sher adds:

> *Revolutions don't always take place on blood-soaked battlefields or glass-strewn streets. They can begin at home, in kitchens and bedrooms, by men who are prepared to listen when their partner talks, to defer instead of challenge, to compromise even when it hurts.*[39]

4

WHAT THE TRENDS SAY ABOUT LIFE IN CANADA

WHAT WE ARE DOING RIGHT

PERSONALLY

Today's young people have been raised in a culture that places considerable importance on good personal development, complete with feelings of confidence and competence. The very fact that we have become so sensitized to self-esteem issues contributes to the anxiety that large numbers of today's teenagers have poor self-images. Such is not the case.

SELF-ESTEEM

Our 1992 survey has probed four aspects of self-esteem: competence, confidence, looks, and being liked. While there are disconcerting differences by gender, the majority of teenage males and females have very positive views of themselves. Eight in 10 indicate they are highly competent and "have lots of confidence." Seven in 10 say they are "good-looking." All but about five per cent describe themselves as "well liked."

Perhaps more telling, however, is the extent to which young people rate themselves positively *in all four areas* — feeling competent, having confidence, being pleased with their looks, and being liked. Nationally, almost six in 10 teenagers score high on all four traits, while close to another three in 10 respond positively on three characteristics.

Fewer than two in 10 indicate that only two or less of the statements describe them accurately.

Differences by region are fairly small. Self-esteem among teens who have come from homes where parents are divorced or separated is not, over all, any lower than other young people.

A report released in June 1992 entitled "The Health of Canada's Youth" suggested that the emotional health of Canadians between the ages of 11 and 15 is worse than that of their peers in European countries. They are more depressed, more lonely, and have more strained relationships with their parents.[1] We would argue, however, that the differences are relative to Europe rather than to poor emotional health. Our survey findings offer a highly encouraging "personal portrait" of Canadian youth.

Such findings certainly don't mean there are no young people with serious self-image problems. As one 16-year-old female from Calgary reminds us, some "teens are turning to substances to make them feel good when they should be able to feel good anytime without the help of drugs."

Further, two important asterisks have to be added to any report that "all is well." The first, as discussed earlier, is the difference between males and females. While a majority of the members of both sexes exhibit good self-esteem, twice as many females as males (22 per cent versus 12 per cent) give evidence of having low opinions of themselves.

The second qualifier has to do with race. Overall, close to one in two teens in all racial groups give evidence of having high levels of self-esteem. But while blacks and whites both score fairly high, natives come out somewhat more moderately, and Asians even lower. More than one in four Orientals and east Indians and Pakistanis give evidence of having low levels of self-esteem, compared to fewer than one in six young people in other categories.

There obviously is work to be done. Still, the news is far from bad. The majority of Canadian young people are growing up with healthy views of themselves.[2]

HAPPINESS

All in all, most young people indicate that they are happy. Asked point-blank, almost nine in 10 say they are either "very happy" (25 per cent) or "pretty happy" (63 per cent). Only one in 10 say they are "not too happy," with just two per cent saying they are "not happy at all." Those levels are virtually the same as those of Canadian adults

| | SELF-IMAGE LEVELS* | | | | |
| | % In %'s | | | | |
	High (4)	Moderate (3)	Low (2)	Very Low (1-0)	TOTALS
NATIONALLY	58	25	11	6	100
Prairies	61	21	12	6	100
Ontario	60	24	11	5	100
B.C.	57	25	10	8	100
Quebec	55	28	12	6	100
Atlantic	53	26	13	8	100
Male	66	22	8	4	100
Female	50	28	14	8	100
Black	64	26	6	4	100
White	59	25	11	5	100
Native	54	34	9	3	100
E. Ind-Pak	52	20	13	15	100
Oriental	47	25	20	8	100
Parents div-sep	61	23	11	5	100
Parents married	57	25	11	7	100

*The four statements: "I am well-liked," "I can do most things very well," "I am good-looking," "I have lots of confidence." The bracketed figures above refer to the number of the four statements that the respondents say describe them either "very well" or "fairly well."

("very happy" 21 per cent, "pretty happy" 69 per cent, "not too happy" 10 per cent).

Differences by gender on this general well-being measure are minor, as are variations by region and marital experience of parents. Racially, whites are slightly more likely than visible minorities to report being happy, rather than "not too happy" or "not happy at all."

Overall, teenagers tend to have the perception that, if anything, life is getting better. We asked them how much they're enjoying life now compared to when they were younger — about the time they started school. More than 60 per cent said that life for them now is more enjoyable, while 20 per cent indicated it's about the same. Only 20 per cent said it's less enjoyable. Among those in the latter category is an 18-year-old male from just outside Ottawa who adds, "Ignorance is happiness."

Again, regional and gender variations are small. Perhaps suggesting the resilience of young people, there is also very little difference between teens whose parents have gone through a divorce and those whose parents have stayed together. However, once more, possibly reflecting the reality of discrimination, including its impact on areas including dating, visible-minority teens are less likely than whites to say that life is becoming more enjoyable.

A biographer once wrote of comedian Woody Allen that "his one regret in life is that he is not someone else." Most Canadian young people do not fit such a description. Self-esteem levels are high. It's clear from the survey that they, like the rest of us, are not without problems and concerns. But the findings do show that, for all the anxiety we adults so frequently have, teenagers as a whole feel emotionally happy and healthy.

The drawing board certainly needs to be revisited. Yet, the findings include many encouraging signs. We've been doing some things reasonably well.

INTERPERSONALLY

We have also done a pretty fair job of passing on to young people the importance of good relationships. They, like us, deeply value friendship and love. They are enthusiastic about their friends and enjoy dating. They fall in and out of love. They enjoy being physically involved with the people they care about.

Like their parents, most plan to marry. But unlike what has often happened to many of their parents, they plan to stay married. Our collective marital record has not dulled their idealism about long-lasting love. Perhaps, if anything, it has only made them all the more determined to be different. Young people believe that good and permanent ties are possible.

More generally, teenagers have also come to believe that concern for others is important. They endorse the idea of equality and decry abuse and exploitation. They insist that steps be taken to ensure the environment is protected so that the present and future generations can enjoy what it has to offer.

True, we are not doing quite as good a job of transmitting important interpersonal values as people did in the past, including honesty, politeness, and generosity. It's also not clear why pronounced gender differences continue to exist, and to what extent the disparity indicts us. Overall, however, we can take credit for the widespread desire young Canadians have for good interpersonal life.

NATIONALLY

To a greater extent than Canadian adults, teenagers endorse the pivotal federal-government intergroup policies of bilingualism and multiculturalism. Although a majority of teens in Quebec want a new relationship with Canada in the form of sovereignty association or separation, a majority of young people in the rest of the country want the province to stay. As they look at other cultural minorities, they tend to favour the mosaic model over the melting pot, and decry racism and intolerance.

The turbulence that has characterized Canada in recent years has dulled the value Quebec teens place on being Canadians. But such has not been the case in the rest of Canada. The net result is that almost one in two young people continue to highly value being Canadians. Among adults, between 1985 and 1990 there was a decrease from 68 per cent to 61 per cent in the proportion who said that being a Canadian is "very important" to them.

One of the pro-Canada types is this 17-year-old male from Ottawa:

Canada is the greatest country to live in, but most Canadians don't know it, or don't show their appreciation enough. The first problem we need to solve is how to make everyone more patriotic. Then solutions to other problems will fall into place.

A 16-year-old female from Winnipeg says:

I love Canada very much. It needs the support of the people who live here. It doesn't matter whether we speak French or English, or Ukrainian or whatever. We are all Canadians first. We should work on pulling our country together.

If nationalistic feelings are not down among teens, the inclination to live in Canada over anywhere else, if given the chance, certainly is. In 1984, Canada was the first choice of 58 per cent of young people; today the figure has dropped to 47 per cent. The 1985-90 decline for adults was from 79 per cent to 72 per cent.

Clearly morale has slipped somewhat in recent years. For many, the country is simply not as attractive as it was about a decade ago. Unity problems, a sluggish economy, and the preoccupation with constitutional reform appear to be wearing thin with many Canadians, young and old. A 16-year-old Toronto male who was born in Poland comments:

> *I don't think I will stay in Canada, because of the Quebec problem and high taxes. I think when I finish university I will make my future in Europe.*

An enterprising 17-year-old white male from New Brunswick tells us:

> *I am a Canadian citizen who was born in Nigeria. I lived in Jamaica for 12 years. I came to Canada two years ago and I don't really like it. I plan to get a university degree and become an accountant, save some money and move back to Jamaica where I will set up my own business and live very well.*

A disenchanted 15-year-old male from Saskatoon is particularly unhappy with taxes: "If the government wants me to pay their damn deficit, too bad. I'm out of the country as soon as I can. See ya in the U.S.A."

Another 16-year-old, a female from Alliston, Ontario, says:

> *Although I'm proud and all of being Canadian, I think in the end I'll probably go to Europe, most likely England or Scotland. Everything just seems so much more laid back there.*

There is one important regional trend exception. In British Columbia, among both teenagers and adults, there has been an increase in *both* the valuing of being a Canadian and the desire to choose Canada over any other place in the world to live. People in B.C. feel that "they've got it good." They plan to stay. One 17-year-old female from "the coast" puts it this way: "I love Canada and I love being Canadian. We have a lot of problems to overcome, but Canada shows a lot of promise as a country." A grade-10 Vancouver student adds:

> *We are a privileged people to be able to be living in Canada where we don't have to worry about when the next bomb is going to drop or where our next meal will come from. The only bad thing about Canadians is that we take more than we give and take it for granted.*

On the bright side, five in 10 young people believe that Canada is a pretty good place to live — a position, incidentally, that is also held by seven in 10 adults. One 15-year-old from Medicine Hat, Alberta, is among the exuberant:

Canada is a great country to live in and I wouldn't want to live anywhere else. Sometimes I think we need more help with the economy, but I'm so glad I was born and raised here.

She is joined by a 17-year-old female of east Indian descent who offers this blunt comparative observation:

Sometimes I wish that children in Third World countries could have the same opportunities as those of us who live in Canada. Canada has done a lot for me. And I am very thankful. I prefer it greatly to my real home.

And from the small southern Ontario community of Cambridge comes these thoughts from a 15-year-old male:

I am very happy to be living in the greatest country in the world. You couldn't pay me enough to move to the States.

For young people such as these, Canada continues to offer much hope. The country's problems have not diminished their belief that resolutions can be found, that life here still has the potential to be as good or better than anywhere else in the world.

	VIEWS ABOUT CANADA							
	% Agreeing							
	BEING A CANADIAN				WANT TO LIVE IN CANADA			
	Teens		Adults		Teens		Adults	
	1984	1992	1985	1990	1984	1992	1985	1990
NATIONALLY	49	45	68	61	58	47	79	72
B.C.	47	48	61	66	53	57	77	81
Prairies	49	48	73	64	58	49	80	74
Ontario	51	51	75	68	57	48	81	71
Quebec	44	30	55	46	57	43	76	62
Atlantic	61	57	78	64	67	55	84	84

GLOBALLY

The "global village" proclaimed by Marshall McLuhan in the 1960s has become a reality for young people and adults in the 1990s. Provided with television, technology, and travel, their awareness of what is happening in the world has been dramatically heightened. We have also made it possible for them to see life with a global perspective. Among such young people is this 16-year-old from Bonaventure, Quebec:

> *Forget Canada, the States, etc. The world should be one. I have no real preferences when it comes to the race I should be with. We are one race — the human race.*

Given their ability to see life elsewhere, today's young people are in a better position than any generation before them to be able to evaluate the good and the bad in Canadian society. They also have unprecedented opportunity to observe societies around the world, and to evaluate them.

Certainly there are some teenagers who are not excited about global issues. A 15-year-old Toronto male says that "Canada should worry about its own problems before other countries," and a 16-year-old Alberta female comments that Canada is "too eager to help Third World countries with their problems before we solve our own." They are joined by some young people who have come from other countries, such as this Philippines-born 17-year-old from Scarborough who says, "I believe that Canada should deal with our own personal problems before we get involved in world issues."

Still, the majority of young people say Canada needs to be highly involved in such issues as the environment, illiteracy, and human rights. Close to four in 10 say involvement is also called for in the areas of arms control, disaster relief, and Third World development. The priority given to world issues differs little across the country.

Despite being only one year removed from the Gulf War, a war that American and Canadian leaders called a "necessary war," some 60 per cent of teenagers *do not* agree that "war is justified when other ways of settling international disputes fail." The figure for adults is also about 60 per cent. As one Brampton, Ontario, grade-12 student puts it, "War is stupid!"

This is the global age, made possible largely because of communication and travel. We know the implications well: the world is experiencing rapid social and economic change. On the positive side, the possibilities for the planet have been greatly enriched. While the precise role Canada will play in global affairs remains to be seen, there is no doubt whatsoever that we have to open our eyes to such globalization if our country is to prosper. Edward Lang, the chairman and CEO of RJR-Macdonald Inc., notes:

> *While Canadians continue the ongoing introspective debate of our future as a country, a rapidly changing world is encircling us. The fact is that our ability to compete internationally will have a far greater impact on our standard of living and future prosperity than any resolve to the constitutional debate . . . One of the greatest gifts we can give our children is fluency in languages. Another is to teach them the fact that in business there are no borders; there are only differences in cultures and customs.* "[3]

To the extent we have helped our young people to see their existence in global terms, we have made a significant contribution.

GLOBAL PRIORITIES	
"To what extent to you think that CANADA should be involved in finding solutions to the following WORLD PROBLEMS?"	
% Indicating "Highly Involved"	
Environmental issues	73
Illiteracy	61
Human rights legislation	57
Arms control	48
Disaster relief	46
Third world development	40
Conflict within countries	32
Conflict between countries	30
Settlement of refugees	29
Overpopulation	26
Troubled national economies	24

WHAT WE ARE DOING WRONG

The survey results reveal many good findings about young people. It is neither true to the data, nor helpful in practice, to declare that there is yet another "crisis" involving teenagers today.

What the findings do suggest, however, is that for all our good intentions, we inadvertently are making personal and social life difficult for teens. Quite unconsciously, we have been instilling certain "cultural contradictions" — ideas that have the effect of sabotaging a good number of the goals to which teenagers aspire. It's as if we've been teaching sprinters how to hit the finish line, while at the same time putting glue on the starting blocks.

The national youth surveys document the existence of at least four centrally important cultural contradictions that are making life difficult for Canadian young people.

I. RELATIONSHIPS WITHOUT COSTS

There is no question that today's teens value relationships above everything else. However, at precisely the same time, they are mirroring Canadian society's unprecedented emphasis on the importance of the individual — personal freedom, personal rights, personal values, personal dreams, personal fulfilment, and personal power.

What is not at all clear is whether young people can have it both ways. Unless a balance is struck between emphasis on the individual and emphasis on the relational, individualism will frequently destroy the very group life that they so deeply value.

THE ROOT OF THE PROBLEM

The background of the contradiction is well-known. Accelerated individualism has its roots in a culture that has been attempting to correct its past wrongs. Canada's movement from an agrarian society to a post-industrial society has resulted in an accelerated emphasis on the individual. The decades before the 1960s were characterized by an excessive emphasis on collectivity that exacted a high price from many Canadians, especially women and cultural minorities. The emphasis on the individual has been an important corrective.

The idea has caught on. Armed with the Charter of Rights and Freedoms, Canadians are insisting on their right to live out life as they see fit. Max Yalden, the chief commissioner of the Canadian Human Rights Commission, reported in March 1992 that complaints to the commission had increased by 100 per cent since 1987. The commission was facing a year-long backlog of discrimination cases requiring investigation.[4] In addition, interest groups addressing every conceivable issue have proliferated in recent years, as people have recognized the political need to give their individual concerns collective clout.

Interpersonally, we have bought into the idea that relationships should *add* to our lives and, if they don't, should be dispensed with in favour of more fulfilling ties. Alternatively, if none are forthcoming, we should bask in positive solitude.

EVIDENCE OF THE PROBLEM

At the attitude level, young people, along with older Canadians, are increasingly insisting on their right to live their lives as they choose. And so it is that 86 per cent place a high value on freedom and 79 per cent on having choices.

But as we have seen, the social warning lights have gone on. Interpersonal values don't fare nearly as well. The figures drop to about 70 per cent for honesty and concern for others, to around 50 per cent for working hard and politeness, and to 40 per cent for generosity. Further, in each case, there has been an endorsement drop of about 10 per cent since the early 80s. What's more, these latter endorsement levels are all below those of Canadian adults, especially people 55 and older.

There's good reason to believe that today's young people, led by males, are discounting the very values indispensable to the good interpersonal life they say they value so much.

Excessive individualism does not stop with the sheer endorsement of valued traits. When asked, in the 1988 survey, about the goals that they consider important to them as they look to the future, eight in 10 cited "a good marriage and family life," along with "success in my line of work." In sharp contrast, just two in 10 saw "working to correct social and economic inequalities" as very important, while a mere seven per cent thought that "being a leader in my community" was a significant goal.

In B.C., for example, one in four teenagers placed a high value on having "plenty of time for recreation and hobbies"; yet less than one in 100 of these gave a similar importance rating to being leaders in their communities. And, don't forget, that's the province where most people, young and old, dream of living one day — including at least one of your two authors. . . .

The centrality of the individual in teenage minds can also be seen in their perception of the key factors that influence their lives. Asked in the same survey for their views of the impact that a variety of possible sources have on their lives, "self" was conspicuous by its presence.

In fairness, nine in 10 young people acknowledged that the way they were brought up was a very important factor. But a close second,

INDICES OF INDIVIDUALISM
% Seeing as "Very Important"

	NAT	BC	PR	ON	QUE	ATL
HIGHLY VALUE*						
Freedom	86	86	86	87	81	90
Having choices	79	82	78	78	81	78
Honesty	70	67	67	69	74	71
Generosity	40	38	37	43	38	42
VERY IMPORTANT IN FUTURE**						
Good marriage and family life	80	78	88	84	72	79
Success in my line of work	79	78	78	81	77	84
Having lots of money	33	37	32	36	25	41
Plenty of time recreatn & hobbies	36	43	28	39	36	33
Working correct inequalities	23	25	20	28	15	31
Being a leader in my community	7	<1	7	9	8	10

SOURCES: *Project Teen Canada 92; **Project Teen Canada 88.

cited by more than eight in 10 teens, was one's own willpower, followed closely in turn by mothers. Sharing third place and acknowledged by about seven in 10 young people were fathers, one's own personal characteristics, and friends. Even the positing of peer pressure is adamantly denied by some. One 16-year-old from Guelph, for example, says, "I'd just like to say that despite my behaviour I never feel pressured, nor do I put pressure on people. I live day to day doing what is right for me."

A few other social factors that likely have more than a little impact on how we "live and move" were virtually ignored. Just 40 per cent of young people said their lives were significantly influenced by what people in power decide — barely ahead of the perceived impact of girlfriends and boyfriends. Teachers, the media, and the state of the economy were seen by just over three in 10 as having an important influence on their lives. God's impact got a surprisingly high 30 per cent rating. Religious leaders didn't fare so well, viewed as having a strong influence by only 14 per cent of teenagers. Even luck scored higher, at 20 per cent.

Results like these suggest we adults are doing a good job of convincing young people they are masters of their fate. We are doing a less than impressive job, however, of introducing them to the importance of their social environments.

Social and economic realities that influence the lives of all of us, young or old, can certainly be altered. But the key to responding to the negative impact of a debilitating family situation, exploitation at work, media mind-making, or the difficulty of finding employment, is first to become aware of its presence and nature. Such blatant obliviousness of teenagers to some of the obvious economic and social factors that affect their lives makes it extremely difficult for them to exercise the very freedom over their lives that they so cherish.

THE CONSEQUENCES

There is good reason to believe that our strong collective emphasis on the individual is poorly preparing young people for both *commitment* to social life and *involvement* in social life.

We want teenagers to experience good interpersonal ties. We want them to be ethical and law-abiding citizens. We expect them to participate in community and national life. We want them to exhibit concern for global matters. Yet, simultaneously, we are preparing them to be highly autonomous, self-sufficient, self-oriented individuals. It's too much to ask. And so it is that a 15-year-old from a small B.C. town finds himself looking at sexuality questions and triumphantly declaring, "It's your body, baby!", only to contradict himself when asked about extramarital relations. He does not approve, because "you are hurting someone else."

Given such a conflict between what is personally satisfying and relationally necessary, young people, like many of us, will frequently fail at social ties. Excessive individualism contradicts the possibility of good relationships. It has the destructive result of failing to instil the commitment required of social life at all levels — friendships and family life, neighbourhood and community, nation and world.

Take marriage, for example. Statistics Canada demographer Jean Dumas recently made the observation that marital relationships have become more precarious as Canadians have moved away from the concept of pulling together as a society and toward an emphasis on the rights of individuals. Such individualism, says Dumas, is leading couples to negotiate unique contracts regarding what they want from a relationship, how long it might last, whether they should marry, and whether or not they should have children.

The only problem with such arrangements, apart from being tenuous, is that they make little allowance for children. Evelyne Lapierre-Adamcyk, a University of Montreal demographer, notes that some unstable unions may not provide children with the nurture they require. "Children," she says, "are in danger of being forgotten."[5]

Another important example of our failure to instil an adequate appreciation for an individual-group balance is the widespread devaluing of generosity. The surveys find that only about 50 per cent of adults and 40 per cent of teens place a high value on generosity. Apparently we mean what we say. After reviewing our charitable donations for 1990, Statistics Canada announced that we gave an average of about $120 over the 12-month period. Canadians are currently giving about three-quarters of one per cent of their incomes to charities — a drop of about 30 per cent from 20 years ago, and about one-third of the proportion of personal income that Americans give to charities.[6]

The willingness to part with dollars, however, is only one indicator of a generous spirit. People, young or old, who are rather "tight" with their money, are not the kind who are willing to give much to the other side when issues arise that call for give and take. It wasn't surprising to hear Victor Goldbloom, the federal commissioner of official languages, tell a parliamentary committee on constitutional reform in early 1992, "We don't live in a time of generosity." He was faced with the formidable task of calling for greater constitutional support for anglophone and francophone minorities.[7]

We see the same style of individualism in our response to environmental issues. Yes, we think we have problems. Yet, something needs to be done. But when adults are asked, "Who do you think has the primary responsibility for protecting the Canadian environment?" more than three in 10 say the government, industry, and conservation groups, close to five in 10 say everybody, and only about two in 10 say individuals.[8] Obviously, at some point, the key to a significant response to environmental concerns will lie with individuals. However, a strong sense of individual responsibility is not apparent at this point in time.

The social and physical costs in Canada of allowing the individual to star in one-character plays are high: minimal loyalty to collectivities of any kind, beyond those that have an immediate payoff for the individual. One wonders what kind of society we would have if the attitudes of this grade-12 Toronto student became predominant:

I am intelligent, aware, and informed. I deserve a say. At 16, I should have the right to be secure. I should have the right not to attend school. I should

have the right to income. I should have the right to be a mother without being
bound by the traditional family or the fear of starvation.

Some young Canadians sense the need for a better balance between the individual and the group, such as this grade-11 student from a small southwestern Ontario town:

It's the IDI's who will ruin our country — the "I deserve it" people who believe
they should get something for nothing. The change in our country has to
start at the roots, with each individual. All the selfish brainwashing has to
stop.

From another grade-11 student in Saint John, New Brunswick, comes this observation:

Canada and the world won't become any better unless people start thinking
as one and working together. The efforts of single individuals won't make
any difference if people can't come together.

A 16-year-old female from Calgary puts it simply: "People make up the world; why can't we all enjoy it together?"

In *Mosaic Madness*, the alarm was sounded concerning the dangers of excessive individualism, but the country has been slow to catch on. One notable exception has been the Ontario Conference of Catholic Bishops. In its pastoral letter on the Constitution distributed to the province's 3.5 million Roman Catholics in January 1992, the bishops declared that excessive individualism has led to neglect of community values and intolerance of others, posing a great threat to Canada's future. The letter called for the Constitution to recognize that social rights and responsibilities are as important as individual rights. "To succeed in reconstituting Canada," the bishops declared, "we must break out of our collective apathy, reach out to others and commit ourselves to the common good."[9]

We believe they're right. Among Canadians young and old, what is needed is the replacement of radical individualism with a relational model where self and society are merged. We have to do a better job of getting the message across to teens that they, like the rest of us, are not islands unto themselves. Rather, we all find optimum fulfilment and productivity in being connected to others. Emphasis needs to be given to the importance of commitment, not to self-gratification per se, but to good relationships as the means to personal and social well-being.

Far from being of significance at only the friendship and marriage levels, such an appreciation for the relational and social is essential to life as it is lived by young people and adults at all interpersonal levels. Intimacy, co-operation, civility, unity, and world peace are all dependent on the precarious balance between the importance of the individual and the importance of the group. David Suzuki, in what he calls "A Declaration of Interdependence," clearly articulates our bond with each other and all of life:

> . . . we are human animals who share the planet with perhaps 30 million other species, our biological relatives . . . Linked in a web of kinship, all living beings are interdependent — using, sharing, cleansing, and replenishing the fundamental elements of life . . . This turning point in our perception of the human place in the natural world, a rediscovery of our home, could transform society from dominance to partnership, from fragmentation to connection, from insecurity to interdependence.[10]

II. CHOICES WITHOUT CRITERIA

It's great to have choices. But what makes choices great is knowing that each has a different outcome, and proceeding to choose the best or better over the mediocre or worst. This holds true when we buy a car or order a meal, get married or have children, join a political party or stop attending church.

The existence of choices means we have to make decisions. Making the right choices is no simple art. As journalist Stephen Waldman reminds us, having choices can have its downside. Choice can erode commitment to anything, from favourite restaurants to favoured marriage partners. Because good choices require time, we may find ourselves simply giving up and becoming inept consumers. Choice can create strain. In Waldman's words, "The more choices there are, the higher the odds I'll make a mistake."[11] At minimum, we typically need a lot of help.

In view of the kind of multi-everything society we have been creating in Canada, young people and most everyone else do not lack for options. What is less clear is that our society is providing much input when it comes to showing teenagers *how* to choose from the many mosaics associated with every sphere of Canadian life.

WHERE THEY'RE TURNING

In an information society like ours, with experts in the wings to provide us with specialized help at every turn, it seems obvious that the acceleration in the number of choices is being met with resources that enable young people to make sound decisions.

But there is good reason to believe that such is frequently not the case. The 1992 survey reveals that, while teenagers face an unprecedented number of life options, their immediate resources for decision-making are extremely limited and of questionable value. When making decisions in such areas as career, school, spending money, and right and wrong, the primary resource for approximately five in 10 young people is parents. About two in 10 turn to friends. In the money and morality cases, close to three in 10 rely on no one. Clergy are conspicuous by their absence in the "right and wrong" instance. When school and career decisions are being made, parents and friends are supplemented by school counsellors in about two in 10 cases.

When facing a major problem, five in 10 turn to friends, four in 10 to parents, one in 10 to no one. In the areas of sexual behaviour, relationships, and having fun, the key resource for most young people is friends. One 16-year-old female from St. Catharines sums up the preference of friends this way:

> *I think teens are more comfortable talking with friends instead of parents because friends know what you're feeling. Sometimes parents tend to forget what it was like for them.*

Perhaps the resources in the career, school, and money zones provide reasonably sound support, especially to the extent that parents, for example, attempt to become adequately informed so that they can give valuable advice and assistance to their daughters and sons. Still, a 16-year-old Montrealer tells us:

> *It feels like the weight of the world is on my shoulders. Young people should not have to decide so soon in life what they want to do "for the rest of your life." More resources must be found to aid in the process.*

However, it's troubling to find that decisions in the important areas of relationships and sexual behaviour are made primarily in consultation with friends, whose competence in at least some instances can be rightfully questioned. And when decisions are made about major problems, covering the gamut of important issues young people face — associated with stress, anxiety, fear, and pain — the finding that six in 10 rely on friends or no one is disconcerting. A 16-year-old from Wolfville, Nova Scotia, says:

I find many teenagers have many problems they don't want to share with their family, but can't solve on their own.

So-called specialists, such as school guidance counsellors, are virtually absent. A Saskatchewan 17-year-old rape victim has this to say:

Our school counsellor is not very good at helping out teens. He is not very approachable and is not well-liked.

Another 17-year-old, from a small southern Ontario community, offers this clue as to why some students are reluctant to turn to guidance personnel:

At my school we can't talk to counsellors about anything important like sex, drugs, and friendships, because they will call our parents and tell on us.

SOURCES OF DECISION-MAKING

"Who do you find yourself MOST LIKELY TO TURN TO when you are making decisions in the following areas?"

In %'s

	PARENTS	FRIENDS	NO ONE	SCHOOL COUNS.	MINS/ PRIESTS	OTHER	TOTALS
Career	55	11	13	20	*	*	100
School	51	22	10	16	*	*	100
Spending money	51	20	28	*	*	*	100
Right and wrong	50	25	21	2	2	*	100
A major problem	37	48	9	2	1	1	100
Sex	8	60	28	1	*	2	100
Relationships	7	80	11	*	*	*	100
Having fun	3	87	9	*	*	*	100

* Indicates less than 1%; accounts for balance of 100% totals.

A grade-12 student from Fredericton comments:

I would like to see the government and adults make it easier on teenagers growing up, by talking openly to teens, respecting teens' feelings, having more courses like Psychology for Living in school, and having discussion groups. They should provide more help for teens who have a really troubled life.

Overall, the survey findings suggest that the wide variety of options facing today's young people are not being typically matched with particularly good decision-making resources.

THE DECLINE OF INSTITUTIONAL AUTHORITY

Critiques of Canadian society invariably have included critiques of our major institutions. A "just society," after all, requires just institutions. And so it is that the post-60s has seen an acceleration in the criticism levelled at government, education, big business, the medical profession, and religion. On the heels of the May 1992 Los Angeles and Toronto riots, police found themselves in the company of politicians and priests in having their integrity and competence questioned.

Over the past decade, there has been approximately a 10 per cent drop in the confidence that young people say they have in Canada's leaders, with virtually no sphere escaping the decline pattern. The drop has been particularly severe for politicians and religious leaders, not quite as severe for educators.

The timing could not be much worse. Precisely when young people are faced with unprecedented options, the institutions that should be able to provide them with insights, information, and direction are, to varying degrees, suffering from a credibility crisis.

Assaults on our institutions, usually led by the media, may be resulting in greater institutional purity. But such moral crusades have also neutralized some of the important contributions of those institutions. The purging has left many young people with large amounts of scepticism and limited amounts of help as they attempt to deal with the exploding number of choices before them. A 17-year-old from Nanaimo, B.C., has this to say:

It's hard to trust a lot of people nowadays. Police officers and priests have been convicted of child molestation. Come on! What's this world coming to? There are a lot of crazy, weird people out there. Who can you trust?

A 16-year-old Montrealer eloquently sums up the institutional malaise this way:

> It makes me sad to see the disintegration of traditional support networks —
> family, community, religion. We have been cut loose from our moorings, and
> in trying to provide choices, our parents have dropped us into a bewildering
> array of pitfalls. We do not need "freedom to make our own way" without
> the support networks of the past. We need a sense of our roots. We need a
> past so we can create a future.

TEEN AND ADULT CONFIDENCE IN INSTITUTIONS

"How much confidence do you have in the people in charge of . . ."

% Indicating "A Great Deal" or "Quite a Bit"

	THE POLICE	THE SCHOOLS	RADIO	TV	COURT SYSTEM	RELIG ORGS	YOUR PROV GOVT	THE FED GOVT
NATIONALLY								
1992	69	67	65	61	59	39	32	27
1984	77	69	–	–	67	62	41	40
ADULTS								
1990	70	55	52	55	43	36	30	13
1985	74	56	–	43	48	50	30	29

The Religion Example Much has been made about the decline of religious participation in our time. Some observers, including many journalists, have shown an almost sadistic delight in announcing another drop in church attendance, or exposing the scandalous activities of yet another priest or televangelist.

Historically, religious institutions have emphasized the importance of personal and social morality. They have been the premier champions of interpersonal values, including honesty and integrity, compassion and forgiveness. Therefore, if religious institutions fail, as has been the case in Canadian society, it is critically important to personal and social life that functional alternatives be found.

On the heels of the May 1992 Toronto riot, much soul-searching took place. People were asking, "Where have we gone wrong?" Invariably, the probes led to reflections on the role of economic and political factors, inadequate education, the changing structure of the family, and endemic racism. But few commentators bothered to raise an obvious question: are the problems of lack of fairness and lack of compassion in any way associated with the decline of religion in this country?

The current national survey findings suggest it is time such a question was raised. For the survey has found that involvement in organized religion, measured by service attendance, is positively related to the endorsing of interpersonal values. Simply put, young people who attend services regularly are more likely than others to value traits such as honesty and caring.

Consequently, the drop in involvement in organized religion means many teenagers are not as inclined to hold such interpersonal values as were their parents and grandparents, who were much more likely to be involved in religious activities.

A 16-year-old from Vancouver who teaches at a Hebrew school tells us that she herself doesn't think God exists. But she goes on to say, "It is important for people to be taught that he does. If not, people don't have anything to be good for."

Looking at religion from a cold, functional point of view, she has a good point. Canadians obviously have the freedom to discard religion and downplay the importance of churches, temples, synagogues, and the like. But in the absence of religion, functional alternatives need to be found. Our findings indicate that equally effective options have yet to be located.

VALUES BY RELIGIOUS SERVICE ATTENDANCE						
% Viewing as "Very Important"						
	Honesty	Forgive-ness	Concern Others	Polite-ness	Hard Work	Gener-osity
NATIONALLY						
Attend Weekly	76	75	69	60	59	51
Never Attend	61	48	55	47	46	34

THE QUICK FIX OF RELATIVISM

There is a very important additional reason making choices has become so difficult. Canadian society has largely discarded the idea of "better" and "best" choices. Nationally, we had a problem. We had to figure out how people of diverse cultural backgrounds could coexist in one country. On the surface, the problem of potential conflict between varied viewpoints and life-styles was solved fairly easily. We accepted the pronouncement of academics — notably anthropologists, sociologists, and philosophers — that everything's relative. That is, we bought the notion that most ideas and behaviour are a reflection of the cultures and personal experiences of people.

According to such thinking, there is no "right" family form, or sexual expression, or religion, just as there is no "right" kind of food, or clothing, or music. What is right and wrong, good and bad, exists solely in the minds of individuals. Folkways, mores, and laws are all socially created. No culture or life-style is superior to another. Terms such as "right" and "wrong," and "good" and "bad" aren't found in the mosaic lexicon.

Most have bought the idea. As of early 1991, 66 per cent of adults agreed that everything's relative. Following suit, 65 per cent of teen-agers, it may be recalled, agree that "what is right or wrong is a matter of personal opinion." We have assumed that diversity in itself is a wonderful virtue and that any opinion is as valid as another.

Viewed as a means to enriched living for everyone, the idea of a culturally diverse society becomes something worth celebrating. We all benefit. Native peoples, French Canadians, and English Canadians are joined by people from all over the world in creating a microcosmic global society that encourages both individual expression and collective reflection. Traditions and ideas are respected, but they are also discussed, examined, and selectively adopted, individually and socially. The result? An enhanced quality of life.

The problem is that our rather blind acceptance that everything's relative — before we have even seriously explored the merits of such an assumption — has paralyzed such a reflective process. If anything, our emphasis on championing the right of individual expression has become so pronounced we are afraid of stepping on one another's toes. Few people want to run the risk of being accused of bigotry, sexism, and the like.

Stripped of the inclination to interact, we find ourselves in the bizarre position of not being able to extract the best from our diverse culture. What we are left with are the consolation prizes of multicultural days, gay-pride parades, and the ongoing admonition to be tolerant of just about everything.

Rather than being encouraged to think and to pursue truth and the best, Canadian young people give evidence of placing limited to no value on such a quest. As Allan Bloom notes in his *Closing of the*

American Mind, relativism extinguishes "the search for a good life."[12] The youth and adult surveys have found that among the traits valued the least are creativity and imagination. Harsh though it may sound, in selling out to unreflective relativism, the fact of the matter is that we as adults have blazed the way in cultivating closed rather than open minds. The national cultural tragedy is that the blind acceptance of relativism has obliterated creative intergroup and interpersonal expression before it has had a chance to take place. We consequently have only scratched the surface of the potential social and personal benefits of our diversity.

THE PLIGHT OF TEENAGERS

The net result for young people is that the shelves of the cultural store are stocked full of choices. But they find themselves without either the resources or inclination to make "the best" selections. Many are perplexed and confused. One 16-year-old from a small Quebec community puts it this way:

> *I believe the world is moving toward a world that is worse instead of better. Bad is good and good is bad. The whole world is screwed up.*

Says another 16-year-old from rural southern Ontario:

> *I feel that Canada has some serious ethical problems. We have lost our standards by which we used to live. Now it's really do what you want, when you want. We receive little guidance from the adults of today, who have largely forgotten what morals are and have become very selfish.*

A 17-year-old male Manitoban echoes those sentiments:

> *Many pressures are placed on today's youth with little instruction given on how to relieve the stress. Young people are receiving our instructions from leaders, but the leaders are directionless and afraid to stand up for right and wrong.*

The Teen Crime Example On a typical weekend in the late summer of 1992, four youths between the ages of nine and 12 robbed a Toronto pizzeria, armed with a .22 calibre rifle. In another part of the city, a 17-year-old used a loaded rifle in the theft of a bicycle from a 13-year-old. One police official observed, "All over Toronto, younger and younger people are committing violent crimes."[13] Considerable publicity has been given to the increase in crimes committed by teenagers. A Statistics Canada report released in late 1991 disclosed that, while charges against adults for all types of crimes had increased by about 40 per cent since 1987, the increase was a whopping 70 per cent for young people under the age of 18. Some 15 per cent of the 60,000 juvenile court cases heard in 1990-91 involved violent offences, up by a third from 1987. The most common was assault, then possession or use of weapons, followed by robbery. Significantly, teenagers are also more likely than any other age group to be victims of violent crime. About one in four victims of violence in Canada are in their teens.[14]

Some observers have noted "the new quality" of youth crimes — the random, mindless viciousness, complete with a penchant for weapons. Of particular concern is why this situation exists.

A recent examination of the issue by the *Toronto Star* cited a number of experts who point to a disturbing lack of ethical certainty in our culture. "Many young people seem to have no clear idea of what is good and bad," the story read. "And for that we have ourselves to blame." Dave Crowe, a Toronto probation officer who has worked with youthful offenders for 25 years, had this to say: "The breakdown of traditional institutions has left an ethical vacuum. Young people are looking for a set of fair rules, but we're not giving it to them." Catherine Challin, a psychologist with the University of Toronto's faculty of behavioural science, commented, "There is so much selfishness, so much dedication to Me. The Me-Generation is raising kids who show the consequences." In arresting an 18-year-old who had robbed eight people at gunpoint, veteran Toronto Detective Sergeant Frank Craddock heard the teen ask, "Do I have to go to jail for this?" Said Craddock, "They don't seem to realize how serious what they're doing really is." He maintains that highly publicized teen gangs are spontaneous, poorly organized groups that are quickly discovered by the police:

> *They're just a bunch of guys who get a sense of power from guns and money. They're macho jerks, guys who want to be big shots. But they aren't very bright, and they can't keep their mouths shut, so they get caught pretty quickly. Whoever shows the most force seems to get the most respect and gets to be the leader. It's as simple as that.*[15]

Most teenagers are not involved in crime. But those who are, in many instances, have seemingly thrown interpersonal norms to the wind. At such time, the message that everything's relative becomes irrelevant, annoying, absurd. We need more. So do young people.

MOVING FORWARD

As teenagers live out their lives, complete with unlimited choices, they are looking for direction that enables them to make the "right choices." They want some "truths," or at least informed bases for making their selections. We have a responsibility to provide young people with good information about the possible outcomes of their choices, and opportunities for reflection and discussion. Unthoughtful relativism urgently needs to be replaced by reflective critiques of the benefits and costs of available options.

Treated as a hypothesis rather than as a given, relativism would undoubtedly be found to have much validity. Against standards such as personal well-being, we would find and do find that many things are indeed relative — the foods we like, the clothes we prefer, the ideas that excite us. On the other hand, we know full well that some things are not relative. Some foods do kill us. Some clothes do not protect us. Some ideas are inaccurate.

David Suzuki again is helpful in reminding us of the perils of abandoning the search for truth. The fact of the matter, he says, is that "certain ideas resonate with truth, certain convictions are inherently right, certain insights originate in the highest planes of our nature."

Joining ecologically inspired biological principles as "non-negotiable goals of a healthy community," maintains Suzuki, are themes such as social justice and equality of opportunity, irrespective of gender or race.[16]

What we are calling for is not a return to the ideological right or to a fictitious past. We also have no interest in seeing a regressional resurgence of dogmatism and intolerance. Far from it. What we are urging Canadians to do is to *think not less but more*. Such a pursuit of truth and "best" has the potential to enrich life for all Canadians.

III. JUSTICE WITHOUT COMPASSION

A third cultural contradiction that requires reflection is the extent to which concern for justice has not been balanced by genuine concern for people. It's true that young people have been increasingly endorsing the ideals of the just society. There is no doubt whatsoever that such a development has been positive.

The goal of a just society was an important corrective to the significant injustices experienced by many Canadians, notably cultural minorities and women, during our first century as a nation. We needed to change, and we have. Considerable progress has been made. Our pivotal twin policies of bilingualism and multiculturalism, along with the Charter of Rights and Freedoms, have succeeded in providing individuals, groups, and institutions with unprecedented equity and freedom. The youth data suggest we will continue to improve.

But while young people are scoring high on their endorsement of justice, they are showing signs of scoring low on social compassion. A significant contradiction is found in their emphasizing justice in the name of caring about people, yet not caring about those they perceive as not following the justice norms. Such a style calls into question the extent to which young Canadians — and adults, as well — are being led by the letter of the law, versus a caring spirit, in pursuing a just and fair society.

A simple illustration. We found that some students were very sensitive to the wording of certain items in our questionnaire. A number voiced opposition to our asking whether their two closest friends were white or non-white. The mere inclusion of the question "What is your race?" led a few to accuse us of being racists. Asking whether or not their mother or female guardian was "employed outside the home" resulted in our being regarded as "sexists" by some respondents. We had complaints about asking teens if they had part-time jobs. Inquiring about religious preferences or parents' marital status annoyed others. Failing to use recycled paper — something, incidentally, that happened only after a costly abortive attempt to do so — also met with their disapproval.

No doubt about it. Young people scored A's for awareness of many of the dominant justice issues. But there were instances where teenagers seemed to think our violating such sacred ideals gave them licence to bring out the verbal artillery, expletives included.

For example, one 16-year-old female from Willowdale, Ontario, wrote beside our race question, "You people are uneducated, and I think the term "race" should be abolished. We are human — that is that." As for our "mother/guardian working" item, she added, "Wake up, this is not the 60s — idiots!" Asked about her perception of the relative power of people in Canadian life, an otherwise civil student from Golden, B.C., declared, "How rude. It doesn't matter; don't be so prejudiced, you hypocritical PIGS!" A 17-year-old Asian from

Vancouver expressed his concern on the one hand about racial discrimination. But in the next breath, he wrote, "If the French want to separate, let 'em separate. If they want economic relations, SCREW THEM!" A grade-11 student from Hamilton says that forgiveness is a quality that is "very important" to her. Yet, to women who want to pursue a legal abortion, she has this to say: "It's murder! If you get pregnant, pay the consequences!!!" A grade-10 student from a small southern Alberta town says that, as a committed Christian, he highly values the idea of concern for others. Yet in disagreeing with homosexuality he adds, "Faggots are gross." A grade-11 student from a small Ontario community unbashedly tells us, "I would welcome back the 60s gladly, with open arms: 'Make love, not war.'" She adds, "And kick the Christians out!!" And finally the failure to instil a sense of compassion alongside one's view of justice can be seen in a devastating comment of one 17-year-old Willowdale, Ontario, male. Having complained about the performance of "Mr. Brian Mulroney," the student concluded, "He should be assassinated!"

RELATING TO THE ENEMY

To examine life in Canada at this point in our history is to observe abundant concern for individual or group rights. We have been highly sensitized to be on the lookout for any sign of discrimination, exploitation, or abuse. There is no lack of legislation, or interest group, or media watchdogs when it comes to ensuring that we aspire to that which is just and fair.

What is far less evident is a spirit of compassion toward people who are not like us — who are majorities as well as minorities, who live in other parts of the country, whose ideological inclinations are different from ours, who are male as well as female, who have abused as well as been abused, who are strangers as well as acquaintances. As journalist George Bain has put it, "Canadians have a lamentably limited capacity to see a national interest broader than the membership list of the occupational, economic, cultural, ethnic, gender, environmental, or other groups with which they identify."[17] Province and region could readily be added to Bain's list.

The mood seems to be one of "I have my rights and other people have their rights. If you stand in our way or my way, then to hell with you." One University of Toronto student leader recently summed up the contradiction in a most telling way when he declared, "People can't be bigots anymore."[18]

Justice without compassion is dangerous. Forget about the need to illustrate with mediaeval crusades or the lynching of blacks in the American south. One only has to look at cyanide in chocolate bars, the spray-painting of fur coats, the anarchist activities of some people on both sides of the abortion debate. As one Vancouver judge declared as he imposed prison terms of up to six months and fines of up to $1500 on eight pro-lifers convicted for contempt of court, "If their behaviour goes unpunished, we may have a society without abortions, but we may end up having a country that is not worth living in."[19] Not that pro-choicers have been known for superior compassion toward the other side. A May 1992 abortion in Vancouver found pro-choice activists chanting at demonstrating pro-lifers, "Get your rosaries off our ovaries," as, according to Canadian Press, they ripped up anti-abortion signs.[20]

Another British Columbia incident is informative. In December 1991, the company Fletcher Challenge announced its plans to take environmental activists to court to make them pay for illegal logging protests in the Walbran Valley on Vancouver Island earlier in the fall. The forest corporation's vice-president Gordon Clark indicated that the company would likely file for hundreds of thousands of dollars for losses caused by vandalism and logging-road blockades. A similar lawsuit announced by MacMillan Bloedel for a blockdale on the west coast of the island resulted in some activists actually complaining that the suit would have a chilling effect on civil disobedience in the forests. Fairly understandably, Clark stated the obvious: "One hopes it will be chilling."[21]

Causes might be just. But if the opposition is trampled and dismembered, it is hard to escape the conclusion that something "just" has been lost along the way. Make no mistake about it: teenagers today are definitely more conscious than ever before of being on the lookout for injustice. It is therefore also critically important to social life that their sense of what is right be tempered by qualities such as forgiveness and generosity. It is one thing for people to fall short of our expectations; how we respond to their alleged shortcomings is quite another. In Canada, we are far removed from the Islamic practice of cutting off the hands of thieves. Yet, in the name of justice, we figuratively are carrying out a fair amount of social amputating of our own. For example:

- Teachers accused of sexual misconduct have their names published and reputations ruined before they ever go to trial.

- Physicians who have had sexual contact with patients are being informed that such misconduct is being greeted with "zero tolerance," including lifetime bans.
- Every minister wearing a collar in public risks being stereotyped as a sexual pervert; needless to say, he is not wise to stroll past playgrounds.
- A parent or relative accused of child abuse finds that, prior to conviction, he is ostracized by his community; there is no place to hide.

Obviously, we in no way condone sexual abuse. But we also do not condone the widespread death of compassion and forgiveness, along with the possibility of new hope and new beginnings. We think it is a sad commentary on life in this country that the proportion of Canadians who regard forgiveness as very important has dropped twenty percentage points since only the mid-1980s.

The call from yesteryear for people to "love your enemy" and "forgive those who trespass against you" was more than a call to lofty living. It was also a call to exhibit qualities essential for making optimum social and personal life possible.

Today in Canada, 72 per cent of teenagers and 69 per cent of adults put a high value on cleanliness. However, when asked about the importance of forgiveness, the figures drop to 59 per cent for teens and 55 per cent for other Canadians. In the case of generosity, the numbers slip slightly to 51 per cent for adults. But they plunge to 40 per cent in the case of teenagers. Such findings hardly speak well for interpersonal relations in either the present or the future.

RELATING TO EACH OTHER

When justice becomes our end in all, it's not only the opposition that's slain; social life is frequently made unpleasant to unbearable. For openers, we find ourselves being more cautious. The surveys have found that close to three in four adults today agree that "one cannot be too careful in dealing with people." Further, some 22 per cent maintain that "a stranger who shows a person attention is probably up to something." Among teenagers, that figure doubles to almost 40 per cent!

Such distrust of people in general can be seen in other youth-survey findings. While 70 per cent of teenagers say that honesty is very important to them, just 36 per cent think the trait is similarly valued by most Canadians. Some 60 per cent indicate that they regard family life as very important, but only 40 per cent think other people feel the same. While a somewhat low 40 per cent say they place a high value on generosity, just 25 per cent think other Canadians so value that attribute. Suspicion, Marxist-style, is expressed by this articulate 17-year-old male from Nanaimo, B.C.:

> *The world as we know it is becoming more and more troubled. It is plainly obvious that the average person is nothing more than a manipulative of the state. Democracy no longer has any meaning, honesty is a word found only in dictionaries, and I really wonder how much longer people can take it all. I also hate to say it, but I feel this survey will have very little weight and was created only to temporarily satisfy the populace and make them feel like they were actually contributing; it's all an illustion, compliments of the government.*

Once in place, caution, suspicion, and distrust only escalate. When we think we should be careful, we treat each other with caution, whether we need to or not. When we are treated tentatively, we respond with equal caution. Whether, in fact, the caution is warranted is irrelevant. Perceived as relevant, caution, suspicion, and distrust have self-fulfilling effects on social interaction.

Having stressed the prevalence of racism and sexism, abuse and violence, we now have our eyes open and our dukes up. We have to be on guard, play good defence. Our level of suspicion has become so high it is downright difficult to express simple civility. It is not just unwise to talk to strangers, it's risky to look at them, and definitely dangerous to care about them. If we attempt to show a little kindness or consideration, people wonder what we're up to. It's no exaggeration; these days, a person needs a permit to look and a licence to care. Individuals working directly with the public have become particularly vulnerable, be they physicians, priests, or plumbers. Witch-hunts have been getting our of hand.

In a recent letter to the *Ottawa Citizen*, Cherri Sleeth, head of the Ottawa-Carleton Community on Child Abuse, noted that many male professionals, including teachers, are afraid to touch children or even to be alone with them. Some opt for work that removes them from children altogether. Sleeth maintains that the fear is potentially damaging to children:

If significant numbers of males move away from work in children's ser-vices . . . the whole nature of the relationships between caring adults and dependent children will be distorted. Children will be deprived of exposure to healthy male models, which is something we greatly value these days. Children will be deprived of the caring, support communications and even protection that normal touching by normal adults affords.[22]

The caution hardly stops with professionals. David Koulack, a psychology professor at the University of Manitoba, points out that parents have to use caution in relating to their friends' children and even their very own children. "It's sad to think that hugs are going the way of the hula hoop," he says, "and that the once spontaneous response of warmth or affection, of comfort or praise, is going to be replaced by measured stiff touches of the shoulder or pats on the head." But, he adds, "I fear this is the way we are headed."[23]

RECOVERING COMPASSION AND PURPOSE

Perhaps the fatal flaw in our post-60s social reconstruction efforts was our failure to lay out a national dream that would enable Canadians of all ages to pursue together what they have been saying they value the most: good relationships and economic prosperity. In opting to emphasize the "just society" over the "best society," we left millions of young people and others with the message that our national objective is equitable co-existence.

If we allow our social life to begin and end with justice issues, such a preoccupation becomes debilitating. Justice becomes more import-ant than compassion, the letter of the law superior to the living of life.[24] Our emphasis on being just and fair has to be balanced with an emphasis on extending ourselves to people who are not particularly like us, and a willingness — in the face of failure and shortcomings — to give each other the chance to start again. The respective options? Social fragmentation and personal despair. The human result? Not particularly enjoyable living.

Such a plea is more than melodramatic rhetoric. We all know that our deepest, most gratifying interpersonal ties — with parents, hus-bands or wives, children — call for us to go well beyond the letter of the law. Aspiring merely to be "just" would make our lives with these significant people emotionally barren and unsatisfying.

Faith Nolan has been politically active since she began to write and perform her music. Born in Nova Scotia and raised in Toronto, she is a fifth-generation black. Although her songs speak powerfully about hard realities — wife-battering, violence against homosexuals, single-parent poverty — she has been described as someone who sees life not only as a political struggle, but as a source of pleasure. She has this to say:

> *People who don't realize you have to have some laughter, joy, and love aren't going to last. You have to have a sense of humour if you're going to deal with painful issues. You have to be able to laugh and have a good time — or you'll burn out.*[25]

An Etobicoke 17-year-old suggests that we all take something of a breather:

> *If we all don't smarten up, we'll end up blowing everyone up. Everyone is so high strung — it's about time for all of us to sit back and relax. Only then will we learn to really care for each other and truly feel as one.*

And comedian Alan Thicke, when told by the CBC to water down his jokes about national unity in hosting the June 1992 NHL awards telecast, commented, "Frankly, I think we're in such a sensitive time politically that we're in danger of losing our sense of humour." Noting that the likes of Jay Leno wouldn't survive on the CBC because his political jokes would result in Canadians having "a collective stroke," Thicke added, "There seems to be a cathartic comedic response that Americans take that Canadians haven't felt free enough or loose enough to do yet."[26]

Social life calls for the letter to be joined by the spirit, the mind to be accompanied by the heart, strain to be offset by laughter.

IV. EMERGENCE WITHOUT BALANCE

There is a fourth notable cultural contradiction. It lies in our wide-spread recognition that teenagers are emerging into adulthood, and our failure to respond to that emergence with the necessary balance between providing them with direction and giving them room. The frequent result is youth's alienation from adults and adult institutions.

The survey findings document a consistent paradox: teenagers supremely value relationships, but frequently do not have good ties with adults.

Ideally, young people should be able to find good social ties just about everywhere. When we think of a little child, for example, he or she does not have a built-in bias against any particular person or institution. Receptivity to positive relations seemingly has no limits.

One would think the starting point for good ties would be the home. High-quality social life, in a perfect society, would further extend outward, encompassing peers, the school, the workplace, the church or its equivalent, a variety of youth groups, and so on. But then again, Canada is not a perfect place.

ALIENATION FROM ADULTS

Enjoyment of mothers and fathers is less than unanimous. While 94 per cent of young people say they receive a high level of enjoyment from their friends, the level for moms is 67 per cent, for dads only 60 per cent. What's more, the enjoyment drop since 1984 for both mothers and fathers is about 10 percentage points.

Symptomatic of fairly common relational problems on the home front, only six in 10 teens say they highly value family life, despite the fact that eight in 10 place that kind of importance on friendship and being loved. Things are a little better in Quebec than elsewhere, yet there, too, things are this side of perfection.

Although differences by gender aren't great, a slightly greater proportion of females than males feel uneasy in the presence of *both* mothers (14 per cent versus seven per cent) and fathers (19 per cent versus 13 per cent). You may recall our earlier finding that females also are more inclined than males to say they have disagreements with their parents. Their tendency to mature sooner, and therefore perhaps experience resistance a bit sooner, may be a contributing factor. One 16-year-old from Castlegar, B.C., sums up her frustration with her parents this way: "I feel belittled by my father and older than my mother."

In the 1988 survey, we asked teenagers for their views about "how older adults tend to treat young people." Approximately eight in 10 said adults generally like young people, while seven in 10 said adults tend to be courteous to them. The figure dropped to five in 10, however, when the issue of respect for the opinions of young people was raised. In fact, about the same proportion maintained many adults are intimidated by younger people. A minority of fewer than four in 10 did *not* think adults as a whole understand young people, and only three in 10 felt adults have confidence in them.

Listen to this 15-year-old from Toronto:

I feel youth are not taken seriously in an adult world. They are smart and sometimes smarter than some adults. I don't appreciate the fact that adults try to analyze us and think they know everything about us. They think they know but don't bother asking US. I also hate adults who are prejudiced toward us because we're teenagers. Even if a majority of teens do something wrong, what about the minority? I think that teenagers should be respected and they will return the favour. In my opinion, my greatest achievement would be to be respected and heard. I feel I am mature and speak smartly. I wish adults would really listen to me and feel my view is important also.

Another 15-year-old, from a small Alberta community, indicates that discrimination against young people is hardly limited to large cities like Toronto, Montreal, and Vancouver:

I think teenagers are really neglected by adults. For example, if we go into a restaurant, some people won't serve us because we are "kids." Or else they will take their time, which is totally unfair. Teenagers should be given more respect.

A grade-10 student from Vancouver, who articulately expresses views on a variety of topics from Quebec's future to abortion and racism, has this to say about her teachers:

When I'm around my teachers, I feel like a little child who has to do what they tell me to do, even though I don't want to."

Another B.C. resident, a grade-11 native who lives in a small community in the interior, says:

I feel personally, as a young adult, that teenagers are treated poorly by the school system. Teachers are supposed to work with us, not be against us. We need to be treated equally, fairly, and given a chance.

A note of interest: the 1000 or so 20- to 24-year-olds who, along with about the same number of teenagers, made up the sample in the 1988 survey, did not differ from 15- to 19-year-olds in any significant way in their view of adults. It seems that merely reaching the age of 20 is no guarantee of "better treatment" from adults. Such individuals may not be teenagers. Yet, in many adult eyes, they apparently are still too young to have their ideas taken seriously.

Findings like these suggest that young people frequently feel that adults don't understand them, don't treat them with respect, and don't have much confidence in them. As one 15-year-old female from a small southern Alberta town puts it, "Most adults think that, to have us, is to just have a lot of trouble."

We are not saying that all is bad when it comes to adult-youth relations on the home front and beyond. Far from it. But the survey findings do indicate that, in a fairly large number of cases — including, perhaps, situations with which you yourself are readily familiar — things are not what they can be and should be.

ALIENATION FROM ADULT INSTITUTIONS

The surveys have documented what most of us have known for some time: the two major sources of enjoyment for teenagers are friends and music. Sports is also a particularly important area of gratification for males. Pets are cherished by many. Further, moderate proportions of 15- to 19-year-olds say they receive high levels of enjoyment from television, VCRs, and — for those who have them — cars. At the bottom? School, jobs, youth groups, and, lastly, organized religion. As we pointed out earlier, these three bottom categories — not coincidentally — are all heavily adult-driven.

What the findings are telling us so far is when it comes to relating to teens, adults are batting zero for two. They themselves aren't high on young people's enjoyment lists. And their institutions and activities aren't faring much better.

THE ROOT OF THE PROBLEM

As we stressed in *The Emerging Generation,* many adults have a simple explanation for why the alienation exists: the problem lies with teenagers.

The Age-Old Thesis You've heard the refrain all your life. Conflict between adults and teenagers is inevitable. Parents whose offspring have grown up are relieved that the experience is over. Parents whose offspring are toddlers acknowledge that tough times lie ahead. People who plan to be parents recognize that having kids has its ups and downs, and one of the downs is having to put up with them when they are teenagers.

According to many, the teenage years are an exacting but unavoidable stage through which children pass on the way to adulthood —

sort of like the necessity of having wisdom teeth pulled. Most of us know it must happen but none of us particularly enjoys it. Our sons and daughters will have trouble with adolescence, are frequently belligerent, callous, arrogant, stubborn, loud, silent, selfish — and those are among the best traits. They alternate between wanting to be treated like children and wanting to be treated like adults. Sometimes, their being semi-children and semi-adults makes them seem semi-human.

If teens blab to the pollsters that life isn't all that enjoyable with mom and dad, then parents, given the chance, find themselves clearing their throats and adding a few more paragraphs to the enjoyment story. For life with teenagers isn't always exactly a barrel of laughs, either. In the 1990 national survey of adults, for example, 90 per cent informed us that, all things being equal, they do receive a lot of enjoyment from their children. But in homes with at least one teenager, all things aren't equal. In such situations, the "enjoyment of kids" figure dropped to 75 per cent, with little difference between moms and dads.

Most adults, however, are not so much resentful of teenagers as they are fatalistic. It's part of the package when one decides to have children. Looking back, many of us probably think we gave our parents and teachers a fair amount to handle when we ourselves were teenagers. Many of us didn't particularly enjoy adults during those years. So why should we expect our sons and daughters to be any different?

The fact that they often prefer their friends to their parents is no surprise. As for not enjoying school, who does? As one senator — awakening after snoozing through much of our presentation — said in response to a summary of the 1984 survey findings we provided, "I didn't enjoy school when I was a kid. Why should they?" Many clergy have come to similar conclusions about the lack of interest young people have in organized religion: it's just something that happens to teenagers.

According to this well-worn interpretation of adolescence, the teenage years are not so much to be enjoyed as they are to be endured. Many a person has been heard to murmur, "I don't envy them," as they look at parents, teachers, and leaders who are dealing with teenagers.

If this were all that could be said, it would seem rational people would not have children at all. A quick cost-benefit analysis would tell them to turn potential bedrooms into hot-tub rooms, offices, sun rooms, and the like. But the adult thesis about young people does not end with despair. It goes on to say there is light at the end of the teenage tunnel. The tough times will eventually pass. By around 18 or 19, for the majority of teens, the miracle of the return to normalcy occurs. No one is quite sure why. It just happens.

One winter, or spring, or fall, quite without warning, the stage ends. Our teens — as hard as it was to believe when they were 14 or 15 — actually thank us for putting up with them. For our part, we suppress a big grin and an enormous sigh of relief, and life moves on to happier things. The postcript to the process is that, in time, intergenerational justice takes place, when they have teenagers of their own. . . .

The Emergence Thesis We don't dispute that the teenage years are not necessarily a utopian period for many adults. But our data document another reality that's also very familiar: the period is not always that great for some young people, either.

Obviously it's popular to pin most of the blame on teenagers. After all, they are the ones who've changed. We're still doing things the same. Basic social science, however, stresses the importance of using an "interaction model" when we try to make sense of behaviour. Translated, if we want to understand people, we need to look at how they relate to each other. If you hear a strange voice, you hope someone produced it. If you complain that a police officer was rude as he handed you a speeding ticket, it would be helpful to know what exactly you said to him when he pulled you over and asked for your ID. Social life involves interaction, or, in lingo familiar to many, "stimulus and response."

If we want to figure out why teenagers act the way they do, it's critical we understand how we relate to them. The premise of the interaction model is that adult behaviour influences youth behaviour; in turn, teenage behaviour influences adult behaviour. The process is dynamic and ongoing.

Because so much has been said, written, and assumed about what has gone wrong with teenagers, we have purposely attempted to emphasize the need to look at how adults deal with teenagers — to be something of advocates for teenagers.

We are well aware that teenagers differ dramatically in how they interact with adults. Our argument, however, is that much of the conflict, alienation, and lack of joy experienced by adults and young people reflects not so much a problem with teens as a problem with adults.

Central to our argument, as presented in *The Emerging Generation*, is that teenagers are experiencing multidimensional emergence. In the course of saying goodbye to childhood, they are engaged in the process of becoming adults. We are not talking merely about physical changes, but also changes along social, psychological, emotional, sexual, economic, intellectual, and spiritual lines. Teens are concerned about their evolving appearance, acquiring significant social skills, wrestling with self-esteem, discovering sexuality, experiencing a wide range of new emotions, coming to grips with finances, learning more and more about what is, reflecting on meaning and purpose.

In the face of such divergent emergence, teenagers require two basic contributions from adults: *direction* and *room*. Much of what they are experiencing is new, and they desperately need information and occasional advice. They also need to know there are limits to what they are allowed to do, at home, at school, in their time spent with each other. Here they are no different from the rest of us. The anthropologist was right: social life requires "folkways, mores, and laws" — conventions, morals and legal guidelines. No one gets an exemption. The alternative is social chaos. Also, there is a time and a place for discipline.

Teenagers do not differ from us in wanting a measure of direction. For example, one female grade-10 student from Golden, B.C., has this to say about excessive leniency toward young offenders:

> *I myself think that teenagers — even myself — get away with murder. Although we are supposed to be young adults, we aren't punished like adults. I think that's wrong. We should at least get punished enough that the message will get through to others who are thinking about committing the same crimes.*

Most parents and teachers don't have to be prodded to provide direction. When teenagers don't respond well, they are often seen as indifferent and even disobedient, unwilling to listen and learn from people who "know better."

In addition to being given direction, however, teenagers also need to be given large amounts of room. It is not just a coincidence that young people place such a high value on freedom. What they are asking for is not the opportunity merely to do whatever they want in an uninhibited and irresponsible manner. On the contrary, in the face of their multifaceted emergence, teenagers desperately need the opportunity to emerge from their childhood shells. They require the freedom to be what they are comfortable being, to act, think, feel, and believe, according to who they are and who they are becoming.

A well-spoken grade-11 student from Montreal offers his thoughts on the need for room, for example, in a familiar setting:

The education system currently promotes technological skills, kills creativity, and squelches all hope of a spiritually fulfilling life. It needs to make some important changes.

A good rule of thumb is this: to the extent that adults are able to find that direction-room balance, ties with teenagers can be enjoyable all the way around. Conversely, any adult or any adult institution unable to find an adequate balance between direction and room will frustrate young people. That's an understatement. They may also seriously *damage* young people.

But don't take our word for it. Try it on your own experiences. For the record, in discussing "the emergence thesis" with adults across Canada for close to a decade, we have invited them to test the argument on their own biographies and see how well it works. The result has made us only more dogmatic on this point. Virtually without exception, people concur. They themselves realize, when they think about it, that the parent, or teacher, or minister, or older friend that they thoroughly enjoyed during their teenage years was a person who could give them input when they wanted it, yet treated them with respect, giving them the room they needed to feel comfortable as budding adults. They didn't have to diminish themselves in the presence of such people. In short, they were adults who gave them direction and room.

The balance, of course, is true of relationships in general. We enjoy friends, marriage partners, co-workers, strangers who don't suffocate us on the one hand or be sponges on the other. We value input, but we also need room to breathe. The only difference with teenagers is that, because they are going through a stage of life when they are coming alive on so many fronts, the need for both guidance and space is particularly acute.

TOO SOON WE FORGET

Unfortunately, we have short memories. Having usually had very mixed experiences with adults when we ourselves were adolescents, we typically buy into the adult interpretation of the teenage years when we hit adulthood — and thus perpetuate the idea that teens are difficult creatures. The two of us stand by our words of almost a decade ago:

> *When we assume adult roles, we feel like adults and we think like adults, complete with the adult myth about teenagers. We consequently tend to* reinterpret *our teenage experience through that framework. We frequently find ourselves taking the blame for how we related to our parents (e.g., "I was really a rotten kid"). In doing so, we tend to remember what was good about them and minimize what was bad. In the process, we absolve them of any responsibility. More seriously, we proceed to use the same interpretation on our own teenagers. The oppressed become the oppressors. The result is that the adult resistance to emergence is passed down from generation to generation, and accorded the status of a virtue.*[27]

Relations between adults and teens are not what they can be. And the longer we take a fatalistic position toward the situation, the longer the myth of inevitable conflict will keep young people and adults from experiencing the quality of life that is possible for both.

It's time we turned this well-worn page.

Part II /
Responding to the Trends

*T*he *second part of* Teen Trends *is about enhancing life.*

Part I has painted a portrait of what already exists. Now we want to grapple with the promise and potential of teen-adult relationships. Each chapter interprets and applies the research findings, in practical ways, with an eye to improving the quality of life exchanged between young people and their parents, educators, religious leaders, media personnel, and other adults who intersect, and sometimes interfere, with teens' existence.

A recent experience my wife and I had on the tennis court illustrates part of the problem in teen-adult relationships.

We went to our neighbourhood court just to hit the ball back and forth. Nothing serious, just a little late-afternoon exercise. People were already playing on the only two courts, so we sat on the grass to wait our turn. A few minutes after we arrived a couple of young guys showed up with their rackets in hand. We chatted a bit. I eventually asked them their ages. They were 12 and 14. The four of us took notice of the posted sign and commented that we shouldn't have to wait much longer.

The sign read:

PLAYERS
Must relinquish courts after one-half hour of play.
The facilities are for the benefit of all community residents.
PLEASE BE CONSIDERATE AND COURTEOUS.

At four-thirty, the players on the first court packed up their gear. My wife and I took their place. As we hit the ball back and forth for five minutes or so, I kept waiting for the two middle-aged men on the other court to let the young guys have their turn.

They didn't.

I'm filled with imperfections, but whenever adults mistreat young people, feelings start churning in me. When it was clear the men had played well past the posted limit, I walked over to their court, pointed to the sign, and suggested it was time for them to get off.

My interference was treated as a breach of tennis etiquette. The adult point of view ruled.

"We were here first. Anyway, they're just kids."

My wife and I hit the ball a few more times and invited the young guys to take our court.

Playing tennis is supposed to be fun. That afternoon it was an emotional ordeal.

We have already established that in the main, young people are turning out like adults. Obviously, adult modelling matters. Behaviour that's neither considerate nor courteous does not merit being reproduced. Sending signals to today's youth that they are "just kids" and accordingly do not deserve to be respected as full-fledged human beings is demeaning. It lowers life. We can do better.

We, your authors, have no illusions about reducing life to fun experiences. Nor are we interested in sitting on mammoth computer printouts and smugly scolding everybody over the age of 19. Institutions and their leaders are not helped by being told, yet again, that they are underachieving. However, we do aspire to shed light on the Canadian experience and, in so doing, lift the level of life between adults and the younger generation. Out of our love for life and concern for Canada, our aspiration is to improve the quality of living for all Canadians.

Day after day and situation after situation, teenagers and adults repeatedly enter life through different doors:

- Teenagers value their friends more than their family. Adults value their family more than their friends.
- Teenagers see their freedom as an expression of their need for increasing independence. Adults are prone to see freedom in adolescents as a guaranteed formula for irresponsible behaviour.
- Teenagers highly value "being respected." Although the majority of adults do not intentionally set out to disrespect adolescents, young people perceive that their opinions aren't worth much in the adult forum.
- Teenagers have easy access to illicit drugs, and all but a very small percentage say no to them. A large sector of adults stereotype modern youth as a group of habitual drug users.
- Teenagers today are burdened with a continual passing parade of local and global problems that never seem to get resolved. Adults look at youth and

think their lot in life is desirable because they are accountable for so few real responsibilities.

- *Teenagers have been handed a very complex world. The cultural consensus of the past has been carved up to accommodate the demands of pluralism and personal preferences. Adults frequently expect the norms of the past to be the status quo of the present.*
- *Teenagers have readily accepted the benefits of their parents' indulgences and enjoy the standard of living to which they have become accustomed. Parents are wondering why their children are staying home longer and getting married later.*
- *Teenagers have hooked their hopes on a set of high expectations that will inevitably tumble many of them into disillusionment. Adults are waiting for their offspring to grow up and are increasingly wondering if they are going to make it.*

When people who live on the same planet compute life on wavelengths that bypass each other, they often develop an inability to see life from each other's point of view. The result leads to confusion and conflict.

The incident on the tennis court may not be common, but it is illustrative of how unhealthy life can be when adults and young people interact. We are particularly anxious to address the prevailing notion that "life has always worked that way." We are equally dismayed when adults view the teenage years as simply a "stage in life that has to be endured." We believe that adults' bowing to the mentality that adolescence is an aberration to be tolerated and the best they can do is survive it is no way for people to live together. We are convinced that living with the attitude that life will be better when we get on the other side of inevitable teenage trauma is a prescription for pain and sorrow during the teenage years.

The chapters that follow are written with the purpose of nudging "what is" toward "what can be."

5

THE ROLE OF
THE FAMILY

*Y*oung people have been shaped by the society they live in. If they could create their ideal world, they would have first-class relationships and a high standard of living.

What is most important to them, however, are relationships and having the freedom to enjoy them. Accordingly, eight in 10 put friendship and being loved at the top of their scale of values. Although family is valued, too, a lower number — six in 10 — say that it's "very important." Because parents value family more than friendship and teenagers value friends more than family, life in the family is set up for predictable conflict.

That doesn't mean young people are particularly negative about family living. Rather, the vast majority of Canadian teenagers are still planning on getting married and staying married to their covenant partner.

On the enjoyment scale, friends tower over fathers and mothers. While 93 per cent of young people say they receive a high level of enjoyment from their friends, the level for moms is 67 per cent, and for dads, only 60 per cent. What's more, the enjoyment of both mothers and fathers has dropped about 10 percentage points since 1984. The situation is a little brighter in Quebec than elsewhere, but still, reality resides quite a distance from the ideal.

We think that things can be improved.

THE ALMIGHTY POWER OF FRIENDSHIP
Friendship is the glue that holds the youth society together. The gratification that friendship delivers is the reason Alexander Graham Bell is the patron saint of the younger generation. Young people grow

up with a telephone attached to their ear because it keeps them connected to what is most important to them. It links them to their social lifeline. The ringing of a phone is even more welcome to most teens than the blare of loud rock music. An 18-year-old Jamaican female from Montreal speaks on behalf of her peers: "What I enjoy most is talking on the phone."

When parents become aware that their teenagers rank friends over family, they get discouraged. Many moms and dads conclude they are failing. At the very least they feel unappreciated to learn that nine in 10 teenagers see their friends as high-level sources of enjoyment while only six in 10 perceive their parents that way.

UNDERSTANDING FRIENDSHIP

Discerning parents will not view the gravitational pull of their teenagers toward the power of friendship as a threat to their own ongoing ties with them. They will understand that the high priority given to friendship doesn't mean young people are entering into alternative life-long relationships. Friendship patterns during the teen years are not shallow, even if they are usually short-term. The relationships have an existential flavour to them. They tune in to the mood of the moment. The quality is intense but often not long-lasting. The teenagers themselves don't really expect their friendships to last a lifetime. They are experiencing life together now. Intimacy doesn't have to continue forever to be genuine. Friendships bring moments of pleasure.

Accordingly, for well-balanced, healthy young people, being alone can be worse than having to write a calculus test. That isn't to say teens always want to be with someone else; they value privacy, too. It is to say, however, they have a deep longing to know that they are cared for, that they can be who they are with someone else who accepts who they are. Peers are naturally positioned to provide this kind of support and experience.

The place and power of friendship in the life of young people is not a new phenomenon. Just think back to your own teenage years. Friends have always played an important role. Earlier chapters document that when past research is compared to the present, friends are becoming more important. In recent decades, teachers, religious leaders, and youth workers have suffered demotions as perceived sources of influence in the lives of the young. Increasing instances of divorce create relational stress in the family and the greater number of women working outside the home inevitably reduces the amount of time children can spend with parents. The consequences are clear: when one sphere of interpersonal relationships makes a gain, other spheres tend to lose. In the case of modern teenagers, it appears there is a transfer of relationship focus from adults to peers.

While the importance of friendship in the lives of young people is not new, there are some developments we as parents need to be aware of, lest we commit the error of projecting our own experiences on the present circumstances of our children. As this book has already made clear, today's young people, in the main, are reflecting the essence of what is around them. However, in some refreshing ways, they are also edging into new territory.

Today's teens are blurring the gender lines. Flowing out of the high value the younger generation places on relationships is a movement toward gender equality. They are relating to each other as human beings before labelling each other male or female. As a result, they are transcending some of the past ways of relating across gender lines. For example, many of today's young people are experiencing quality friendships with members of the opposite sex *without* the ingredients of romance or sex. Genuine gender equality is on the horizon.

As parents, our own patterns from the past can blind us to what is really going on with our teenagers. Think about an everyday happening in homes across the country. The phone rings. Mom picks it up and learns it's Jeremy calling yet again for her 17-year-old daughter, Jennifer. The two of them talk for about 45 minutes. Jennifer's laughter is frequent. She obviously enjoys Jeremy. During this time mom begins to think *romance*. She begins wondering, How serious is the relationship? What's Jeremy really like? Is he trustworthy? How long will it last?

Jennifer eventually hangs up. Attempting to act nonchalant and spontaneous, mom asks, "What were you and Jeremy talking about for so long?" Jennifer responds, "Oh, nothing much. He's a friend. We were just talking, that's all."

Mother and daughter separate. Jennifer is enjoying friendship. Mother is still thinking romance.

The fact that young people are blurring the gender lines and enjoying platonic relationships does not mean healthy sex drives get shut down. After all, today's teenagers are experimenters and their hormones are active. But who would argue against the idea, especially these days, that beginning with friendship is the best approach to love and commitment? While there is no virtue in being naive about what can happen when members of the opposite sex enjoy each other, when misconceptions are the rule between parents and their teens, problems are inevitable. When there is ambiguity or concern, honest discussions about what parents are thinking and what teenagers are experiencing can be very useful.

Let's give young people credit. They are leading the way when it comes to valuing and experiencing relationships. And they are building more friendship into romance. Consequently, when those romances crash, they often want to retain something from the relationship and continue as friends. It may be idealistic and a scenario for increased emotional pain, but it is a step forward from the old way of being dealt a broken heart and never talking to the person again.

Another pattern is emerging, too. From their birth many modern young people have known only a multicultural environment. The evidence says they are less racist, more inclined to accept diversity, and disapproving of behaviours that sanction discrimination. As a result the young are looking at each other and seeing less colour. For more and more teens, friends are friends, whatever the colour of their skin. Today's youth are being released from the tendency to stereotype others who are different from themselves. In groups they simply see people, other human beings. The prevailing attitudes of the young should produce a more humane and level ground society.

The future will also bring tensions. As increasing numbers of young people commit themselves to marriages that cross ethnic lines, members of the older generation may shake their heads and withhold their approval.

EMBRACING THE FRIENDSHIP REALITY

Nothing is gained by blaming yourself for your child's lack of enjoyment of your company. In fact no one is to blame. It's far more constructive to accept the reality that friends take centre stage in the life of your teen, and most of today's teens. Avoid the trap of insisting on a "family time" when your teenagers already have plans to do something with their friends.

An even smarter move is to extend the reach of your family to include the friends of your children. Rather than fighting the gravitational pull between them and their friends, develop a reputation among your teens' peers as parents who welcome them in your home.

Institute an open-door policy. And often that means the fridge door as well as the front door.

Families with teenagers and the budget to cope with the demand are always watching for good deals on cases of soft drinks. They recognize the connection between the hunger in teenagers' stomachs and the cravings in their hearts. They understand that the "language of food" sends out signals that say, "I like you. You are welcome here."

Open-door homes are places of acceptance. The welcome mat stays out, and people show up again and again. Open-door homes are places with lots of laughter. We're not suggesting parents condone party damage, but they needn't make a big deal about a few spills on carpets. Instead of a lecture after the damage is done, they invite the group of friends to a Saturday Clean the Rec Room Day. When they want to make the "you must learn to be responsible" point, then as well as letting the "culprits" do the work, they suggest they also buy the shampoo. But when the work is done, they make sure the pizza is delivered on time!

The open-door policy doesn't take away the parents' prerogative to close the door sometimes. To keep healthy, families need time by themselves. Some cultures encourage an open door; others endorse family practices that are more closed. Some family styles are simply more exclusive than others. There are no absolute right and wrong patterns. The balance between an open door and a closed one varies from family to family.

PEER POWER

Computing the friendship factor and then anticipating how life works is relatively simple. Because friendship is both the top-rated value and the number-one source of enjoyment for young people, it naturally follows that teenage friends will wield power in one another's lives. They both exercise peer power and are subject to its influence. Often, the exchange of influence is positive. Having friends who are active in sports and enjoy the outdoors usually fills leisure time with wholesome activity. Other times peer power is negative. Being part of a group that hangs around malls may lead to trouble of one kind or another. Whether positive or negative, teenagers and parents must deal with the dynamics of peer pressure.

Whether it is an innate drive to protect one's children or an inherent fear that sources outside the family bring destructive influences, parents are notorious for being down on teenage peer power.

This pessimistic posture toward peer power sends a double-negative message to both your children and their friends. And when you think about it, sending the signal that you don't trust their friends also implies you don't trust your teens, either. This sets life in the family on a downward slide.

Fighting the force of friendship will in the end be a losing proposition. A counter-strategy is to encourage your children to exercise good judgment when choosing their friends. Reinforcing the potential of *positive peer power* is a better long-term game-plan.

When you become a mother or a father, two things are guaranteed: pleasure and pain. The guarantee of pleasure comes early when the children are young. Parents are not only needed, they have the power and are in control — not just physically, but emotionally. As the children get older, however, there is a power shift. Particularly in the emotional realm, teens exert more control over their parents than parents do over them, and this is where things start to get painful.

Parents feel threatened by *negative peer power*. Suspecting that your teen's friends are shoplifting and doing drugs is bad enough, but knowing that, at least for the time being, those same friends have more influence on your child than you have is profoundly disturbing. Simply realizing friends wield a negative influence over your son or daughter blows dark clouds over any home.

The pain parents feel comes in many forms, but most often it is induced by a sense of helplessness. Lying awake in the early hours of the morning waiting to hear the key turn in the lock, suspecting sexual activity that is far too premature, dealing with underachieving at school, knowing that hard-earned money is being wasted, smelling alcohol on successive weekends, absorbing announcements such as, "I don't believe in God anymore and I'm certainly not going to church," aching with the awareness that what used to be a group of friends has turned into a gang, and picking up the phone to find it's the police on the other end of the line — these are the recipes for pure parent pain.

Knowing what's going on but not being able to do much about it triggers a unique kind of agony. The helpless cry of a parent whose daughter had run away from home captures the anguish: *"I can't help and I can't stop caring."*

PARENT POWER

Because friendship is so powerful in the life of young people, decreeing to a son or daughter, "You are never to talk or spend time with your friend again," seems a tremendous risk. But when life is out of control and severe damage is on the horizon, there is a place for "tough love."

Writer Mordecai Richler's view of living with limits as a Canadian applies on the family front, too. On a recent television interview, he protested, "I will drink only so much bad Canadian wine for my country." For the sake of sanity, and for the protection of those who have gone too far, there are times when parents should stand up and say they've had enough.

Even though teenagers are often determined to go their own way, parents have power, too. Consider the following table. The data is a response to the question, "Who do you find yourself most likely to turn to when you are making decisions in —?"

	% Indicating Parents	% Indicating Friends
Spending money	48	18
Relationships	7	75
Sex	8	55
Having fun	3	81
Right and wrong	45	22
School	45	20
Career	48	10
A major problem	31	41

The parent domains are clear. Although the low level on "having fun" is rather particularly embarrassing, teenagers do seek counsel and direction from parents in several important areas. When it comes to spending money, issues about what's right and wrong, school concerns and career decisions, parents have open doors into the lives of their teens.

At least two parenting principles emerge from the data. First, when it comes to being involved in the life of your teenagers, walk through doors that are already ajar. Enter into the life concerns of your teens at the points of least resistance. And once you have entered, journey into the other areas normally reserved for their friends.

Second, parents should not expect to be the only source of influence in their teenagers' lives. Astute parents will understand that teens are on a journey from dependence to independence, and will expect the influence of friends and other adults. At the same time, there will be no surprise when the long-term marks of parental influence prevail.

An important footnote: For adults who desire to stay in touch with the younger generation, the bottom-line message is, *Relate at all costs.* Do whatever necessary *not* to breach the relationship.

Several years ago, I was on a plane and sitting next to a man who told me he had three teenagers. I was explaining some of the main findings of our initial research. This man grew increasingly impatient. Finally, he turned in his seat so he could look me in the eye and asked, "I'm interested in what you're saying, but have you figured out how to handle them?" My response then still stands: "The issue is not so much how to *handle* the younger generation but how to *relate* to them.

An 18-year-old female from the Maritimes expresses what all parents would undoubtedly hope their teens would say: "I have a great relationship with my parents and my life is pretty good. My parents are there for me when I'm in trouble."

MAKING ROOM FOR FAILURE

In family life, as in most aspects of life, nothing is perfect. We must include a place for failure. Comparing family life to playing baseball will invoke some fresh thinking. The two have numerous similarities.

Like baseball, family life is a team sport. In the traditional family, dad is the pitcher and mom is the catcher. In the roles of life, it's dad who throws the fastballs and curveballs. And mom, she's behind the plate, calling the signals.

The younger children stay close to home plate, handling the ground balls in the infield. Mom and dad like the little ones near enough to keep an eye on them. The teenagers need more room. They chase down the fly balls in the outfield. They often invite their friends to help them play their game.

Even a casual observer of winning baseball teams soon realizes that the teams that do well have bench strength. A team without a strong bull pen and a core of pinch hitters doesn't do very well over the long season. In today's complex and often perplexing world, families, too, need bench strength. Neighbours, colleagues from work, adults from religious organizations, teachers from school, and family friends are all people who may be in positions to make some key contributions.

Certain families need more back-up than others. Families that have been fractured for one reason or another face life without a full line-up. Single parents are forced to play more than one position. Every day in our country, unfortunate accidents and premature deaths leave people aching and alone. A family can be fractured forever in a single night of violence and abuse. Members of dysfunctional families often find themselves covering bases for one another. Stress and strain dominate the family scene. Too often, families stumble badly in their efforts to survive, and so need an expanded roster.

On a more positive note, another similarity between family life and baseball is that most of the game is non-violent and slow-paced. There are lots of routine ground-outs and fly balls. Even when there's a hit, home runs are not the norm. Putting the ball in play and just getting to first base is what usually happens. Of course, in almost every game, there are occasional flurries and extraordinary action; a brilliant double play, a catch off the wall in the outfield, a bases-loaded strike-out, and extra innings are all dramatic. But over the long season, the umpires get most of their calls right and there's not much complaint. Even with 95-mph pitches and bats swinging through curve balls, baseball games see little intentional violence.

In family life, alarm clocks go off, most meals are eaten without arguments, clothes are washed and sometimes get ironed, toilets get flushed, televisions get turned on and off, videos are rented, homework gets done, problems are discussed, decisions are made, and bills get paid. Along the way are birthday parties, tears and laughter, and the occasional bottle of champagne. Before we realize it there are only 34 shopping days till Christmas. Certainly problems invade and upset, but in the main, there are many more days when we are healthy than sick. A lot of family life is routine.

But in the family, just as in baseball, no one bats a thousand. The best any member of the family can muster is a healthy average. Obviously, some members of the family have higher averages than others. But not even dad or mom gets a hit every time they go to the plate. In both baseball and in the game of life, people make errors. There are wild pitches. There are both strike-outs and walks. There are fair balls and foul. And one predictable pattern for teenagers is forever contending that foul balls are really fair. They are always pushing to make the playing field bigger.

When baseball was dreamed up, the idea of three strikes before you're called out was a real winner. Imagine a family not allowing their children more than one strike. Everybody loses.

THE MOM-OVER-DAD PHENOMENON

If we assess who's getting more hits on the family playing field, we've got bad news for dads. Signalling a lack of acceptance and feeling put down, a 16-year-old male and an 18-year-old female explain respectively, "When I am around my father, I feel I have to look normal," and, "When I am around my father, I feel belittled in all I do." Adding further to the scenario, another 16-year-old male reveals, "When I am around my father, I feel overpowered."

For whatever reasons, today's teens are more willing to turn to mom than dad for both caring and counsel. Whether young people are looking to share what has gone wrong or what has gone great, they are simply more ready to turn to good ol' mom.

	How much value	Source of enjoyment	Source of influence	Turn to when facing problems	Look to for moral guidance
ATTITUDES TOWARD PARENTS AND FRIENDS					
In %'s					
MOTHER	62	68	75	36	39
FATHER	62	59	66	15	23
FRIENDS	83	93	59	26	30

SOURCE: *Project Teen Canada 88*

We've already looked at why some of the ratings for friends are so high. Similarly, there are explanations for the scores of mothers exceeding those of fathers.

Think about life within the family. The last time dad said he wouldn't be home for the weekend, did anybody in the family have an anxiety attack? But what if mom unexpectedly left a note saying she's going away for a couple of days? Wouldn't the response be different?

Most conventional two-parent families would cope if mom was not on the scene, but just barely. Mothers tend to be the lynchpin both in family relations and in keeping the household together. Even if she spends as much time at the office as dad, she spends more time looking after the house — preparing meals and ensuring there are groceries in the fridge. In addition, most mothers are more involved in the lives of their children.

Contrary to what many contend, and even with 61 per cent of mothers with young children working outside the home, dads are not flocking to the "new father" movement, which calls for men to be nurturing and emotionally demonstrative dads.[1] As a result, it should come as no surprise that mom gets most of the attention from teens, who value relationships. They've grown up interacting more closely with her, and dad has been perceived as distant.

Father is still commonly portrayed as the primary breadwinner, the one in charge, and the provider of wisdom. He does more recreation with his son than with his daughter, but seldom interacts in a deep meaningful way with either.[2]

Why are dads perceived as distant? Again, conventional wisdom says women, natural nurturers, are more sensitive to the emotional needs of their children. But conventional wisdom alone is too simplistic to explain the total situation.

Elements of the modern world, such as industrialization and mass transportation, have been the primary architects of the fractured family. During the Industrial Revolution, fathers were removed from the primary-care activities they shared with their wives in more agricultural/cottage-industry economies. Likewise, women were removed from the income-producing activities and given sole responsibility for child-rearing. Modernization and urbanization fractured families along the father/children line of relationships.[3]

In much of the western world of today, the average father leaves for work around 7 a.m. and is home sometime around 6 p.m. Consequently, many children are, for all practical purposes, fatherless. We've accepted it as the norm.

In Canada, as in many industrialized countries, dads are home only when there is time to spare from the office or plant floor. For the father flirting with the idea of being more than a marginally involved parent, he has to deal with one of the cornerstones of our corporate culture: active parenting is okay only if the job allows it.[4]

One-dimensional working dads are almost precluded from tapping into the emotional needs of their children. That doesn't make men actually less nurturing or less emotional, but too often we accept social strictures that don't allow that side of men to be expressed. Both children and fathers lose out.

The case for co-parenting — where both wife and husband have significant interaction in the physical, emotional, and spiritual development of their children — is becoming stronger all the time. Still there are obstacles to overcome. Journalist Vivian Smith argues that "it is not easy to just pick up how to be a good father when women still dominate the field, when the workplace is not supportive and when other men know as little about it as their own fathers did." Breaking socially entrenched patterns is difficult. Writing on the subject "Fathers' new roles aren't easy to rehearse," Smith cites her husband's experience: "When he takes our son and daughter to the park, invariably someone will come over and say, 'Oh, baby-sitting the kids today, eh?' as if he had someone else's children foisted on him. He replies that no, these are his children. He is no secondary, stand-in parent."[5]

If dads choose, they can make some moves today. What would a conversation between son and father be like if the father asked serious questions and really listened to the answers? Why can't daughters go on fishing trips, too? What adjustments would it take in fathers for teens to perceive dad sometimes as an advice receiver rather than an advice giver, or an approachable friend instead of head of the house.

Concerned fathers can begin rocking a few boats in the workplace. Employers need to hear more often an employee say he can't work the weekend or stay late because he has a date with his daughter. A father needs to be able to say good night to colleagues without apology when his son is waiting to go to the hockey game.

Fathers will have to step out of the fairly rigid social straitjackets they have inherited. But for those who choose, the current climate supports the "new father" movement, which encourages dads to reach beyond their societal-given role as breadwinner and give a higher priority to their divine-given role as parent.

NORMAL ISN'T NORMAL

What happens when children move into adolescence is quite predictable. They begin to devalue the treasures of home, simply assimilating them as their personal right of existence. But just because teens value friends more than family, we mustn't conclude that they are anti-family; they simply accept the family as a fact of life. In practice, the home is reduced to a house, a mere launching pad to the outer world where real life happens. Life with the family becomes more of a reference point for other activities rather than a focal point for centre-stage living.

As parents we start feeling used. Our home has been turned into a hotel — and we don't like it that way. The home we treasure appears to be just a place for the kids to eat and sleep and take long hot showers — with free maid service thrown in.

In family life the laws of normal living are broken. Reflect a little on your own experience.

Think about the last time you were invited to a friend's house for an evening meal. There were probably a few moments of conversation and maybe an appetizer before your friend excused him/herself to go to the kitchen and put the finishing touches on the meal. Then, when the call came for you to come and eat, you moved without a moment's hesitation toward the table. Normal life works that way.

Now think about life in the family. The day has been mostly routine. Not overly hectic, pretty close to ordinary. Breakfast in a flurry, getting the kids off the school, and making your way to work. The demands at the office are reasonable, the errands you planned to do over lunch got done, and it only took five minutes longer than usual to get home. A quick look at the mail, a browse through the paper, three incoming calls for the kids and it's time to make supper. You are a little surprised that your son has already done his duty and set the table. As you cook, you think a little bit about the office and wonder about calling your folks tonight. Twenty minutes later you call everyone to the table. Not a muscle moves. You call again. Still no response. Anger starts to build. You think to yourself, What's wrong with those kids, don't they realize I've worked hard all day? You call a third time, only this time you shout.

Family life works that way.

A scene from an old episode of the television sitcom "Family Ties" makes the same point. Alex and his mother have been arguing. As the battle dies down and things are close to being resolved, Alex innocently looks at mom and says, "I think of you as my mother . . . not a person."

It must be noted that the above scenarios are scripts for families with the advantage of two parents and a double income. The plight of single parents and the tensions of families living under the strain of unemployment or other hardships only further exacerbate the "normal" family situation.

Like it or not, regardless of their form and circumstances, all families face the frustration of redefining what is normal — that is, normal for family living. And that includes understanding and surrendering to the realities of what constitutes "normal" for adolescents.

In the outside world, most often life is reciprocal. The way you treat people is the way you get treated. When you ask a colleague at work to cover your phone while you're away from your desk, the request is generally accepted with a nod of the head.

In the family, life may be less courteous and more reactionary. While dad is taking his morning shower, another member of the family flushes the toilet. Dad comes into the kitchen yelling, "How many times have we asked everyone in this family not to flush when someone is in the shower? Can't people in this house be more considerate?" The request to turn down the sound pulsating out of a television showing rock videos is often ignored or responded to with, "What's the problem? It's not loud!" How many parents would be open to the suggestion that music you don't like always seems too loud?

There is another phenomenon to compute into this business of living together in families. Simply stated, the family is the place where we allow ourselves to be the most human. Adolescents assume that "once a member of the family, always a member of the family," and they feel free to be their real, sometimes rotten, selves. The situation is tinged with irony. Parents who extend the great gift of psychological security to their children create a place of safety in their homes. Whether we are old or young, feeling safe frees us from the requirement to perform. When children and young people know they are really loved, they not only feel safe and secure, they develop a deep inner sense of belonging. They can also become presumptuous. They start taking their preferred status in life for granted. They excel at being human. They forget to be grateful. They are blinded to the importance of contributing to the source of their strength.

In the family, you are what you are.

THE FORCE AND FEAR OF FREEDOM

Parents of teenagers don't need to read psychology texts on adolescent development to know that the drive for freedom in the younger generation is as basic as breathing. However, knowing that teens value freedom highly is one thing. Living with the expression of that freedom is quite another. The freedom-seeker frequently becomes a freedom-fighter, and the results are explosive.

FREEDOM'S MULTIMEANINGS

There are many reasons for this phenomenon. In general, the communication over the freedom signal is both sent and received on a faulty frequency. When most parents are putting limits in place, they are motivated by a desire to protect the people they love. But the message teens receive is not on the "protect" or "love" frequency. The message they hear is, "I want to control you."

During the past few years, we have probed the freedom issue with both adults and adolescents. To young people the question has been, "When you say, 'I want to be free,' what do you mean?" With adults, the question has been, "When you hear young people say, 'I want to be free,' what do you think they mean?" With a few exceptions, the responses have consistently revealed that on the subject of freedom, adolescents and adults are on different wavelengths.

Adolescents mean. . .	Adults think they mean...
Let me learn	No rules
Let me make some real decisions	License
Give me the right to voice an opinion	Reckless
Accept me	Lawlessness
Trust me	Irresponsible
Treat me as an adult	Destruction
Grant me independence	Disaster

I will always remember a young women of about 17 who got to her feet and confidently declared, "To me freedom means more guidance and less restrictions." She was offering a framework for the responsible use of freedom. It's critical to make a distinction between those who are in their early teens and those in their mid- and late teens. The younger teens have a flair for irresponsible freedom. Their drive for freedom means the unrestricted right to do what they want with whom they want for as long as they want. For their own protection, younger teens need more restrictions. Until they start exercising good judgment, they need rules. They need imposed limits to protect them from some of their less than wise inclinations.

Many parents fear that the irresponsible use of freedom will result in deep damage to their children. And certainly, some teenagers have abused their freedom and turned well-intentioned trust into behaviour that has dealt them a lifetime of tragedy.

But the responsible use of freedom propels young people into orbits of healthy growth. The development of children and teenagers who are not allowed to make real choices is stifled. Instead of learning to become responsible human beings and moving toward healthy autonomy, their social, emotional, moral, and intellectual growth is retarded.

FINDING THE DIRECTION–ROOM BALANCE

A posture that straddles the distance between too much freedom and excessive control is reflected in this principle: *as few rules as necessary and as many choices as possible.* The approach is neither permissive nor overbearing. Rules protect young people as they learn how to live. Appropriate choices give them learning experiences so they can progressively exercise good judgment over more important matters.

Another freedom-related parenting principle will, if practised, save a lot of pain on the home front: keeping perspective on what is more important and what is less important. When it comes to negotiating life with today's teenagers and responding to situations that are less than ideal, go *major on the majors and minor on the minors.* A few examples of what matters might be major and what ones minor:

Major	Minor
Sexual promiscuity	Consistent refusal to tidy bedroom
Doing illicit drugs	Too much time on the phone
Pathological lying	Earrings in young men's ears
Abusive language	Punk hair-styles
Violent behaviour	Too much makeup
Unrelenting disrespect for other family members	Disagreements about spending money
Disregard of curfews and other agreements	Arguments while negotiating curfews and other agreements
Getting picked up for drunk driving	Getting a ticket for speeding

Families who understand the difference between the majors and the minors will have a better time living together. Obviously, each family will have to find its own way through the freedom maze.

Reducing the parenting role with teenagers to a simple formula is impossible; the task is too complex. Learning all the right techniques is not the secret to effective parenting. We might view parenting as an art form. Of course skills are involved, but more importantly, the job requires a certain artistry. It lies in knowing when to act and when to silently observe.

But despite the honing of parental intuition, living with teens can still be an exasperating affair. This is especially so when the dancing partners of friends and freedom get in sync with each other. When this adolescent alliance is linked with what might be termed "teenage pretzel logic" unpredictability reigns. Consider the following scenario:

Gordon is out with his friends and is fully aware that his curfew is 11 p.m. At precisely 11:32 p.m. he looks at his watch and it suddenly dawns on him that he is late. Gordon announces to his friends that it's already past his curfew and he has to leave immediately. His friends offer him something to think about: "You're already late, which means you're already in trouble. So, what's the rush?" Gordon acknowledges a certain amount of logic in that argument and settles back. He reasons he's already in trouble, so why not stay and enjoy his friends a while longer?

In pretzel logic, two hours late is the same as 45 minutes. The logic also creates a lot of misunderstanding and guarantees big trouble.

No one disagrees that teenagers are on a turbulent journey. Life is profoundly complicated for them and for us. *They* are travelling from dependence to independence, from a family focus to personal autonomy. *We* are speculating about what will come next. *They* are scrambling to make some sense of who they are and what they would like to become. *We* are wondering if they will make it on their own. The transitions are often traumatic.

SOME PARENT PITFALLS

Parents' intentions in the upbringing of their teens are almost always honourable. No parent ever says to herself, "I'm going to do all I can to destroy my son." Such projections are nonsense.

Still, although parents do not intend to stand in the way of the growth and development of their offspring, they often set up obstacles, retarding the very aspirations they have.

OVERPROTECTION

Overprotection is one. The tendency starts early and has unrelenting sustaining power. "Don't go outside without your coat done up, or you'll catch your death of cold," is a typical protection posture. We might legitimately ask when was the last time a young person died from going outside without her coat buttoned.

The parental inclination to protect is as natural and instinctive as breast-feeding. A certain amount of parental protection is both admirable and life-affirming. But overprotection can be life-denying. It retards development. Instead of transferring responsibility to young people, it denies them the opportunity to be responsible and precludes the importance of being accountable.

The tendency to overprotect can be curbed by parenting that *encourages healthy autonomy*. It is to allow the younger generation to take steps toward progressive independence. For us as parents, the inclination to shelter children is often prompted by the instinct to guard what we value. Whether the warning is to be careful crossing the street or a lecture about drinking and driving, we are fearful our children will get hurt. But excessive protection can also be harmful.

For teenagers, being released from overprotection will have two implications: they will be given age-appropriate choices and they will need to be ready to deal with the consequences of their choices. Parents are right when they put a daily monitor on their young children's progress at school. Sitting alongside nine-year-olds to be sure they get their homework done is age-appropriate parenting. Continually asking teenagers in junior high school if they have done their homework or whether or not they need any help with their assignments is also a good game-plan. But using the same unrelenting style with high school teens falls into the category of overprotective parenting. Fifteen- and 16-year-olds already have 10 years of school experience. If they have not learned to assume a major part of the responsibility for their educational destiny, it is time for a memorable learning experience. Rather than nagging about the homework issue, the time has come for intermittent reminders along with comments about consequences. High school students who continually choose to ignore homework assignments end up failing courses. The consequences are real. They face the necessity of taking a course or two during summer school or finishing their high school careers after their friends have already graduated.

Young people who have to wrestle with the consequences of their decisions along the way end up better equipped for long-term living. When young people's everyday experiences with life foster progressive self-determination, they are travelling on the road to healthy emergence.

OVERCONTROL

Parental overcontrol is a close cousin of parental overprotection. It is also a dangerous game. There are predictable results. One is an overreaction of mammoth proportions.

Why does a 17-year-old woman, denied dating privileges, assert her independence by getting pregnant? What makes a teenager who lives in an overzealously religious home suddenly announce he "no longer believes in God" and refuses to attend worship anymore? Why do some young people whose parents rule their homes like military generals express their autonomy by shop-lifting? How is it that an adolescent with a high IQ brings home a report card with failing grades? The answer is obvious. Overcontrol and the blocking of pathways to healthy emergence can cause volcanic-like eruptions in teenagers. When you understand the adolescent psyche, you will better understand that the teenagers' responses are predictable.

The other consequence of parental overcontrol is passive, non-thinking, unresponsive sons and daughters. When parents dominate their children, they take on responsibility themselves, instead of assigning it to their offspring. When young people have their decisions made for them by their parents, their development is retarded. When they're not allowed to work out solutions to their problems, they end up ill-equipped for life beyond the home. Instead of being released to pursue their potential, they get shut down, pathetic. When parents are asked if they'd intended to produce such a species, they respond with a vehement *no!* But the harsh reality remains: overcontrol means closing down the pathways to healthy development.

Responsibility may be an old-fashioned idea, but it belongs in the modern world. A thinking parent can counter the temptation to overcontrol by committing to a form of parenting that cultivates a sense of responsibility in their teenagers.

One of the major dynamics between parents and teenagers that can foster responsibility centres on the matter of *trust*. The challenge for parents is to run some risks of trust without being excessively gullible. The challenge for teens is to handle their parents' vote of trust without behaving in a manner that generates mistrust. The breakdown between the generations often comes because parents start from the position of distrust. Many parents can be heard saying to their teens, "Prove you are trustworthy and then you will be treated that way," while teenagers on the other hand lament, "You aren't even giving me a chance to prove I *can* be trusted." Although there are risks involved, life will work better when parents choose to trust first and only move to impose restrictions and take away privileges when trust has been breached.

There are many ways to signal trust in today's teens. Handing the car keys to a 16-year-old who has just got his or her licence and wants to drive over to a friend's house is an act of trust. Asking the same 16-year-old to chauffeur his or her young sister to the dentist sends the same message. When mom and dad are away for the weekend, allowing their senior teenage sons and daughters to invite a few close friends who are known to the family over on Saturday night says, "We have confidence in you." Asking young people to shop for groceries and, on the way, to electronically withdraw money from the family bank account, strongly announces, "We believe in you. We trust you."

In the midst of controversy when parents are fearful and teens are pressing for life to go their way, honest and brave parents will think back to when they were teenagers in the same situation and ask, "How would I have liked to have been treated by my parents?" It may sound idealistic, and we agree that it is. But what's wrong with trying to pass along some ideals that our children can then hand on to our grand-children?

OVERINDULGENCE

Parents who don't believe in giving gifts to their children are to be pitied. But so are parents who lavish their children with gifts. Overindulgence is not the preserve of the rich and affluent. Indifference to repeated emotional outbursts, tolerating antisocial and unacceptable behaviour and never letting your teenager suffer the consequences of his negative behaviour are all forms of overindulgence.

In a country like Canada, supplying youngsters with an excess of material things is one of the most common forms of indulgence. The practice not only creates unrealistic expectations in young people, it dulls their ability to feel gratitude and appreciate life. Overindulgence by making things too easy and protecting the young person from reality, instils a faulty value system.

Overindulgence fosters a mind-set that says, "I expect to live in the fashion to which I have become accustomed," and feeds a mentality that asserts, "I'm entitled." I'm entitled to a job that is equivalent to my educational attainments. I'm entitled to a bigger house and better car than my parents have worked hard to achieve.

When a teen is both overindulged and overprotected the consequences can be disastrous. The formula is predictable:

OVERINDULGENCE + OVERPROTECTION = I'M ENTITLED

The higher ground for parenting is instilling values to live by. The real issue here is modelling. If the aspiration is to instil an attitude of gratitude rather than entitlement, then Thanksgiving in the family will be more than just an annual statutory holiday. When there is a parental desire to transmit the value of honesty to young teens, 13-year-olds will pay adult prices at restaurants that say "children's prices apply to those who are 12 years of age and younger." In two-parent families, if mom and dad want to convey gender equality as an ideal for life, then their behaviour will counter some of the male and female role stereotypes that have ruled the past.

Modelling is articulating in words and demonstrating by deeds what we would like our children to reproduce in their own lives. Directly stated, "To bring up a child in the way he [or she] should go, travel that way yourself once in a while."[6]

EXTENDING THE STAY AT HOME

When young people are afflicted with overindulgence, overcontrol, and overprotection, their movement toward autonomy is slowed down. Specifically, adolescence is extended and adulthood is delayed. A practical consequence for many young people is that they are staying home longer and getting married later.

The intent in identifying the pattern is not to blame parents for "doing it wrong." Youth themselves are also major contributors to the creation of their circumstances. And in many instances, young people are quite content to delay wrapping their arms around the realities of responsibility and independence. But without a doubt, many members of the older generation are not impressed that modern youth are taking longer to become independent.

Norman's parents were so happy when their 27-year-old left home that they announced the occasion by buying an advertisement in an Edmonton newspaper: "Marvis and Oliver are proud to announce that their son Norman has finally moved out . . . after more than 27 years." When interviewed, Norman, an engineering student, said he's adjusting to life without the cooking and cleaning services of his mom. But he admitted, "I'm eating out a lot."[7]

The story is amusing, but the incident is indicative of a social trend. For whatever reasons, increasing numbers of the younger generation are stalling on the way to full autonomy, "hovering reluctantly in the passageway to maturity."[8] They are functioning as fledgling adults. Being on their own is almost more than they can cope with. For whatever reasons, many do not develop the attitudes and skills necessary to launch into independent lives. And those who are unable to maintain their independence over the long haul are like homing pigeons. After they have left home for a period of time, they come back. Parents are having to adjust to the fact that the empty nest isn't empty after all.

The results are being registered in the increased number of young adults 18 and older who are still living at home. In 1981, the figure was 808,000; by 1986 it increased to 1,058,000. The figures continue to rise.

The pattern is also reflected in the average age young people are getting married:

	Female	Male
1975	22.4	24.7
1985	24.6	26.7
1989	25.7	27.8[9]

There are a multitude of reasons for the trends. Contributing to the patterns are high levels of unemployment, unwed mothers choosing to keep their babies, marriage postponement, gender role complexity and confusion, baby-boomer control of the workplace blocking entry to desirable careers, the cost of housing in metropolitan centres, and other financial pressures. And clearly the excesses of parental overindulgence and overprotection that foster attitudes of entitlement in youth are also accentuating the pattern. Young adults who live with "I'm entitled" mind-sets are inclined to hang on to the standard of life to which they've become accustomed rather than launching themselves into the unknown.

The leave home–return home pattern, as well as the reluctance-to-move-out pattern, is laden with problems. Instead of a young person's being stimulated to grow by having encountered a new environment, returning home can usher in the return to old ways. It's a rare parent who can resist the temptation to parent when an adult son or daughter re-enters the nest. The stage is set for the son or daughter to lose their equality yet again. Instead of relating, as in "I am an adult, you are an adult," when children return home, there is a tendency to fall back to the stage of "I am the adult, you are the child." Everybody loses.

A while ago, a mother approached me to seek counsel about her daughter. Linda was 23, working full time but still living at home. The mother confessed that Linda rarely helped around the house and refused to pay board. There was also a debate raging between the mother and the father about whether or not Linda should be asked to move out. After sketching the situation, the mother asked me what I thought. I answered with a question. "As you assess the situation, what will be most helpful to your daughter's development?" The mother paused for a moment and then said, "It's time for Linda to move out, isn't it?" My response was to affirm her conclusion, adding, "Have a long discussion and give her three months' notice."

The counsel may sound too harsh. And in particular situations it may be untimely for a 23-year-old or even a 27-year-old to go out and sign a lease. We have given today's youth a complicated world, and it takes time to sort out all the options. Down-sizing unrealistic expectations into realistic ambitions doesn't happen overnight. Even young people with impressive educational credentials may face major obstacles in finding appropriate employment. A young person who chooses to chase a dream of becoming a musician or artist will probably need the resources of a parent patron for longer than just a little while. In the end, parenting decisions are judgment calls. And while there is no inherent virtue in putting young adults out on the street, when the time is right, there is merit in encouraging them to fly on their own.

Too frequently, older Canadians fail to treat younger Canadians with basic human respect. They relate to teenagers as if they are still children, and many do the same with adults in their early twenties. For whatever reasons, older adults seem reluctant to let adolescents and young adults grow up. Rather than being welcomed into adulthood with its ensuing privileges and responsibilities, younger Canadians are being blocked from entering the adult world.

When we probe people on the specific messages they are receiving on the subject of being fully adult, they speak clearly. Collectively, they communicate the following:

In Canada, you are fully adult when you have finished your education, are holding down a full-time job, paying taxes, and are preferably married with at least one child. When all the criteria are met, maybe by the time you reach 30, you are accepted by the older generation as fully adult.

YOU WAS NEVER MY AGE

Even though we are fully aware and ready to acknowledge that today is not the same as yesterday, when debates rage between a parent and a teenager, one of the great adult temptations is to reach into the past, clear our throats, and utter, "When I was your age . . ." The Broadway musical and film *West Side Story* got it right. Doc, the drugstore owner, in a hassle with a member of the Jets, blurts out, "When I was your age . . ." The teenager returns, "You was never my age."

As parents, we are inclined to reach into the past instead of dealing realistically with the here and now. Whenever we are inclined to say, "When I was your age . . ." we will be wise to keep in mind that today's world is not a replica of yesterday's. Consequently, life for today's teenagers is unique. They are faced with challenges and difficulties earlier generations have not had to deal with. Today's youth are writing first-time history.

Parents who are plugged in will accept the fact that "When I was your age . . ." assumptions cannot work. They will see their children's points of view and compensate for the new realities. And when that happens, life in the family will be greatly enhanced.

6

THE ROLE OF
EDUCATION

*A*dults *who associate drudgery and stress with going to work will be able to empathize with the feelings many young people have about school. Although approximately one in three find school an exhilarating experience, the majority of high school students walk into their classrooms with little enthusiasm.*

Although teenagers readily endorse the importance of getting an education, less than half say they enjoy their educational experience. More than three quarters point to the school as a source of considerable strain.

When young people identify the source of their enjoyment at school, it's friends. Even before the first bell rings, they plan to touch base with a friend or two. What is disliked most are classes and homework. There are more students who say they enjoy the lunch break than students who say they enjoy their teachers.

But that's the downside. The findings also point to promising prospects. Teachers are positioned to make a difference. While teachers may not be enjoyed as much as friends, 60 per cent of students nonetheless feel positively toward them. The same proportion maintains, "All in all, my teachers are genuinely interested in me." And about 25 per cent say that classes and learning are what they enjoy most about school.

School is a mixed experience for students. Certainly there are problems, but there is also crucial learning going on. What's more important, the findings point to the potential for school to be a richer experience for all involved.

THE CURRENT SITUATION

Although the very idea of school generates a deep sense of gratitude for Saturday and Sunday in many teenagers, it is far from an afterthought. School is centre stage to their perception of what is important for their long-term living. It may be a surprise to some, but when high school students were asked how the government should arrange their priorities, education ranked in the number-one position. Placing education above health care, a total of 78 per cent said education should be given high priority. Most of today's teens readily accept the message in the government's Stay in School TV ad:

Dropping out is no way out.
More education = more freedom.

While young people affirm the importance of getting an education, they also indicate that school is a source of high anxiety. When asked, "What common problems bother you?" 75 per cent identify "pressure to do well at school;" 72 per cent said what they were "going to do when they finished school" also troubles them. And if enjoyment of the school experience is a trade-off for today's students, the predicament is grim. Only 43 per cent say they get a significant level of enjoyment from their involvement at school.

MIXED REVIEWS

One afternoon, while driving in my car, my attention was captured by an interview on CBC radio with a 16-year-old grade-11 student named Linda. She lived in southern Ontario where, at the time, the teachers were on strike and the schools were closed. Linda was obviously an enterprising young woman, because in response to the strike, she had organized SOS (Students Opposed to Strike). At the time of the interview, the strike had been going on for 10 weeks. Linda explained she had made a formal presentation to the trustees, and the response was only, "We are doing all we can."

Showing strong initiative and concern, Linda had also set up tutoring centres. When the radio interviewer asked how her efforts had been received, she said the teachers she had talked to had told her, "What you do while we are out of the classroom won't count."

The interviewer continued to probe. "What have you learned about adults during these weeks?" was his next question. By this time

I had pulled my car to the side of the road and was taking notes. Linda's answer was precise:

My experience has taught me three things. First, adults are hard to talk to. And second, they don't really listen to us. And because we're teenagers, they don't take us seriously. I find it really frustrating to be treated that way.

Linda's experience with the adults within the educational institution is deplorable. Her experience is echoed in the comments of a grade-10 student from Vancouver who, as well as offering her perspective on Canada's future, abortion, and racism, added, "When I am around my teachers, I feel like a little child who has to do what they tell me to do, even though I don't want to."

Expressing open dissent about school, a 17-year-old woman from Ontario declared, "You did not give enough emphasis to our wretched school system which is screwing everybody as bad as the government!! Thanks for the opportunity to bitch mildly."

Yet, painting a one-colour picture misrepresents many of the positive things happening in the schools across the country. Recently, I spoke informally with a veteran guidance counsellor. He talked about his previous week:

Life in the school isn't what it used to be. I don't mean to say that the past few days have been normal, but neither are they all that exceptional . . . I helped arrange a funeral at our school this week. Two of our senior students, who are co-habiting, lost their baby. The baby was born severely handicapped and lived for just two days. The whole thing was hard and sad. The one bright spot was that, without any of the teachers making the suggestion, the students in the school took up a collection to pay for the cost of cremating the baby . . . Over the years, I've seen so many changes. The kids today are a lot more open about life. They've opened me up. I've changed for the better. I'm more forthright, more honest, more compassionate.

As we parted company, I thought that it would be a privilege for my own children to have contact with such a man.

Other images and remembrances come to mind.

After a consulting session in a high school, I remember watching an exchange between a male principal and a female student. She would not have won a popularity contest. Her social skills were obviously low. I also knew that the principal was already late for a meeting, yet he allowed the interruption and stopped to listen. He gave his complete attention to the young woman. As the two of them talked there was eye contact. Smiles were exchanged. As they separated, the principal reached out to touch the student's arm as he pointed in a specific direction down the hall. I could easily imagine that over the supper table there would be a spark in that young woman's eyes as she told her family, "I talked to my principal today . . ."

You can't help but be impressed with teachers when you know they work night after night preparing fresh lesson plans. When you realize there are vice-principals who follow up their disciplinarian decisions with notes of encouragement and teachers who take initiative to set up extracurricular groups for students going through divorce at home, you want to propose a toast to today's educators.

Still, criticism of our schools is a common theme in our culture. The following critique is an excellent example:

> *We have been disquieted by the common complaint that the graduates of our schools have often failed to attain an acceptable standard in English. University and secondary school teachers complain that their students are unable to express ideas, either orally or in writing, in lucid, accurate, and fluent English. The criticism is echoed by employers, who complain bitterly that young persons make errors in spelling, punctuation, and grammar, and cannot express themselves logically and clearly in speaking, even in the idiom of debased English that they commonly employ.*

In a formal reply, English teachers stated:

> *We feel that the criticism is justified, but that teachers are not to blame, inasmuch as they have large classes and insufficient time for the correction of written work.*

Sound familiar? Disquieting, perhaps, to know that the above is cited from the 40-year-old "Report of the Royal Commission on Education in Ontario 1950."[1] During the past half century, have we made any progress?

HIGH EXPECTATIONS

When we focus our lens on education, we are dealing with a sphere that continues to have status in Canadian society. In fact, we place such a high social value on the younger generation's getting an education that we are quite ready to pay highly for it. If you are a home owner a quick check of your property tax assessment tells the story.

Historically, Canadian youth have been shaped by three major institutions. Family, church, and school have been the major forces in forming self-images, transmitting values, conveying beliefs, and generally equipping young people for life.

Earlier chapters have detailed the prominent place the family has had and will continue to have in the workings of Canadian society. Even though the rigours of modern life have produced stress fractures in the family, adapted forms of the family will remain as the basic building block of life in the future.

Nevertheless, schools have taken over a number of social domains that, only a decade or two ago, were not part of the curriculum. And it's not as though families held a plebiscite and voted to hand over more of life to the school. It simply has worked out that way. For example, what started as extracurricular courses in family-living skills grew to include sex education in the regular program for all students. In more recent years the mandate has included AIDS education and clear instruction about "safe sex." Some parents see these developments as an infringement of their exclusive territory. But most parents breathe a sigh of relief and hope their kids are getting what they need to cope and make informed choices.

As already noted, religious institutions were more prominent in the past than they are in the present. Today, only a small minority of youth take advantage of their services and see them as a place to belong. Because of the demotion of organized religion in the culture, the school remains as the one social institution that systematically gathers society together. Especially for young people from homes filled with turmoil, the school is the only adult-managed environment where they can experience life with predictability.

Government decision-makers have seen the school as a container into which they can pour the solutions to many of society's ills. The reality of drug problems on the streets has brought drug education into the schools. Social shifts have had ramifications for schools; increasing numbers of women working outside the home has created a demand for day care and after-school programs. The cultural push to press kids to seize every opportunity and to grow up in a hurry has some children lining up for class not long after they have learned to walk. Employers, too, have expectations for schools. They want ready-made employees equipped for the rigours of the modern workplace. Yet, the place of technological change that rules much of the workplace is far faster than institutions can ever hope to keep up with.

All these additions without any real deletions equals a crowded curriculum. Schools still need to deliver the basics, but the extras are putting them on overload.

In reality, the expectations of society exceed the ability of what schools can feasibly achieve. As a single institution, the school cannot and will not be able to meet all the needs of their students, as well as respond to all the concerns raised by society. Schools and their personnel cannot be a catch-all cure-all system for the rest of society.

Educators need to stop pretending they can achieve all they are being asked to do. They should push responsibility back toward the family, into the workplace, and to other sectors in the society. Our intent of raising these matters is to acknowledge the pressures being exerted on today's schools. Still, there's a tension. Educators must be called to the highest level of competence possible, yet we also realize that "we can no longer ignore the social context in which our children are raised.[2] In the final analysis, it is the ingredients of the social context that are poured into our schools.

Talk with educators and they will convince you that violence in the school environment is increasing. One in three teenagers believe that violence is a "very serious" problem in our schools. But we can't just point the finger at educators and accuse them of giving up on good old-fashioned discipline. "Troubled youth reflect a troubled society," not undisciplined or incompetent schools.[3]

The data spell out levels of violence in Canadian society that are disturbing, to say the least. When today's teens were asked if they knew anyone who had been subject to an act of violence, apart from what they'd read in the paper and seen on TV, the percentages who had were as follows:

Physically attacked at school	45
Victim of gang violence	35
Physically abused at home	42
Sexually abused	39

Allowing incidents of violence in schools, gang or otherwise, is voting for a reign of terror. Educators must not tolerate such behaviour. Nor should the rest of us tolerate physical, sexual, or other forms of abuse in the society at large. The source and stimulus of the violence that occurs in schools flows out of the culture that cradles the school. When there is less sanction of violence in society, there will be less violence in our schools.

In the meantime, we need to stop blaming our educators for the social ills taking place in schools.

SOME KEY DIVERSITY ISSUES

Although our schools are not to blame for social ills, they can make some critical contributions to the culture that cradles them.

We have already established that schools are high-level problem places for students. Pressure at school is the number-one concern of teenagers. Why is this the case? It should be less so. Fewer than one in two admit to school's being a place they really enjoy. Why should the educational experience be such an ordeal for so many? Educators will show more wisdom when they respond to their context — the circumstances within which they teach the curriculum. They will raise everyone's learning curve when content and context are woven together, when the curriculum is reconfigured into solving some of the pressing problems of life.

The education experience should be enjoyed. And it's true that most young people do look forward to starting school. Our surveys have also found that students are more positive about their technical-school and university experiences than they are about their high school ones. Why? For starters, the curriculum that the technical schools and universities provide may be fresher and more in touch with young people's interests than what is provided in high schools. As well, students may find they receive more "room" and greater respect. Are there not ways to make high school a richer experience for both teenagers and their teachers?

DIVERSE DREAMS

To most young people, Canada is a land of both *promise* and *propaganda.* In some ways, youth are like most adults: they simply assume the opportunities and privileges of the past will continue and increase in the future. They place their faith indiscriminately in the principle of progress. They are ready to buy in to the prevailing propaganda.

The reasons are clear. Parents have aspirations for their children.

They want them to achieve the highest levels possible. Modern youth are hopeful. They are idealistic and have high expectations. This is especially true with regard to their assumptions about the value of getting an education and reaping the rewards of their efforts.

One of the privileges of being young is that, with relatively few responsibilities and unchallenged expectations, there's no need to be realistic. For example, when young people compare their educational intentions with what their parents have attained, their aspirations far exceed what they are likely to experience.

YOUTH EDUCATIONAL EXPECTATIONS COMPARED TO PARENTAL EDUCATIONAL ATTAINMENT		
In %'s		
	Youth expects	Mother attained	Father attained
Some high school or less	3	42	47
Graduate high school	11	31	20
Some vocational	7	6	6
Graduate vocational	24	9	8
Some university	5	3	4
Graduate university	50	9	15

Some cultures have caste systems formally entrenched in their social structures. In Canada, we have a sort of educational caste system. We extol the virtues of a university degree and relegate everything else to second-class status. Young people set their sights accordingly. At least 50 per cent of 15- to 19-year-olds expect to pursue their dreams and graduate with a degree. In reality, only 15 per cent even get in the registration lines. We are guilty of cultural overpromising. Young people are being duped. The same pattern is true for those who plan to pursue post-secondary vocational studies. Approximately half of those who hope to keep going to school actually make it to a community college or vocational campus.

The harsh reality is that before most young people turn 20 they have to deal with the disillusionment of their educational dreams. We would be better off to tell the truth — that only a small minority of young people need to go to university or ever will go — and work harder at enriching the alternatives to better serve the majority. Too often, a typical adult response to a disillusioned older teen has been, "Well, welcome to the real world. It's time you grew up!"

And it's true — dreamers set themselves up for disappointment. Nevertheless, they are only setting their educational sights on what society has told them to strive for. But how, ask parents, can appropriate doses of realism be doled out without crushing young people's fragile idealism? For young people are indeed idealistic, and their optimism is often unrealistic. Adults need to be careful not to push today's vulnerable youth into pessimism.

DIVERSE EDUCATIONAL ALTERNATIVES

Elitism seems to be the rule of the day. Without our being conscious and deliberate, the social conditioning of the past will continue shaping the future. We will unrelentingly hold up university as the only really valuable education to pursue. But in response to the real-life problem of educational elitism, many adults can make moves to dignify a wide range of educational alternatives.

Without demeaning the value of a university degree, it will be important in the future to give new status to community college diplomas, to trade school and apprenticeship programs, to technical training, and other pursuits. Young people will not only be better served, but society as a whole will benefit.

One difficulty to overcome rests with educators themselves, all university graduates. Not only do high schools systematically sort students into hierarchical streams, teachers are naturally tempted to try to educate students in their own image. Without consciously resisting the inclination to do so, teachers are almost programmed to slot students who have the smarts to be university-bound into the upper echelon of their perceptions. The rest are relegated to second-class. Without an intentional commitment on behalf of educators to both enlighten the understanding of parents and to alter their old ways, the problem will remain, and young people will continue to tumble into disillusionment.

DIVERSE CULTURES

Because educational institutions gather in the culture, schools cannot ignore the diversity of our multicultural society. Our educational institutions in Canada need to help make multiculturalism work.

In the history of our young country, we haven't had a lot of practice at making it work. Problems still remain and tensions continue to exist. Who would argue that, in Canada, minority groups have been constrained by the power of the majority? Our past has not been perfect. But sometimes, good intentions to affirm the concerns of minority groups lead to excessive sensitivity, which impinges on the privileges of the majority. A sort of reverse discrimination.

The following excerpt, from a letter sent from a school board's administrative office to its high school principals, is an example. The intent of the letter is to give guidelines for commemorating Remembrance Day and honouring those who died while at war:

> *Remembrance Day gives us the opportunity to appreciate the qualities of endurance and courage and devotion to the principles of freedom within our community. We must express a sensitivity to the fact that for many students the word "remembrance" has a very familiar meaning. Staff would be aware that some students may not want to share their memories.*
>
> *Symbols of remembrance may be very different depending on the culture where a student comes from (for example, crosses may not be meaningful to Iranian, Israeli, or Sri Lankan students, and others who do not have a Christian background). In our multicultural society, it is advisable to use only appropriate symbols, such as flags, poppies, and wreaths, rather than symbols pertaining to any particular faith.[4]*

The administrator's sensitivity to our multicultural society is commendable; the rights of minority groups need to be acknowledged and protected. And it's easy to see why he might urge school principals not to use "symbols pertaining to any particular faith, which in this case happens to be the Christian cross, and to restrict themselves to flags, poppies, and wreaths. However, we believe the restriction is without good reason.

Eighty-five per cent of adult Canadians identify themselves as either Catholics or Protestants. Young people between the ages of 15 and 24 are hanging on to their religious identities, too — 77 per cent Catholic or Protestant; three per cent Jewish and other world religions. The historical death of Christ has been such a prominent event in the world that the cross has become a universal symbol for death. In the future, crosses may be banned from Remembrance Day ceremonies, but they will still stand in Flanders fields. Is not the better alternative to acknowledge the place of the cross in the culture and explain both its religious and historical meaning? Besides, Remembrance Day is a national event, not a religious occasion.

But whether a special day is national or religious, when those in the majority are asked to surrender what has meaning and value so that those in the minority will not be offended, the request endorses reverse discrimination.

A better alternative is to encourage a multicultural society to understand and gain an appreciation for what is meaningful — from all points of view, not only our own. Learning to respect one another's beliefs and living peacefully with one another's differences is a social necessity in today's Canada.

If we are limited in our public expression to only what everyone can endorse, the content of our public communication will be innocuous. Further balkanization and fragmentation in the country will be assured. The challenge in the public forum is to facilitate healthy majority-minority interplay. It calls for understanding, not judging.

SHARED CALENDARS

In December 1991, using ambiguous language about "community and sharing," the principal of a public school banned the singing of Christmas carols by his 600 students. Even though the school constituency is estimated to be two-thirds Christian, some staff argued that the non-Christian students would be upset by the wording of the carols.

The incident is an example of small-mindedness. Canada without Christmas carols is tantamount to conceiving Bangkok without Buddhist monks. Singing "Silent Night" and "Hark the Herald Angels Sing" is part of the Canadian Christmas experience. Cleansing the culture of Handel's *Messiah* is an act of cultural impoverishment. "Christmas with its glorious festival of love, joy, peace, generosity, family and music . . ." As one of the "great festivals of human existence," Christmas should not be reduced "to Rudolph the Red-Nosed Reindeer."[5]

What will such decision-making, as expressed by the school principal, do to community life? When we gather together, do we want to be restricted to only those activities that the entire community can unreservedly endorse?

When parliament passed the policy of multiculturalism, the goal "was not simply to permit myriad cultural groups to coexist; the dream was that the various groups would bring the best of their heritage together and produce a nation richer because of its cultural diversity . . . Like a mosaic art piece mounted on a wall, our different parts can add up to a unified whole."[6]

It is worth saying again. A healthy multicultural, multifaith society extends to understand the other person's point of view. In a truly multicultural society, Christmas and carols with a Christian flavour, Rosh Hashanah and Yom Kippur which have special significance for Jewish people, Ramadan for Muslims, and Divali, the Hindu Festival of Lights, should all be given their place on the shared cultural calendar.

The student experience in the school should be a rehearsal for life after graduation. If the school can be an environment where we can make multiculturalism work, then we can project an enhanced future for all of life in Canada.

TEACHERS CAN MAKE A DIFFERENCE

Educators get paid to teach the curriculum. Administrators and teachers sign contracts to fulfil specific tasks. The obligations are clearly spelled out, and their first responsibility is to meet the stated criteria so that students can both learn and apply their learning to their living.

But educators who want to enhance their effectiveness will discern the implications of knowing, that as persons, they are a central part of the curriculum. Enlightened teachers will understand the culture of their clients and see the fusion between their person and their pedagogy.

A POSITION OF OPPORTUNITY

Almost two in three teenagers claim to have confidence in teachers. The same number believe that, all in all, teachers are "genuinely interested in them." There is strong evidence to conclude that young people rate teachers more positively than adults generally. This is particularly apparent when understanding and respect are the themes being evaluated.

Clearly, teachers have garnered a favoured position with young people. However, that is not to say that all students are having positive school experiences. The previously mentioned differing attitude of high school, vocational, and university students is revealing. High school consistency rates on the low end of the satisfaction scale. Approximately one-third are having an extremely positive encounter, another third are having a "not so good, not so bad" experience, and other third are prime suspects for dropping out.

Often, teachers either give their primary attention to those who are excelling or to those who have almost given up. If the above assessment is accurate, a case could be made for teachers to give special attention to the middle third. Those students who are excelling will continue to do well whether or not they get specific assistance. Those who have already tuned out and turned off probably need far more assistance than a classroom setting can provide. Doesn't it make sense to give extraordinary attention to those students in the "not so bad, not so good" category? They are the ones who can be motivated to give a better effort.

ATTITUDES OF STUDENTS TOWARD THEIR SCHOOLING			
In %'s			
	High School	Voca-tional	Uni-versity
LIKE SCHOOL "I like it very much"	23	36	43
COURSES "Very Interesting"	23	39	43
WORK ASSIGNED Meaningful & Important "Most of the time"	32	59	54
IMPORTANCE FOR LATER IN LIFE "Very Important"	41	56	48

TAKING ON CHALLENGES

Today's teachers have their hands full. Not only do they have their own aspirations to pursue, they are monitored by the expectations of the society at large.

NURTURING AN APPETITE FOR CRITICAL THINKING

The complexity and the lack of consensus in the modern world has heightened the importance of being intellectually discriminating. Compared to the past, in order to live well, we must think more. In his book *Handbook for the Positive Revolution*, Edward de Bono uses a simple metaphor to show the importance of cultivating the skill of clear thinking:

It is not enough to be intelligent. Many highly intelligent people are poor thinkers . . . Intelligence is like the horsepower of a car. It is only a potential.

Thinking skill is like driving skill . . . There may be powerful cars that are driven badly. There may be highly intelligent minds that are used ineffectively.[7]

In the journey through life, when today's teenagers shift into neutral, they think less. Instead of appreciating the importance of critical-thinking skills, intelligence is a low-ranked value in a high-demand, complex world. The realm of the heart (affective domain) is so powerful in the make-up of modern youth that the realm of the head (cognitive domain) is minimized.

That is not to say today's young people are intellectually inferior or that they score lower on IQ tests. Rather, it is to contend they are intellectually selective. They choose when to turn on their minds, but unless they are prompted to flip the switch, they would rather feel than think.

Consequently, educators are called upon to turn young people's minds on and nurture their appetites for critical thinking. If youth don't acquire the skill and develop the habit of thinking discriminatingly while they are at school, they will be ill-equipped to live in the world we have given them. The perspective Piaget offered on the goals of education are still right for the present:

Education is to form minds which can be critical, can verify, and not accept everything they are offered . . . Education is to create men [and women] who are capable of doing new things, not simply repeating what other generations have done — men who are creative, inventive and discoverers.

INSPIRING THE EXPRESSION OF CREATIVITY

The movie *Shirley Valentine* includes a scene that admittedly projects an unfair caricature of a school principal. The scene is framed as a flashback as Shirley relives one of her traumatic school memories. Shirley is put down and embarrassed by her principal in the presence of her friends. Her reflection as an adult on the impact of the event is disturbing: "I was never really interested in school after that."

Easy to say, "Oh, that was just a movie." But it's true that students can get more easily turned off than turned on. Most children enter elementary school with a creative flair and freedom of expression. But too often it's all downhill from there. The correlation is depressingly predictable: the longer children go to school and the higher they climb academically, they will usually be met by a corresponding decline in the creativity teachers and professors use to communicate the content of their programs.

Our modern world discourages creativity. Affluence dulls the drive to be creative. Having money propels us to acquire rather than create. Sophisticated technology that's too difficult to understand, let alone repair, leaves us with no other option but to call an expert or install a replacement. Even the movie industry fails to score high on creativity. When a film is a popular success, its plot formula is repeated, and we are subjected to a long parade of sequels. Think about what Rocky I, II, III, IV, and V are saying about creativity.

Should we be surprised that today's teenagers place appallingly low-value levels on creativity and imagination? Only four in 10 give a thumbs-up rating to their importance.

Creative people make a difference to ordinary living. Clever twists are put into the routine. They make non-smoking announcements on airplanes by saying, "This is a non-smoking flight today. Anyone caught smoking will be extinguished!" Passengers smile. Some laugh out loud. Life tastes better that way.

Effective teachers inspire creativity in their students. They keep their students second-guessing about what comes next. They reward the unorthodox and aren't all that concerned about colouring that swerves outside the lines. They actually encourage healthy non-conformity. Creative schools are places where surprises happen. In one school, on the first day of spring, without an announcement over the PA, teachers greet their students coming back for afternoon classes by serving them ice-cream cones.

Increased creativity in our schools would cause fewer students to express sentiments such as this one from an 18-year-old male: "What I like most about school is when it's over." Or this from another 18-year-old male: "What I like most about school is the student cafeteria."

Without creativity life is a sterile, black-and-white affair. Creativity gives it colour. Albert Einstein may have overstated the case, but his orientation for this moment in history is right: "Imagination is more important than knowledge."

EDUCATING FOR THE TWENTY-FIRST CENTURY

Teaching to cultivate critical-thinking skills and to inspire creativity will provide some of the basic equipment today's teens will need for

living in tomorrow's world. Bold problem-solving, innovative decision-making, and utilizing means and methods to resolve increasing
technological and moral complexities that haven't even been
thought of yet will all be a part of our future.

In the present milieu, however, schools are subject to unending
streams of scrutiny and criticism. Educator Marc Tucks offers this
perspective: "The problem is not that schools have gone to hell in a
handbasket; it's that the nature of the economy has changed dramatically in the last 20 to 25 years and the schools have not changed with it." [8]

Futurist John Naisbitt points in the right direction: "In a rapidly
changing work environment, no single job skill will be more important than the ability to think and communicate. No one school subject
will serve future workers better than learning how to learn." [9]

Could it be that schools have simply been too satisfied with the
familiar? Have educators been content with communicating facts and
handing on information that, although it allows students to pass
examinations, does not equip them for life?

Many observers have distinguished between "getting an education" and "learning for living." Information may be "the oxygen of
the age," but education as information only will not meet the demands of today, let alone tomorrow. Cultivating the competency of
"learning to learn" will be an ability that will serve students long-term.
Producing psychological stamina in students, many of whom will be
pressed to undergo several career changes in their lifetime, will equip
the younger generation for life.

In the 1990s and the twenty-first century, students will have lots of
information, but what they will really need are the skills to use what
they can access. In simple terms, it's one thing to know how to add,
subtract, and compute fractions in a classroom. It's quite another to
be in a restaurant where you have to add up the bill, compute the
PST, add the GST, and then calculate an appropriate tip. Applying
facts and information to new contexts demonstrates an understanding of causes, and offers choices in order to act on the consequences.
There is a great difference between receiving information and using
that same information. When information is understood it not only
means young students are getting an education, it will also enable
them to make a living.

Institutions are notorious for being slow to change. Undoubtedly,
the drag from the past has many schools locked into teaching an

obsolete curriculum. The public also continues to evaluate schools on past standards rather than freeing them to pursue future needs. The three Rs are still non-negotiables, but why would anyone be asked to retain the multiplication tables in her or his head when inexpensive and accurate calculators are so close at hand?

POSTSCRIPT: DON'T EXPECT TO BE RESPECTED

From a teacher's point of view, it may seem logical to conclude that, when one nurtures an appetite for critical thinking, inspires the expression of creativity, and educates for the twenty-first century, students would respond with affection and respect. Affection maybe, but a teacher can't expect respect.

The reason is simple. Respect for authority in the culture at large isn't what it used to be, and once again students are mirroring the prevailing attitude. In the past, people were respected because they were older or because they held responsible positions in society. That was back when children obeyed their parents, voters had regard for elected officials, laity esteemed clergy, teaching staffs respected administrative staffs, and students respected teachers.

Like it or not, respect for positional authority, whether personal or institutional, has eroded. Today, regardless of who you are or what you do, respect is not granted automatically. Respect has to be earned. Regard has to be deserved. And just like adults, teenagers are unimpressed with people who simply parade their older status or remind others of their revered position. In the school environment, just as the administrative staff have to earn the respect of the teaching staff, so teachers have to earn the respect of their students.

Life works best when people in the same environments have mutual respect. And when those who have position and power are the first to send the "I respect you" signals to those for whom they are responsible, that is when life works exceptionally well. Whether in the classroom or the workplace, the dynamics of respect in today's world are reciprocal. If you don't give it, you don't get it.

The data clearly inform us that young people are not used to receiving signals of respect from many of the adults in their lives. Yet, 75 per cent of teenagers say they highly value "being respected." This is a sad state of affairs. For when teenagers, like adults, are treated with respect, they not only respond with respect, but they are also open to being influenced.

Connecting the relational drive of the youth culture with the erosion of respect in society produces two key prerequisites for effective teaching:

PERSONAL RAPPORT + EARNED RESPECT = EFFECTIVENESS

COMPENSATE FOR THE COMPULSORY

Discussion about how to create "mutual respect" school environments do not make it on to very many staff meeting agendas. Unfortunately, there are still some schools whose motto is My Way or the Highway. For students, schools are the epitome of a controlled environment. Schools are institutions in which conformity is compulsory. The ringing of a bell as the signal to go directly to the next class does not turn classrooms into prison cells, but it's worth noting that until young people are sixteen, it is illegal not to attend.

Teachers who empathize with students' needs will seek to compensate for the compulsory. They will understand that compulsory environments contradict the adolescent drive for freedom and wisely conclude that unless it is absolutely necessary, they will not fight this inevitable drive.

Accordingly, staff meetings with prudent educators will hold discussions about how to increase the number of choices their students are offered during a normal school week. They will actively build student choices into their pedagogy, into curriculum, classroom experiences, and the totality of school life. When possible, instead of simply assigning the same project to the whole class, a list of alternatives will be offered. Students will be encouraged to suggest what they would like to do to fulfill the requirements of some courses. Alert educators will seek to channel the energy of the young into expressions of responsible freedom.

HUMANIZE THE INSTITUTIONAL ENVIRONMENT

Educational institutions, with their sanitized hallways and desks in straight rows, desperately need to be humanized. They need to be personalized. And the potential for warming up those cold and sterile places rests squarely on the shoulders of the educators, who day after day and month after month share life with their students.

Specifically, teachers are the humanizers, the personalizers. But unless they are more than just human photocopiers churning out curriculum content, they will keep on depositing their monthly cheques but will miss the big fringe benefits of their profession. They will miss the human interaction, the personal touch between themselves and the learners in their lives.

Teachers who humanize their environments will intentionally take time to relate to the teenage students around them. They will understand how dominant the friendship drive is in youth culture. They will realize that the students sitting in the desks in front of them are harbouring attitudes that silently state, *Relate to me, then teach me.*

Unfortunately, because of sexual-abuse incidents, the decline of trust, and increasing xenophobia in the society, teachers' unions continue to counsel educators, Don't touch! Don't put yourself in the position of being charged with harassment or even sexual abuse. Every profession has a few members with twisted minds. But the question that educators should ask is, are we going to let these few not only control us but also dehumanize our profession?

We don't stop going to medical doctors for physical examinations just because there are a few abusers in that profession. Teachers who are committed to humanize their institutions will communicate care and positive regard for their students, and that could include reaching out to touch an arm or squeeze a shoulder.

Teachers who respond to individual students humanize their environments. For instance, just taking note of a student who is absent can send the right message. When the student returns, before beginning the class, the teacher can approach her desk and ask, "We missed you yesterday. Are you all right?" The message sent to the whole class is that you are important and I care about you.

Collaborative learning is another way to humanize institutional environments. We have already established that teenagers are social creatures who feed on friendship. Doesn't it add up that they will learn better when they're able to talk with each other rather than when they are told to sit in silence and figure things out on their own?

Teachers who make an effort to affirm the various forms of co-operative learning will not only enhance their students' social skills, they will also increase their group process competencies. The interpersonal dynamics will serve the interests of both teachers and students. Positive word will circulate around the school about teachers who excel at using group process learning.

Fewer students will be left lamenting with this 15-year-old female from the Maritimes: "What I like least about school is having to sit at a desk all day."

One effective way for teachers to communicate that life is meant to be a co-operative affair is to model the message. Teachers who inform their students that "today's approach to the class was put together in a working session with colleagues" sends the message teachers are human beings and need help, too.

CARVE OUT A POSITIVE REPUTATION

Every teacher in every school develops what is usually a well-deserved reputation — a very personal, spelled-out ranking.

Students grade their teachers on far more than how they teach. They scrutinize the way their teachers dress, check out what kind of cars they drive, and speculate about their private lives. "He's tough but fair." "She'll believe anything." "She's somebody I could talk to." "He's arrogant and never wrong." "I think he's going to bed with her." "Don't take a class from him — boring!" One thing is certain. When students look back at their school experiences and think about their teachers, they will remember them far more for how they treated their students rather than for what they taught them.

It probably doesn't happen, but in teachers' colleges and faculties of education, it would be beneficial for teachers-in-training to think ahead about what they would like their students to say about them. Carving out a positive reputation before showing up in the classroom will have an impact on the attitudes of students.

Carving out an individual reputation is one matter. The collective reputation of the educational fraternity is another. And the way contract negotiations are being conducted is a realm where the whole educational system is failing.

Think about the process. Teachers' unions and trustee negotiators represent their interests behind closed doors until the talks reach an impasse. The next phase is to take the issues into the public forum. Each side uses the media to hurl accusations at the other. Unless there is a resolve, the teachers launch a work-to-rule campaign and the trustees threaten a lock-out. And sometimes teachers go on strike and squander their professional reputations walking the picket line. When that happens, teachers, administrators, trustees, parents, and students all lose.

What gets communicated to students during these times? "Teachers are in it just for the money. We don't really matter." Strikes and withholding services damage the collective reputation of educators. When young people are reduced to commodities and used as pawns at the bargaining table, the whole learning process is damaged. Surely there is enough ingenuity among intelligent people to figure out how to solve problems in private and to be guided by principles that reflect a commitment to the higher purposes of true education.

As ideal as that may sound, however, strikes are often necessary — and a legitimate component of Canadian labour relations. So, when negotiations break down and teachers feel compelled to strike, can they take some action to ensure that picket lines don't trample the reputations they have cultivated with their students? Are there ways for the administration to meet regularly with student representatives to brief them and discuss how they're affected? Can students carry out some extracurricular activities on their own on school property during a strike? Strikes are meant to be resolution mechanisms, but can the mechanism be employed so that teachers concerned about their contracts can also express concern for their students?

Perhaps education should be decreed an essential service. Then, when negotiations break down, an arbitrator would be appointed to impose a compulsory settlement. Teachers would thus be spared the indignity of walking the picket line and sending negative messages to their students.

GIVE UP HIDING BEHIND THE MYTH OF OBJECTIVITY

Teachers do more than just teach and facilitate formal learning. They embody life for their students. How they handle themselves in contract negotiations and who they are as people all have impacts. In a way, teachers *are* the curriculum. Their persons, inside and outside the classroom, deliver many messages to their students.

A teacher cannot spend significant time with a class of students without disclosing his or her personal biases. When people live in the same environment for months at a time, they influence each other. Parents are concerned about teachers' expressing their opinions, especially if those opinions are related to beliefs or life-style matters. The response of some to the problem of proselytizing has been to champion valueless teaching. But valueless teaching is impossible. With their presence and through their teaching, educators both implicitly and explicitly convey values in the same way television sitcoms send out their not-so-hidden messages.

What are the alternatives?

Teachers should be encouraged to teach with a sense of mission, to live with energy and enthusiasm. The last thing today's teenagers need is more vagueness and disguised neutrality. At the same time, proselytizing of any kind in the classroom is off-limits. A teacher expressing a personal opinion and owning it as such is one thing, but seeking to persuade and convince a student to hold the same belief is another. When teachers do offer an opinion or belief, they need to present it as only one perspective among many. Young people usually already are aware of many aspects of their teachers' private lives and won't be surprised to hear what their teachers think and believe.

School ought to be a forum to make informed choices. Students need to be aware of alternatives in order to make their moves toward autonomy. Instead of striving for value vagueness, teachers should express their preferences on a wide range of issues, providing they don't do so with evangelistic zeal. Adopting this code and living this way is more honest.

Piaget was right once again when he observed, "As teachers are, so they will teach." Teachers cannot teach without communicating views and transmitting biases. Accepting that and then employing limits is a far better approach.

CARE FOR PEOPLE AND DEMONSTRATE
A LOVE FOR LEARNING

Recently, I listened to a teacher talk about two touchstones in her life as a high school student.

As a totally normal and healthy 16-year-old, she fell in love with her French teacher. He never knew the level of her affection, and the whole affair was nothing more than teenage fantasy. One day, however, the teacher she secretly adored lectured her and embarrassed her in front of her classmates. She was devastated, more deeply hurt than the teacher could imagine.

A couple of days later, while she was still feeling emotionally scarred and betrayed, that same French teacher happened to meet her in the hallway. He stopped her and said, "I owe you an apology. It was unfair of me to lecture you the way I did." Reflecting on the incident, the woman realized that day in the hallway, Mr. Johnson had restored her faith in humanity.

The second touchstone was different but just as memorable. This time the subject was history, and it was one of those afternoon classes when heads were nodding and interest was waning. The teacher laboured on, but knew she was losing the attention of the whole class.

In a moment of frustration and passion, she exclaimed, "Everyone, look at me! Don't you realize, blood was flowing in the streets of Paris!"

Teaching with a care for others and a love of your subject is the combination that will instil learning that will last a lifetime. But to be considered a successful teacher, there is a test that must be passed: have the students learned what they have been taught? Whether or not the curriculum has been covered, whether the pedagogy has been conventional or unorthodox, whether the learning experience has been enjoyable or a gruelling ordeal, *until students have learned they have not been taught.*

Canadian schools have been subject to reams of criticism. And much of the negative appraisal is backed up with a wide range of international research. New Brunswick premier Frank McKenna charged that "Canada, despite all its spending on education, has one of the highest drop-out rates and one of the highest levels of illiteracy in the industrialized world." Citing a 1988 international study comparing 23 countries, McKenna pointed out that Canadian students fare worse as they get older. Specifically, the study ranked grade-five students in sixth place, but by grade 12, those same students had sunk to twenty-second place.[10]

A comprehensive two-year study by the Economic Council of Canada was equally disheartening. The study concluded that Canadian educators are "among the best-paid in the world, and students stay in school longer, yet academic results are mediocre compared with international rivals." The study was particularly alarmed at the inability of the educational system to prepare young people for employment. "While some countries have adapted school systems to meet the needs of a changing world, the council found Canada has done relatively little to prepare or encourage its students to compete.[11]

Educators have to own their results. Blaming the students or discounting the reliability of the comparative studies is an inadequate response. When students don't get passing grades, neither do educators. The fact remains that, until students have learned, they have not been taught.

At the end of the year, not all educators watch their graduates walk across the stage to receive their diplomas from the same perspective. Those who place themselves at the centre of the learning experience are inclined to look at their students and think, I was your teacher. I taught you. Educators committed to student-centred learning have a different focus. They think, You were my students. You learned from me. The difference may seem small but the impact can be profound.

Educators who aspire to excel and are tuned in to this generation of students will be ready to assume three personal identities.

First, they will see themselves as competent *professionals*. At a time when young people are suspicious of most forms of authority, the effective educator will perform at a level that engenders respect. A display of professional competence and a manner, not cold and calculating, but clear and visionary, will allow educators to walk into their classrooms and stand before their students conveying the message:

We are the teachers, our role is to teach.
You are the students, your role is to learn.
Let's excel at it together.

Committed teachers will intentionally instil in their students a love of learning and a desire for truth. They will set higher standards for themselves than their systems require of them.

Effective educators will also be ready to assume a *para-parent* role in the lives of their students. They will take time to listen and send out signals that every person in their presence is significant. They will understand that teens' needs for rapport with adults is frequently unmet, and they will not be afraid to get personal. Although they will be careful not to counter what they know parents and guardians desire, para-parent educators will make positive contributions to the character formation of their students.

Effective educators will also see themselves standing alongside their students as *human beings*. There will be a clear awareness that even though the teacher-student roles are different, educators will be content to see themselves standing on level ground beside other human beings. They will know we are all learners, and they will like it that way.

7

THE ROLE OF RELIGION

The majority *of young people in Canada are sending a sobering message to those who value organized religion. Attendance continues to decline and participation in youth groups is low. Relatively few teenagers place much value on religious involvement. In the minds of the vast majority of young people, religion is something that is marginal to everyday life.*

Still holding on to their religious legacy, however, young people expect to use the services of the country's religious institutions for ceremonial purposes — marriages, births, and deaths.

But there is light in the darkness. The surveys also document that more than 80 per cent of young people identify themselves with Canada's major religious groups, with around 20 per cent actively participating. More significantly, teens exhibit a high level of receptivity to matters spiritual, including meaning, purpose, and life after death. There's also an extraordinary interest in supernatural phenomena. In short, although not planning to show up for regular worship services, the majority of Canada's youth are open to experience the spiritual.

The times signal difficulties for those who value conventional forms of faith. But there are also opportunities to be pursued.

AN ENDURING PLACE FOR RELIGION

Historians would agree that it is impossible to understand present-day Canada without examining the role religion has played. Populist views of society tend to be less historical and more pragmatic. Many Canadians see no need or place for religion in the modern world. Others are even inclined to censor religion, keep it out of the public forum altogether. We would argue that a case can be made to support an enduring role for religion in today's society.

VALUE DURABILITY

Very few Canadians would disagree that organized religion is being pushed to the sidelines. An indication of the marginalization of religion in modern Canada is evidenced in whom young people turn to when they are making decisions. Only one per cent indicate they would turn to religious leaders for counsel on the subject of sex, and only two per cent would consult with a minister or priest about right or wrong. But disregard for the role of religion has implications for society at large. At stake are three of the chief values of our society: honesty, forgiveness, and generosity.

Consider the following data:

VALUE ASCRIBED BY FREQUENT WORSHIP ATTENDERS AND NON-ATTENDERS		
% Viewing as "Very Important"		
	Honesty	Forgiveness	Generosity
Frequent Attenders	76	75	51
Non-Attenders	61	48	33

Frequent worship attenders are affirming the values of honesty, forgiveness, and generosity at significantly higher levels than those who do not attend.

Some may question the importance of these findings. Does it matter if we become a less forgiving and less honest society? Are the implications of declining levels of generosity positive or negative?

We believe that a decline in these values is profoundly important. Honesty, forgiveness, and generosity are not just values, they are virtues. A society that lacks them is in danger of becoming a hell on earth.

One of the advantages for young people who are regularly involved in religious institutions is that they acquire knowledge systematically. Like learning mathematics in school, youth who participate in formal religious structures learn about ethics, morals, and values in an organized manner. Involvement in catechism sessions, confirmation classes, and other religious-education endeavours all serve to construct a framework for their moral instruction and faith development. What can result is an organized conscience and the construction materials for building character. Like putting together the pieces of a jigsaw puzzle, there is the possibility of piecing together a picture that has harmony and clear design. Even if participation in religious institutions is abandoned later in life, a person still has a framework in place to give guidance for making decisions in life that follows.

To contend that involvement in a structured religious life allows young people to systematically affirm their values and ethics is not to say young people who aren't involved end up valueless or immoral. However, it is to state that, unless young people get a formal and systematic setting to figure out their values and beliefs, they will have no other alternative but to assimilate what is important to them in an ad-hoc and laissez-faire fashion.

Without formal input for their value-shaping and character-formation, young people are susceptible to adopting what is implicit and undefined. They are prone to embrace as their own what is appealing in their friends, what they see paraded on television, and what is modelled by their parents and other significant adults in their lives. The process is often more unconscious than conscious, more accidental than deliberate. Without specific instruction, they are vulnerable to assimilating values in a vacuum and accepting unexamined beliefs. If young people who regularly participate in formal religious structures face the task of putting jigsaw puzzles together, then those who absent themselves from formal involvement face the challenge of creating modern art and then describing what they have concocted.

Whether or not young people participate in formal religious training, values and beliefs are most effectively transmitted when they are both taught and caught. Accordingly, young people are best served when they are taught by trustworthy people who model what they teach. Although there have been recent highly publicized exceptions, religious institutions continue to be places where young people have access to good teaching from fine-living people.

There is a qualification that deserves careful consideration. In this discussion linking the values of honesty, forgiveness, and generosity with religious involvement, we need to acknowledge that they are being affirmed as attitudes rather than as explicit behaviours. You might ask, then, "Is the behaviour of people who regularly attend places of worship more honest, forgiving, and generous?" The answer is that if the behaviour isn't distinctive, it ought to be. And in the end, if those who make theoretical claims do not also live out the evidence of their theory, then both the theory and those who espouse it are fraudulent.

But whether or not the behaviour of regular attenders is distinctive, key questions still remain. If our religious institutions have been one of the main shapers of our cultural values in the past, what will be the sources of our value formation in the future? What will those values be? Even if the role of formal religion were to be relegated to the past, it would still continue to serve as a reminder to find adequate replacements for the future.

CHOICES WITH CRITERIA

For young people, living in the world we have created for them is almost overwhelming. The complexities of modern living can make teenagers feel as if they have to embark on the journey of life without a road map. Whether they are standing at a counter choosing a flavour of ice cream, deciding what video to rent, considering career choices, making life-style decisions, contemplating their beliefs, or wondering whether or not a full-fledged marriage is necessary, Canada's youth are confronted with a world that is profoundly complicated.

As we have already cited, young people are faced with an increasing array of choices. A good example is found in the federal government's Royal Commission on New Reproductive Technologies. In a first phase report entitled "What We Heard," a total of 119 questions were raised relating to modern reproductive issues. A sample of the questions include:

Do we want to control the kinds of family forms that are acceptable in Canada?

Should donor insemination, as a "low technology" procedure, be available outside the medical system for women?

Should access to new reproductive technologies be restricted to heterosexual married couples, or should it be available to single and/or homosexual women who wish to bear children?[1]

The complexity of these issues is staggering. As a society, we haven't been here before. How we respond will have long-term social implications. As we head into uncharted territory with so many human consequences, it is important to be guided by clear moral criteria. Otherwise decisions will be made by the loudest voices or subject to the mood of the moment.

One gift religion can offer to a culture are clear criteria for consistent and coherent decision-making. Understanding what orthodox religions have concluded throughout the centuries can serve as invaluable reference points for decision-making in the future. Censoring the historic views of religion out of modern debates is short-sighted and immature.

CONSCIENCES WITH CONVICTIONS

Anyone who breathes also believes. Whether or not people are conscious of it, everyone operates with a hierarchy of values, a code of ethics, moral standards, and a system of beliefs. The real test is not what people verbally claim about their beliefs and values and ethics, but what is most often expressed in their behaviour. The value of honesty translates into telling the truth, forgiveness as an operative value is giving people second chances, and generosity is shown by how people spend their time and use their money. In the end, external behaviour flows from the essence of internal convictions.

Because so few young people in the 1990s are regular participants in formal religious structures, they are missing the opportunity to consciously construct their spiritual framework. These young people need specific assistance. The influence of the family has been and will continue to be primary in this realm, but youth today also need other adult input to assist them in constructing consciences with well-reasoned convictions.

A world where people lack consciences with convictions would be a dangerous place. Coherence would be impossible. Decisions would be ad hoc and inconsistent. Life would be lived randomly rather than with specific design. And in the end chaos would prevail.

Because religion is no longer the dominant guidance system for developing consciences with convictions, other sources of influence have come to assume that role. Young people are vulnerable to a wide array of cult and other "conviction managers" who cultivate opportunities to relate to them.

Whether or not we live with specific faith commitments, surely we are mature enough to appreciate the critical contributions religion has made to our past so that the essence of the good can be brought into the future.

SPIRITUALITY WITH COMPASSION

Simply developing a clear set of convictions will not be adequate for living in the modern world. Affirming strong convictions alone will likely lead to excess. And we know from experience that religious people can be harsh. They can get so caught up with their convictions and sense of legal justice that they pre-empt the flow of their compassion. When that happens, people are put down and judged, and religion is given a bad reputation.

On the other extreme, religious people can be so accepting and compassionate they stand for almost nothing. They tend to drain the ideal of love of any real substance, and eventually they become both unprincipled and innocuous.

Healthy spirituality is a balance of *uncompromising conviction* and *unrelenting compassion.* Conviction invites people to take a stand and build their lives on principles. Compassion solicits empathy and prompts people to view life from the other person's point of view. When the two virtues co-exist, strength and beauty stand side by side. When conviction and compassion converge, they counter the drive to seek justice without compassion. The double commitment produces a concern to seek what is best for the collective good rather than simply driving for self-concern.

Young people will be invaluably helped as they are able to observe adults dealing with the creative tension that comes when there is a commitment to both conviction and compassion.

REFLECTION WITH PURPOSE

Throughout the course of history, religion has consistently raised the traditional meaning questions about life.

Who am I?
Why am I here?
What happens after I die?

These questions have always been a part of the philosophical pursuit, and in the spiritual quest for meaning, they have been central.

Life that is rich is lived deeply. Watching "Cheers" or "The Simpsons" on TV doesn't begin to even open the door to the quality that can be discovered in reflective silence. And the benefits of spiritual meditation are accessible to everyone.

The following selection from a church bulletin entitled "Fasting and Feasting" frames life with depth and substance. If one is so inclined, pondering the meaning can nourish one's inner life:

> *Fast from criticism, and feast on praise,*
> *Fast from self-pity, and feast on joy,*
> *Fast from ill-temper, and feast on peace,*
> *Fast from resentment, and feast on contentment,*
> *Fast from jealousy, and feast on love,*
> *Fast from pride, and feast on humility,*
> *Fast from selfishness, and feast on service,*
> *Fast from fear, and feast on faith.*

The contemplative writer Henri Nouwen suggests that reflection has a practical purpose that can contribute to a more creative present: "In our chatty world, in which the word has lost its power to communicate, silence helps us to keep our mind and heart anchored in the future world and allows us to seek from there a creative and recreative word into the present world."[2]

As previously proposed, adults who work with young people will serve them well if they invite them to take time to pursue the fourth R — reflection. The practice will give young people time to ponder some of the complicated decisions they face and perhaps foster an inner spirit that will generate both conviction and compassion in their day-to-day living.

A SOCIETY IN TRANSITION

Regarding the role of religion in life, Canadian society is in transition. And as the shifts take place around them, young people are pretty much doing what adults are doing. Although only a minority of today's youth are active participants in organized religious life, the majority are retaining their religious identities. Embracing the religious organizational affiliations of their parents, young people are the recipients of family-transmitted religion. They are accepting what is being passed on to them from the previous generation and, in particular, their parents. Accordingly, eight in 10 are self-confessed "religious somethings." In keeping with the religious demographics of adult Canadians, all but four per cent of that total call themselves either Protestants or Catholics. Consistent with the adult pattern, eight in 10 believe in God, and the same number believe that Jesus is the divine son of God. Just as today's Canadians are "ethnic somethings," most adults and youth in the country are also "religious somethings."

Although Canada is becoming both a more multicultural society and an increasingly secularized society, the Judaeo-Christian view of life continues to be the primary orientation for the vast majority of Canadians. It is often assumed that people of visible minorities who've immigrated to Canada identify only with religions other than Christian. Certainly, that is true for the majority, and an increasing multiculturalism is contributing to the creation of a multifaith society. However, of those teenagers who make up the visible minorities, 26 per cent who were born outside Canada and 44 per cent who were born in Canada identify themselves as Christians — either Catholics or Protestants.

The experience of a 17-year-old Laos-born woman who now lives in southwestern Ontario illustrates the point: "I am still searching for the religion that suits me."

Acknowledging the make-up of Canada's current religious climate, what follows seeks to be sensitive to the religious diversification that is emerging in Canada. And it specifically applies to those who are working with young people within religious institutions. But because the Canadian demographics are predominantly Christian, the recommendations particularly apply to Christian churches. Nevertheless, the ideas will relate to all religious settings. Adults who work with young people in Boy Scouts, Girl Guides, 4-H clubs, and other community youth groups will also find principles to guide their strategies and programming.

YOUTH'S SEVEN RELATIONAL LAWS OF LIFE

Whether adults work with today's youth within religious structures or other settings, it will be crucial to function within the laws of life that control the youth culture. Just as it is impossible to live in this world without embracing beliefs of one kind or another, the dominance of friendship in today's youth culture means there is no escaping the relational laws of life, either. If you hope to influence the younger generation or minister effectively among them, you must deal with the friendship factors that rule their lives.

'WHO' IS MORE CRUCIAL THAN 'WHERE'

Wise youth workers look beneath the surface. They look beyond what young people do, and ask *why* they do what they do. And they soon figure out the motivational patterns of the younger generation aren't all that complicated. The power of friendship is in control.

The real-life scenario works this way. The youth group leaders plan a special weekend retreat. The program has all the right ingredients, including an inviting locale and exciting activities. But the members of the group are still reluctant to commit to coming. When asked if they're going to, the responses sort into two main categories — "maybe yes" and "maybe no."

Some leaders get frustrated. Other leaders understand that the reluctance to commit is not tied to where the group is planning to go or for that matter what they are planning to do.

The real issue is *who* is going to be there.

Tuned-in leaders operate from the premise that equality is a myth. They know that some individuals have more power than others and, thus, the ability to exert influence. They observe the group to determine who they are.

Discerning youth leaders make deliberate moves. And they count on the power of their relational leverage to influence the influencers to sign up first.

PEOPLE ARE MORE IMPORTANT THAN PROGRAMS

Historically, programs have been to youth workers what curriculum has been to school teachers. They have controlled both the content and flavour of a gathering of young people.

In the modern era, the potency of relationships impinges on the role programs previously played in youth ministry. Programs that used to be the primary tools in the youth worker's arsenal have been demoted. Today, people are more important than programs.

In practical terms, when a church, or any organization that desires to initiate a venture involving young people, the first question that must be asked is, do we have suitable adults to give leadership, that is, adults who are able to build rapport and surrender their time? The priority is not to deal with the specifics of the program, but to recruit leaders who can attract young people to the program.

Because the power of the personal is more potent than the attracting force of the organizational, it is crucial for the informal to augment the objectives of the formal.

ORGANIZATIONAL STRUCTURES MUST BE WARM

When young people do show up inside organizational structures, if they don't build relationships there, they will simply go elsewhere. They will go where they experience relationships.

There are two major sources of organizational warmth. The first is the physical environment. A sterile church basement is a turn-off. A colourful, comfortable room with a stereo and soft carpet is more inviting. So is a pizza place with loud music!

The second, and more important source of warmth inside an organizational structure exudes from the people who are present. Effective youth workers have very long arms. They have the ability to reach around everybody there and give out group hugs. They implicitly and explicitly send out the message "You are welcome here. Everyone in this place is valuable, whether you're in a foul mood, overweight, or your face is obviously under an acne attack. You are accepted."

THE TOUCH OF A PERSON IS MORE POWERFUL THAN AN IDEA

For young people, the experience of friendship is lived out inside the affective domain. Friendship warms the heart and triggers inner feelings. Unfortunately, the dynamics of friendship can cloud or even completely bypass the cognitive domain. In other words, young people don't generally perceive their friends as sources of intellectual stimulation.

Astute youth workers will align their thinking with effective educator strategy and be prepared to relate first and teach second. Stated in another way, they will plan to first enter the "heart" doors of young people, and then go through their "head" doors. Effective youth ministry incites two-way traffic between teenagers' hearts and heads. In the flow of healthy life there are experiences to both stir the heart and ideas to engage the mind.

Youth workers with their eyes open to reality will compute that the touch of a person is more powerful than the persuasion of an idea. Influence travels across the bridge of relationships. It flows person to person. The consequences are rather easy to predict. A youth worker who is intentional is effective. That is, someone who has a specific agenda to convey can have more impact in a one-on-one conversation at the doughnut shop than by organizing a conference and bringing in a speaker, however excellent, who is unknown to the group.

RESULTS TAKE TIME

One of the realities of relational ministry is that making an impact on young people takes time. Building rapport and establishing trust doesn't happen overnight.

This is frustrating for ambitious youth workers, many of whom are young themselves. They want to get things done now so they can get on to the next event. They aspire to alter the course of history in a weekend. Consequently, they are inclined to lead with a microwave mentality.

But youth ministry is not the place of service for people who require instant gratification. Carving out personal beliefs, establishing ethical codes, consolidating value systems, deciding whether or not to seek and know the God of the universe, and spiritual decision-making are all serious matters. They not only deserve careful consideration. They take time.

Youth expert Dean Borgman offers a solid perspective: "An amateur youth worker wants newness, bigness, and instant success. Professional youth workers look at the results of their impact when the young people they have served are 25."

INFLUENCE IS LIMITED TO A FEW

Another inescapable relational law of life is that one person's influence is limited to just a few young people. Consequently, a team of adults is required to work effectively with a large group.

If a group has eight to 12 participants, one or two adults can create a quality experience for those involved. If there are aspirations to give growth experience to a group of 25 to 30 teenagers, a team of four or five adults will be necessary.

This relational law doesn't preclude large audiences of young people gathering for special events. Clusters of friends are ready to travel almost anywhere — if they can go with each other. However, when the pattern involves gathering the same group of young people at the same place for a similar purpose, the right ratio of adults to youth is necessary.

Whenever influence among young people is the focus of conversation or the subject of ministry strategy, there is one constant reality to keep in mind: young people in relationship with each other have a profound influence on each other. Articulating the impact of social links between today's youth, a 15-year-old female confesses:

I grew up with my parents as scientists and thinking that there's no other way. But now I have a boyfriend who is very Christian, and it bothers him that I haven't accepted Jesus Christ into my heart. He's really made me think about everything. One of the biggest decisions I've ever had to make.

RELATIONSHIPS ARE AN END IN THEMSELVES

In defining the relational laws, we have been processing the implications of friendship as being both teenagers' number-one value and their highest source of gratification. This reality has profound implications for youth ministry. In a sense, young people are deifying friendship. As a result, relationships often become ends in themselves. As young people feed on friendship, they taste what is for them the ultimate of life. Their desires are fulfilled. There is no motivation to look for more.

But from an adult perspective, which projects life with a sense of mission, there is more.

Particularly for adults motivated by religious commitment and working with youth in spiritual contexts, there is a desire to encourage young people to increase the strength of their beliefs. Whether that means discussing the Bible, the Koran, or other sacred writings, as well as praying and worshipping together, young people will benefit as they study and express their responses.

At another level, motivating today's teens into practical service deserves a high priority. Whenever youth workers get together and share their perceptions, one of the common themes that emerges is that today's teenagers are concerned about the state of the world they have inherited. As we've already noted, youth today are compassionate creatures. They care deeply. And they are ready to respond when they see they can make a difference.

Prompted especially by churches that give a priority to youth ministry, every summer, in remote communities and in inner-city settings, youth workers and teenagers can be found working side by side painting houses and clearing trash. Young people are paying their own way to travel to underdeveloped nations to dig latrines and pound nails for better housing. Earlier this year, 75,000 young people denied their unrelenting appetite for food and raised money for the world's poor by participating in World Vision Canada's 30-Hour Famine.

Canada would be a better place and people's needs would be met if, across our country, youth groups were also conceived as baby-sitting societies. What would happen if teenagers who regularly gather in religious and community youth groups were challenged and enabled to give at least one night a month of free baby-sitting to a family straining under inordinate pressure? Young people would experience what it is to be givers — and neighbours would know what it is to be loved.

COUNSEL FOR THE COMMITTED

Allow us to speak directly to those who are living with a religious commitment and an ensuing sense of mission in life. Not everyone agrees that such a commitment is desirable. Even those who are drawn in that direction will disagree among themselves on how a sense of mission should be expressed. The splintering of the Christian church throughout history and the presence of other world religions in modern Canada guarantees diversity. Learning to live with our differences and even appreciating them will continue to challenge us in the future. Surely, in areas of beliefs and personal preferences, we must give permission to others to affirm their particular views, as well as take permission to lay claim to our own.

OFFER A FAITH THAT WORKS

In the modern world, what works has worth. What doesn't work gets discarded. And if young people perceive that their faith doesn't work, it will get discarded, too.

To retain those young people who are currently participating inside religious organizations, it will be important for their involvement to make a difference to their daily living. If those same young people are to be motivated to invite their friends to join them, their confidence in what they're doing will have to soar.

Simply stated, the faith journey for young people needs to:

- Encourage their experience with the supernatural
- Equip them to interact with the real world and the range of people who intersect their lives
- Give them a coherent sense of themselves.

The spiritual involves the vertical. An encounter between the divine and the human. The decisions of faith are meant to be personalized. And in the exchange between the human and the divine, something transcendent takes place. Beyond the boundaries of the physical, the realm of mystery is explored. And along the journey, one can move from the hope of believing to the experience of knowing.

The spiritual also involves the horizontal. Faith is about loving your neighbour and living together in a society. It is about the practical righting of wrongs and pursuing a more just future. When disparities between the rich and the poor are addressed and the vulnerable are being protected, spiritual work is being done.[3] The spiritual also embraces what is immediately important. For the young, faith will work when it includes friendship and gives a framework for the expression of responsible freedom.

The spiritual also involves the internal. The spiritual domain speaks to the issue of coming to terms with the real you and constructing a healthy inner self. Faith that works for young people will deal with the reality of inner darkness. At the same time, it will affirm the importance of loving yourself enough — but not so much that others get demoted.

COMPLEMENT THE CULTURE

Fighting the prevailing forces in the youth culture will be exhausting and, in the end, a losing battle. The dynamics of youth culture are too powerful to subdue. To stand in their way will be like trying to stop the flow of water from a small mountain stream. While it is possible to build a make-shift dam that will force the water back up stream and stop the immediate flow for a short while, before long the water will create more pressure than the dam can contain and find another way down the mountain. The same is true for the forces that reside in the younger generation. If these natural drives are stifled and stymied, eventually they will surge their way into the flow of life.

Wise youth workers will harness the forces in the youth culture. Rather than fighting what is inevitable, unless principle is being jeopardized or moral compromise is required, they will go with the flow.

As we have noted, freedom is a highly ranked value and force to be reckoned with in every healthy teenager. Yet, religion has a reputation for being restrictive. There are very few images that link religion and freedom naturally together. Religion is more likely to be associated with lack of freedom. How will we respond?

First, youth workers will figure out what they themselves think and believe about freedom. Then they will be able to communicate insightfully about the subject of freedom in conversations, in five-minute talks, in twenty-minute formal addresses, and in two-hour discussions. Those who are pro-active in dealing with freedom issues will connect with teenagers' interests, dispel the notion that taking faith seriously denies the freedom of choice, and send the message that religion is for the real world.

Our survey affirms what experienced youth workers already know: friendship and music are the highest sources of enjoyment for young people. Accordingly, going to a live concert with a friend is as close to heaven on earth as young people can get. Just as computing the friendship factors in youth ministry is critical for success, figuring out how to use music as a resource will also be important. Integrating music into youth-ministry programs will not only attract young people, it will tell them you understand them. Listening to song lyrics and watching videos, analysing as a group the explicit and implicit messages, can help young people understand what is influencing them. Youth workers who take the time to tune into youth music and thereby become musically literate, will be in a position to relate more effectively.

A third response will be to carefully explore the realm of the supernatural. Young people do not have God grudges on their shoulders. They are not anti-religious. Rather, out of the legacy of their heritage and the input of their world, they are supernaturalists. Eight in 10 believe God exists, seven in 10 say some people have psychic powers, six in 10 believe evil forces exist, five in 10 accept the idea of extrasensory perception, four in 10 think they can make contact with the spirit world, and three in 10 expect to be reincarnated.

Accordingly, a 17-year-old woman in grade 12 writes: "I believe in the higher spirits, but not God or any set religion."

A 16-year-old man in grade 11 from Nova Scotia states: "I have my own type of religion that keeps me going."

Young people are predisposed to the supernatural, and although they don't intend to turn to organized religion to actively pursue their interest, they are not negative about spiritual realities. When we want to get in touch with people, step number one is to meet people where they are. Therefore, if young people are open to the supernatural but have no intention of going to formal worship, then begin with, "What does it mean for you to believe in the supernatural?"

Discovering the answer to that question will be an enlightening experience for adults bound by strict orthodoxy. Astrology, extrasensory perception, contact with the spirit world, and reincarnation have not historically been considered conventional in western spiritual thought. Adults who are secure and mature enough to suspend their personal belief biases and try to understand another's point of view will be effective. Those who simply exhort or send judgment signals will not get a serious hearing.

In assisting young people to figure out their beliefs, where the discussion starts may be more critical than where it ends. Unless the interaction starts where people are in the present tense of their thinking, it is unlikely it will even begin.

COUNTER THE CULTURE

The data clearly show that the current cultural mood has invited young people to wrap their arms around relativism, a philosophy that truth in the areas of beliefs, ethics, morals, and life-style alternatives is a matter of personal opinion. Accordingly, we should not be surprised that close to seven in 10 teens have concluded, "What's right and wrong is a matter of personal opinion," and that six in 10 believe, "All world religions are equally valid." As an 18-year-old black male explains, "I take the good points of each religion."

These relativized views held by today's youth represent one of the current cultural shifts. Prior to the 1960s, when truth was accepted as an external reference point for values and morality, and organized religion was more influential, young people were faced with life that was more prescribed and less complicated. Lines for expected behaviour were straighter, and categories for what was right and wrong were clearer. For today's generation of youth, life is more like a maze.

When relativism reigns, the consequences are subtle but predictable. When truth claims are discarded, absolutes are abandoned. The objective is brought under the control of the subjective. In the areas of values, ethics, beliefs, and life-style alternatives, certainties are exchanged for uncertainties. *Maybe* is substituted for *yes* and *no*. Good and evil are a matter of opinion. Beliefs are the private property of the individual.

Contending that truth exists and that it can be known does not give any individual, or for that matter any organization, an exclusive corner on truth. Individuals and organizations who come to the conclusion that their way is the only way have transcended their humanness. In order to become absolutist about truth, it is necessary to deny the subjectivity of one's human perspective. Regardless of the desire or the diligence to have the final word, the mind of the Creator is neither totally accessible nor completely comprehensible to the perceptions of those who are just created. For those who take truth seriously, the tension is to hold firm to those convictions that are clearly defensible, while still remembering that being human has its limitations.

Still, there are enormous differences between people who start with the assumption that truth exists to be discovered and those who believe that the best they can do is form personal opinions. When applied to values and ethics and morals, truth-seekers look outside themselves to find standards and convictions. In the end, opinion-makers look inside themselves for the final word. On the one hand, those who pursue truth and its implications for personal direction find criteria and time-tested standards that are beyond themselves and shared by others. On the other hand, those whose final appeal is their own opinion are inevitably pulled toward individualism and selfism. As we have already noted, there are long-term consequences for both individuals and society as a whole.

The whole mood of relativism is one that takes away permission to hold and express strong convictions unless those views support the tenets of relativism. Being passionate about tolerance, openness, and the individual's right to think and choose as he or she desires is given social approval. But, particularly in the context of interpersonal relationships, being passionate about a conviction that might infringe on someone else's prerogative is almost precluded. The long-term result invites passivity. Eventually a generation is created that is comfortable with contradictions, relaxed with ambiguity, and above all, accepting and non-judgmental. Consequently, except for a few of the younger genera-tion who rally to support the enduring causes in the culture or other monetary social crusades, we have cloned a quiet generation.

While being judgmental is not a virtue, neither is being soft on truth. Modern attitudes toward sexuality are a case in point. Com-pared to three decades ago, we are a sexually permissive society. Accordingly, eight in 10 teenagers approve of sex before marriage when people *love* each other. When the relational qualifier is *like* each other, six in 10 flash a green light. In Quebec, nine in 10 approve of an unmarried couple living together, and eight in 10 cast their ballots in favour of having children without being married.

When you consider the past role and current official position of the Roman Catholic Church in Quebec, individualism has tri-umphed. When the implications of *love* are compared to *like*, it's easy to conclude that the youth culture is ruled by relationships rather than what was formerly extolled as a moral principle.

A 19-year-old female states life the way it is for her: "If two persons are in love, they don't need anyone's permission to have sexual relations."

The response to AIDS-education campaigns has been to acclaim the wisdom of "safe sex." Surely in a society that champions choices, we can also imagine a couple exchanging marriage vows at an altar with the underlining message: "Say *no* to sex until you choose to say *yes* to marriage."

When it comes to being religious and applying the tenets of faith to the realities of life, calling young people to counter some aspects of the existing culture should be the norm. Whether the concern is to convince young people to believe that truth exists, that materialism is not worthy of worship, that care for the environment is first of all a spiritual issue, that global disparity has moral implications, or that selfishness is destructive, instilling a temperament in today's young adults to counter some of the prevailing cultural norms is the right thing to do.

CREATE SAFE PLACES TO PURSUE THE SPIRITUAL

At best, religious institutions can expect approximately 15 per cent of the country's young adults to continue entering their doors. It doesn't take a calculator to compute that 85 per cent of the younger generation are out there, figuring out how to live without the benefit of a cohesive spiritual perspective.

It would be a tragic mistake to just lament the numbers, for that would be to misunderstand the temperament of today's youth. The survey shows that half the generation look at themselves and conclude they have spiritual needs; four in 10 admit to having some interest in religion, but do not see themselves as very religious, and six in 10 believe how we live will influence what happens to us after we die. They just don't plan on getting out of bed on Sunday morning to make their way to worship.

Describing himself as a person who attends church once a year or less, a 16-year-old Montrealer says, "I am a Christian, spiritual, participating in my mind, alone with my prayers."

Unfortunately, we are living in a time when certain revelations have shown that religious institutions aren't necessarily safe places. Allegations and convictions of physical, sexual, and emotional abuse have not only lowered the confidence in religious leaders, but made people wonder whether or not they are safe to seek solace inside the religious world. Violence and abuse is never justified, and it is especially deplorable when people are victimized inside institutions that exist to serve and heal. Still, why should incidents of betrayal by a decided minority of religious leaders and their institutions cause us to shun religious structures? We don't avoid doctors and hospitals just because a few in that profession are being hauled into court by patients who contend they have been sexually abused.

Nevertheless, rather than just decrying the situation, designing structures that protect young people from further exploitation will be important. Requiring increased levels of accountability and exercising good judgment rather than simply being naive about what could happen will be important in the coming years.

Creating safe places involves more than just guaranteeing physical protection. Young people will not be well served unless they are also in touch with adults who understand their need to ask questions and openly deal with their doubts about the faith they have received from their families. Young people need places where it is safe to search.

When children are young, they simply parrot their parents in beliefs and behaviour. To *own* faith, however, teenagers frequently must push against those who've been informing them.[4]

For young people, the journey into scepticism about the claims of religion is more often the norm than the exception. And with even more predictability, as teenagers scramble to consolidate their religious convictions, they are likely to at least temporarily reject the conclusions of their parents.

While they are wondering, "Who am I and what do I believe?" one of the first conclusions they come to is, "I am not my parents and I do not believe as my parents believe." A less traumatic interpretation of what is happening is to realize that teenagers experience a "tension between inherited and personalized faith." They are asserting their individuality and moving toward their "own chosen faith."[5]

Religious leaders, youth workers, and parents will experience less stress themselves and be in positions to support young people in better ways as they:

- realize that questioning and sometimes rejecting God can be a normal part of young people's spiritual growth
- allow children and, in particular, teenagers to question and debate religious issues
- take comfort in the knowledge that a challenged and rebuilt faith is often the strongest faith of all.[6]

James Fowler, who pioneered the study on how faith grows, contends that rebellion coincides with the blossoming of cognitive development.[7] In the case of teenagers, they are starting to see contradictions in simplistic views of God — rewarding those who behave properly and punishing those who disobey.

Teenagers are in the process of computing some of the complexities of life, but their simple views are inadequate. Healthy questioning and honest searching can lead them to the next stages in their spiritual development. Tragically, this period of time can also lead to personal drift and a lifetime of spiritual indifference.

Young people will feel safe when religious structures are places where they feel they can receive uncensored acceptance. They will be attracted to people and places where questions are welcomed, doubt is understood, and the freedom to choose is affirmed. It is only when young people are genuinely allowed to search that the real discovery can be celebrated.

EMPOWER YOUTH TODAY

In a Peanuts cartoon, Charlie Brown represents life from the youth point of view when he exclaims, "Having potential is a very heavy burden to bear." Far too often in religious circles, young people are collectively deemed to be "the future." They are labelled as "the church of tomorrow." The data leads to the conclusion that unless increasing numbers of young people also become "the present," there will be fewer and fewer participants in organized religious life in the future.

Young people who are involved today need to be empowered today.

One of the historical virtues and continued commitments that flows out of organized religious life is that assistance is given to people who have extraordinary needs. As a result, communities are served, compassionate ministries are provided, worldwide ventures are supported, and money is given away to many different causes.

We have already noted that approximately half of today's teenagers are working part-time. Consequently, many of them not only have spending money, they also have discretionary income. Just as adult participants are encouraged to give a portion of their hard-earned money to their faith communities, young people who are attenders should be encouraged to give, too. But in return for their participation, young people will benefit if they are also given the responsibility of designating a portion of those monies that their faith community will give away to outside concerns. The task of processing the decisions of how much to give to what causes will both foster a sense of responsibility in young people and sensitize their social consciences. Even in religious circles, money is power, and giving youth some decision-making that relates to money is a form of empowerment. The initiative will also tell the younger generation they have a role to play in the present.

In principle, adults will better serve both today's youth and the future of institutional religious life if they will consciously "hand on" rather than "hang on" to positions and decision-making functions under their control.

AVOID OVERPROMISING AND UNDERPROMISING

Unfortunately, formal religious environments are not always safe for young people's *spiritual* health.

Specific ministry to the young is often separated from adults and expressed in contained environments. Youth groups on a special night, retreats that happen on weekends, and camp settings that take advantage of the atmosphere of creation are frequently places where young people are gathered. These environments can increase effectiveness, but they are also potential danger zones for ministry manipulation.

A concerned father recently told me about the experience of his son. David was a healthy and energetic, spiritually sensitive senior teen who also had a short-fuse temper. His spiritual journey had been an up-and-down affair. During the summer, just before his last year in high school, David attended a week-long church-sponsored camp. The spiritual style in the camp was to call people to clearly decide whom they were going to serve. David's sensitivity prompted him to seek the assistance of one of the camp counsellors. The youth declared his desire to serve his God, but he confided that losing his temper had previously been a major problem, one that had alienated him from the God he wanted to love and serve. The counsellor simply assured David that if he would surrender his temper to his heavenly Father, God would take care of the problem. In that moment, David did everything he could to make his total response to God.

David's father reported that, after his son returned from camp, he was a model teenager for nine days. "He even read his Bible and some other devotional materials he'd been given at the camp." Then the father's eyes glazed over with tears as he explained, "On the tenth day, David's Bible and the other pamphlets were in the waste basket in his room. It turned out he lost his temper at school and that also caused him to decide to give up on God. That happened ten years ago, and David has never picked them up again."

Obviously, religious overpromising is a pitfall. Youth ministers should also be alert to the opposite problem of religious under-promising. For if the message is that pursuing the spiritual doesn't make any real difference, then why should teens bother? The proper tension is to lift up the theory of what the teachings of faith promise without overstating the claims and setting young people up for eventual disillusionment and ultimate rejection.

The Christian view of God and the faith expressions of other world religions repeatedly call for the transformation of humanity. What all religions should avoid is models of faith that create expectations, which, in the final analyses, are really calls for dehumanization.

Effective ministry is more like a dance than a march. There are very few straight-ahead easy answers, no magic-wand solutions. Especially for teens who have such a long distance to travel in life, pat formulas are woefully inadequate to answer the complexities of life and the inner quest of the human spirit.

PURSUE INTEGRITY WITH A PASSION

The 80s were scarred with scandals. They crossed all sectors of society, spanned a range of ideologies, and circled the globe.

In the early part of the decade Tomas Peters and Robert Waterman penned an influential book entitled *In Search of Excellence.* "Excellence" became the buzz word of the era. But before long, junk bonds in the business world were linked with fraudulence, Ben Johnson and Pete Rose disgraced the sports world, Jim and Tammy Bakker embarrassed the religiously committed, politicians in Canada, the United States, Germany, and Japan proved to be deceitful. Excellence proved to be good in theory, but reality told another story. By the end of the decade, Peters co-authored *Thriving on Chaos.* The contrast is indicative of the hopes and disillusionment people experienced in the intervening years.

During the last decade, religious leaders in Canada have been subjected to parallel predicaments. From Newfoundland to the north, from central Canada to the West Coast, those who have superb theories about faith have proved to be impostors.

The heart cry of the 90s is *integrity.* People are aching to put their trust in people. They are looking for connections between theory and practice, for coherence between words and deeds.

Religious leaders and those who belong to faith communities desperately need to exude integrity. Both the culture and balanced theology will allow religious leaders to be human and extend a reasonable margin of error, but in the current milieu, there is little tolerance to calculated hypocrisy.

Meanwhile, for the sake of the country and for the sake of the younger generation, it is time for the religious to be truly religious.

TODAY IS NOT LIKE YESTERDAY

Canada has a rich religious history. Political analyst Ron Graham recently invested a year of his life to examine the place of religion in Canada. In the introduction to his book *God's Dominion*, Graham, a self-confessed sceptic, assesses the prominent role religion has played in the country's history:

> *No student of Canadian politics and history can ignore the extraordinary impact God has had on those who have come here. Spirituality governed the aboriginal tribes of America before the Europeans. Bishops dominated French Canada from Laval to Leger. Religion ruled the issues and parties of English Canada. Denominations shaped our education system, our social services, many of our laws, even the ethics of our business elites . . . No less an authority than the Bible gave Canada its designation and motto, from the seventy-second psalm: that God "shall have dominion also from sea to sea, and from the river unto the ends of the earth."*[8]

There is a line of continuity from the nation's historic roots that extends to the first line of the 1982 Canadian Charter of Rights and Freedoms: "Whereas Canada is founded upon principles that recognize the supremacy of God . . ."

A treasured religious history is one matter: sustaining organized religious strength is another. As young people make the transition from home to school or work, many of them also depart from the ways of their parents and discontinue their involvement in organized religion. Those who translate their religious affiliations into regular and active participation in structured religious life are in the minority. As a result, only 15 per cent of those in their senior teens or twenties are regular attenders inside religious structures.

Expressing the disenchantment of her generation, a 15-year-old female says, "I see myself as religiously aware, but I don't like the way my church handles religion. Not much is offered for youths in church. Therefore, many don't follow it."

While it's true that identity with historic religious organizations remains high, those who just affiliate have a "snack bar" approach to religion. Consequently, members of the clergy are repeatedly requested to serve as short-order cooks, performing baptisms, weddings, and funerals.

Although those who do attend regularly are sources of encouragement to clergy and laity in Christian churches and other religious communities, there is also a disconcerting tendency among the young to be "circulators" rather than "participators." They are all too ready to worship in a particular place without digging in for the long term. Based on fluctuating interests and desires, the young who are committed are often ready to shop and shift.

Still, active involvement in communities of faith can be critically important for young people. Figuring out what you believe and consciously consolidating your spiritual formation is an inherent part of growing up. Establishing a frame of reference for moral decision-making and developing a philosophy of life is essential for living with coherence in our complicated world. Teenagers who do participate in religious youth groups build relationships with peers who are compatible with their own ways. They also have access to adults who both care for them and can provide spiritual counsel. Yes, there've been instances of abuse and exploitation within religious structures, but that is no reason to censor all religious organizations. Exceptions need to stand as exceptions instead of being turned into norms.

Cultural dominance sets a society up to experience the dynamics of social stigma. If you are not a member of the majority, you are usually still subject to the cultural control of the majority. In the past, this cultural dominance was decidedly in the hands of those who viewed life through a Judaeo-Christian lens. The church used to be centre stage and highly influential, but no more. And because good relationships with peers is so important to young people, the minority who do participate in formal religious life often feel inferior and culturally intimidated.

Many teens who are regular members of religious youth groups cope with the social pressures by compartmentalizing their private spiritual lives from their mainstream public living. They attend on the weekends, but during the week, they keep their participation a secret from their non-attending classmates. Only a small percentage of the attenders take a more aggressive stance and regularly reveal their spiritual commitments.

In the coming years, it will be important for those who don't and those who do to learn to respect each other. Whether we are exchanging life as adults or adolescents, extending a wholesome regard toward each other without the necessity of agreeing with each other will enhance life for everyone.

In the 1950s, Saturday night was special. Week after week, the vaunted Toronto Maple Leafs would have their showdown with the mighty Montreal Canadiens. Foster Hewitt's gravelly voice would call Canadians from coast to coast to join him for "Hockey Night in Canada." The event was far more sacred than going to church the next morning. Maurice "Rocket" Richard and Tim Horton were not just hockey players. They were heroes, to be admired and emulated on the local rinks.

During the 50s and into the 60s, involvement in formal religious life in Canada was like playing for the Leafs. In the hockey world, the team was not only winning Stanley Cups, the dynasty was respected. On the religious scene, there was more stigma attached to *not* going to church that there was to be a regular attender. God was not only acknowledged as a historical reference point, he was assumed to be relevant to what was going on in the world.

As methodically as if they planned to fall and fail, the once mighty Maple Leafs stumbled from respect to ridicule. Religion, too, was bodychecked to the sidelines of society. Being serious about religion lost favour with the majority, and religious institutions surrendered their prominence in the culture.

The Maple Leafs are allowed to still play in the league, but before the season starts everyone knows they'll be fortunate to make the playoffs. The same is true for religion. Our multivoiced pluralistic society has granted the right for churches, temples, mosques, and synagogues to play in the game of life, but in the back of everyone's mind is an awareness they won't be real competitors.

Faithful Maple Leaf fans keep believing and hoping their team will make a comeback and regain their former glory. A change in ownership, different management, the acquisition of new players, yet another coach, and adjustments in style and strategy all raise such hopes.

Those who live with deep faith commitments have good reasons to plan and pray, to believe and work in new ways, to pursue innovative strategies, and also to hope.

8

THE ROLE OF THE MEDIA

*L*ed *by television, the media are having an unprecedented influence on young people. Far from simply providing entertainment, the media are turning today's teens into the best-informed young generation in history. But beyond just entertaining and informing, the media help shape reality for Canadians young and old.*

The media are today's primary mind-makers. Caught up with a preoccupation to present the new and dramatic, and used as a stage for interest groups to parade their causes, the media have created a problem-prone world for teenagers. Today's youth feel weighted down with the burdens of modern life.

Providing information and creating perceptions are central functions of the media in any society. In Canada, however, information and perception have an important twist: they tend to come via our neighbour to the south. As a result, our concerns and our fears, our looks and our laughter, our heroes and our hopes are mostly American-made.

Young people tend to trust what they receive. Confidence in the media exceed confidence in government, religion, and the courts. Only confidence in the police and the schools are able to match the trust placed in the media.

Even though confidence levels in the media are high and intake amounts are inordinate, young people are reticent about admitting they are being greatly influenced. Only eight per cent maintain that their lives are influenced "a great deal" by the media, while 28 per cent give the media a "quite a bit" influence rating. Another 41 per cent think the media only have "some" influence on their lives. The remaining 22 per cent go as far as to say the media have "little or no" influence on them.

People in the media, particularly the electronic media, are powerful people in the culture. The media's access to the minds and emotions of today's youth, placed alongside the technologically sophisticated forms of communication at their disposal, means people in the media are in a position to make a unique contribution to Canadian life.

THE UNEQUALLED PERSONAL POWER OF TV

Anyone who questions the pervasive place television has been given in the daily routine of all Canadians has simply to take an evening walk through any neighbourhood in the country. The blue hue from the set flickers through the panes of living-room windows. Television is the modern hearth.

Consequently, today's youth grow up with TV channel changers in their hands. If food consumption equalled the intake of television, almost every member of the teenage population would be obese.

INORDINATE INTAKE

In the media world, the release of a new movie is like publishing a book in an expensive hard-cover format. The question for the consumer is, when will it be available in paperback, or when will it be released on video?

With the cost around eight dollars, going out to a movie translates into an expensive date for teens. Why not wait for the video? Better still, watch TV — it's free. But the low cost and easy accessibility are not the only reasons we've become a television society.

In the past 40 years our lives have been rearranged to accommodate our viewing habits. Today, there is a television set, sometimes two or three, in 98 per cent of Canadian homes. Viewing patterns reveal that the TV schedule plays a major role in the arrangement of most people's schedules. Television is the prime controller of leisure time.

The existence of satellite dishes has pushed the pervasiveness of television into the remote areas of Canada. A recent study concludes that "the Inuit, once among the fittest Canadians, are turning into a generation of couch potatoes." A study commissioned by the Department of Health and Welfare indicates that the Inuit have become "junk-food junkies, increasingly leaving behind an itinerant life-style on the tundra for a comfortable chair in front of the television screen." In that time the average Inuk in Igloolik, a community of about 1000 people, has become "fatter, weaker and less fit . . . Television has become a staple of life. In 1970, there were only a few TV sets. In 1990, 134 of 139 households in Igloolik had at least one TV."[1]

The implications of the pervasiveness of television are far wider ranging that just physical conditioning. The media's levelling effect on Canadian youth is illustrated by its influence. When asked to name his "favourites," a 17-year-old male cited the following:

ATHLETE:	Michael Jordan
SPORTS TEAM:	Chicago Bulls
MUSIC:	Hardcore rap
SINGING GROUP:	Led Zeppelin, Ice T, Public Enemy

And where is this young man from? Inuvik, NWT.

Some readers may resent these claims and contend they are overstated. Like it or not, the cultural and personal consequences for the majority of Canadians who spend in excess of 20 hours each week in front of their TV sets is enormous. And teenagers come close to reflecting the adult viewing patterns:

Daily Television Viewing

In %'s

1-2 hours	—	42
3-4 hours	—	37
More than 5	—	21

In monitoring TV-watching trends, Statistics Canada concluded that, in 1990, Canadians were glued to the tube for an average of 23 hours a week. That amount was one hour less than in 1986. Including the amount of time spent watching videotapes, teenagers consumed approximately 18 hours a week of TV.[2]

Television intake is well documented. What is less clear is why the levels are so high. Even though television is part of the daily diet for all but three per cent of Canada's young people, only 61 per cent claim to receive "a great deal" or "quite a lot" of enjoyment in exchange for their viewing time, a decline from 68 per cent in 1984. For almost half of today's youth audience, it appears that watching television simply puts in time.

Essentially, we use television to entertain ourselves. Whether our desire is for sports or drama, game shows or just a little laughter, our high levels of TV consumption mesh perfectly with our cultural devotion to leisure. Our insatiable appetite for entertainment and the instant availability of diverse television programming create a natural cultural fit. Television becomes our cheapest and best form of escape. With the flick of a switch and the changing of a channel we can travel to another continent or vicariously enter the drama of our favourite soap. In the words of one cultural observer, "In effect the family rec room can become a diverse dramatic world of heroes and hookers, singers and monsters."[3]

DENIAL OF INFLUENCE

We know about the intake and something about its reasons. But what about the impact? On this topic, the majority of young people are like adults: they are reluctant to acknowledge that watching TV for 20 hours a week has significant influence on their lives.

The survey shows no more than one in 10 teenagers are ready to admit that their TV intake influences them "a great deal." An additional three in 10 accept the reality that their media intake influences them "quite a bit." In the case of the remaining 60 per cent of teenagers, four in 10 acknowledge "some" influence and two in 10 contend that the media have "little or no" impact on them. Yet, when asked about the impact of television on others, 55 per cent of teens believe watching violent TV shows tends to make people more aggressive.

The most obvious contradiction between what teenagers are ready to admit about the influence of television on their perceptions and what is really happening shows up when those same teens state their views on Canada's social problems. In the 1992 survey, when young people were asked to identify the country's social problems, in order of importance they listed, "AIDS, the environment, child abuse, and drugs." What issues have repeatedly been in the headlines during the past year?

Why, when compared to the youth perceptions in 1984, do young people of the 90s perceive "racial discrimination, violence against women, and unequal treatment of women" as far more serious problems? The answer is simple: they are exposed and influenced by what the media present as serious problems.

Furthermore, why is American Michael Jordan of the Chicago Bulls the favourite athlete of Canadian teenagers? Have they seen Michael take jump shots in basketball stadiums in Toronto or Vancouver? Hardly. The answer, of course, is the influence of television. Canadian youth are more affected by what they watch than they are ready to admit.

Whether young or old, we are all influenced by a variety of sources. However, because the majority of young people deny being significantly influenced by television when they are actually influenced in major ways, they are left living with vulnerabilities. No matter what our age, such denial means we are subject to inputs that are outside our consciousness. Consequently, our ability to consciously control or deliberately respond to what is influencing us is minimized. It is a dangerous way to live.

Alerting young people to problems and sensitizing their consciences to issues of societal concern is an important function of the media. We would not want to propose that either reflecting or creating culture is necessarily a bad thing. In fact, reinforcing norms can be beneficial. Television can reflect and reinforce many of the best qualities of our culture. For example, watching programs that support an anti-drug message are helping to form a drug-free society. The effects are obviously beneficial for everyone.[4]

But there are other norms incessantly paraded across the small screen that deserve a second look. How many bald male newscasters have you watched lately? Do people in wheelchairs play the main characters on shows about romance and power? Why do men age gracefully in TV-land, and women, if they age at all, do so in a state of horror and crisis? Unfortunately, "in a visual, post-literate culture, television does make the body shape relevant to the successful conveyance of ideas.[5]

Producers and directors are very aware that viewers sit in front of their sets with "zappers" in hand. Yet, they know that even hypnotized people cannot be forced to do anything against their will. Always alarmed about what might trigger a zap to another channel, television specializes in distorting reality. "Glamorously dramatizing social problems, selling sensational stories like hawkers at a circus sideshow," script writers and producers create their version of reality.[6]

Monitoring viewer patterns, television programmers are not overly intimidated by the zapper. The shows become shorter and more enticing. Perhaps a bit more sex to capture the zapper holder and keep the pace up so the viewer won't be tempted to tune in to the competition. One study warns of the consequences. "Teens swim in an electronic sea, mesmerized by the ever-changing spectacle of strange and colourful shapes and sounds. Enrapt, they readily forget the danger of drowning . . ."[7]

THE PERSONAL CONNECTION

Researchers studying the pervasive influence of television technology have tried to understand why we feel so connected with the box in the corner of the room. One investigation suggests that television is best understood as a relational force. Television connects us with other people. The drama of the characters living out their lives on the set of "Beverly Hills, 90210," the mix of compassion and comedy in the scripts of a "Mash" episode, the sheer escapism of watching other people's crimes and catastrophe connects us in a very real way with the people and the plots.[8]

Television uses the same techniques that make interpersonal communication so persuasive. The TV society is a relational society. We feel emotion for the characters in our favourite shows. On newscasts, it's not the content we trust as much as who is delivering it. We feel the rush of victory when the athlete we most admire crosses the finish line first. The power of relationship, then, is one of the key reasons TV is the almighty tool of information and entertainment.

When evangelists Swaggart and Bakker lost their credibility with their viewers and supporters, what mattered was that they lost their relationship of trust. In their instances, the messengers were an indispensable part of the message, and when the senders tumbled the receivers abdicated. Accordingly, the power of television is not so much the content that is being communicated but the way the individual sitting on the couch connects with the individual facing the cameras.

The morning we awakened to the news that Barbara Frum had died, we felt as if we'd lost a friend. Although we never knew her personally, she'd earned our respect. Throughout the day and into the evening news, the plaudits rolled in, extolling Barbara's unique talents. Her colleagues applauded her virtues, profiled her strengths, and shared a few anecdotes. The major networks headlined her life on the late-evening news and, Barbara's program, "The Journal," featured her accomplishments with affection. In the morning, newspapers across the country portrayed our Barbara as an outstanding Canadian, a caring person, and a distinguished professional.

Still, within a few days the newspapers that profiled Barbara's achievements were stacked in a corner or taken to the garage. By the weekend they were discarded. Inevitably memories of Barbara will fade. They will be replaced with other faces, more interviews, and tomorrow's news. Life will roll on, and the media won't miss a beat.

Our attention will move on, too. As in the past, we will tune in to what comes next. Radio, television, the daily newspapers, magazines, and feature movies, these are the media that elevate some things to importance and relegate other matters of life to insignificance.

In the modern world, television is the most powerful medium. One of the many tributes to the late Barbara Frum summed it up best: "It's worth remembering that the strongest link between people is not created by satellite or high technology, but by the day-to-day contact with the people around us. Barbara Frum, who worked in one of the most sophisticated high-tech mediums, understood that."[9]

Combine the powerful draw of relationships, which is especially inviting to young people, with the wizardry of special effects, the drama of carefully selected music, and the display of emotions and life-styles, and television can reach a form of high art. But the same combination of ingredients are alarmingly manipulative.

Using a dazzling range of rhythms and sounds, the music industry, even in its formative stages, had already captivated young people. Tapes and Walkmans came along and put new movement into walking. But the music industry went further. They imprisoned their audience with alluring high-powered videos. For more than 10 years MTV has virtually handcuffed young people to their television sets. The strategy was simple but consequential. By making it possible for teenagers to get their musical fixes without going to a concert, they used the power of music to become even more powerful. Modern technology and high-cost productions allow teenagers to reach out and touch. Relationships are created that are almost live. And with religious fervour, many young people bow down and worship at the feet of their stars.

And it all happens in the comfort of our homes. But even though music videos are so compelling and provide such enjoyment, teenage viewers are not helplessly hypnotized by the TV. The image of a couch potato sitting mesmerized by one channel, or maybe two, went out the window a decade ago. Now with satellite transmission, cable networks, movie, weather, and specialized sport channels, the average viewer is much more interactive. Nobody is the prisoner of bad programming anymore. Today's viewers can interrupt their viewing and break it into smaller units.[10] The modern way makes what was powerful in the past more powerful in the present. How else can anyone explain 20 hours a week?

In a recent newspaper column, Rick Salutin scripted a little sanity for members of the media:

I just think the media are full enough of themselves right now. They have inordinate power. They play a role today akin to that of the church in the Middle Ages: interpreting reality and justifying the status quo, while occasionally issuing limited challenges to it. Chances are they're even more influential than the church ever was. It's bad enough without congratulating themselves and declaring their own centrality and power in the world they are supposed to be merely describing. I don't even care if they're right. A little humility would be good for them.[11]

UNPARALLELED CULTURAL IMPACT

Not everyone is convinced television deserves the status it appears to have. Some people have a love-hate relationship with their sets. They can be heard to cynically remark, "In the old days we used to go to three channels to conclude nothing worth watching is on. Today we have to go through 30 or 40 channels to discover that nothing worth watching is on."

Still, we continue to watch. And the impact is profound. Both consciously and unconsciously, at both the personal and societal levels, media makes an unparalleled cultural impact.

CREATING VISUAL LEARNERS

Before television, books were a popular form of entertainment. Sometimes the reading allowed vicarious adventures, or engaged our minds with puzzles, or taught history in the context of fiction, but whatever the text, books used to be more important than they are today. TV has replaced them, and there has been a cost. Today, only 18 per cent of teenagers say they enjoy reading "a great deal."

Television's ability to project images into our minds and dump facts onto our laps has diminished our patience with reading. In a fast-paced manner, television asks us to swallow images whole. Its mode of presentation requires viewers to absorb what is presented with very little time for digestion. As one author notes, with the advent of television, "People who saw reality every evening in their living room suddenly lost patience with the slower rhythms and glancing allusions of the novelist."[12]

And so, television has created visual learners. Consequently, young people, who are products of the television society, think differently than those who lived before the advent of television. In the past, society leaned more toward the literary. When people read more and watched less they naturally developed their abilities for reflective and analytical thought. The great novelists of the nineteenth and twentieth centuries wove complex plots, created multidimensional characters, and swept their reading audiences in and out of emotional storms. Novelists created worlds and populated them with characters by stringing words into paragraphs, paragraphs into chapters, and chapters into books. The reader had to absorb the words, process the meaning, calculate the nuances, and translate the message or emotion.

With the introduction of photography in the 1800s, the arrival of movies early in the next century, and the accessibility of television today, people have learned to receive messages differently. Instead of having to read and interpret meaning, they see an image and know what it represents without having to process words to get the message. The amateur videotaping of Los Angeles policemen beating Rodney King is an example of the power of the visual. What people saw on TV with their eyes was more convincing than the ruling the court brought down. The members of the jury tried to use words to explain what really happened, but the camera had the final word with the public.

Rather than having dictionaries, with ideas and definitions in their minds, today's youth have video screens in their heads to interpret the world around them. Daily doses of television reinforce the already entrenched pattern of visual perception and understanding. Is it superior or inferior to other ways of thinking? The answer to that question remains a matter of debate, but the modern way of perceiving has changed how young people learn and how we can effectively communicate with them.

There are many critics in the culture who pontificate about the decline of literacy. Business people, journalists, and educators all lament the declining levels of comprehension and competence. According to writer David Rutherford in the *Toronto Star*, what is often overlooked is that in today's world, where television is so pervasive, "visual literacy is at least as important as learning how to read . . ." The modern way may not be better or worse, but it is different, and it brings its unique strengths and weaknesses into the mainstream of modern life. Learning and responding to visual input is but another change that demands a pro-active response. Rutherford concludes that we struggle to make yet another shift to something else that is new. "While ignorance of the written language severely limits our ability to cope with the world, an inability to recognize ideas when expressed visually means that their subtle insinuations will go unchallenged by critical thought."[13]

Teachers in our schools are recognizing dramatic differences in the thinking processes of many of their students. Some seem to have less of an ability to think through ideas logically. They respond more to stories and illustrations about history than they do to a cataloguing of the facts of history. As writer Jerry Foresburg explains, "They come into the classroom expecting to be entertained. Teachers want to engage in dialogue and discussion. Students want to see a performance.[14] Today's youth are indeed affected by their world.

IMPINGING ON RELATIONSHIPS

Part of the power of television is that it is relational. In communication dynamics, TV connects senders with receivers. In newscasts, the transmission is from high-profile personalities to ordinary Canadians. In dramatic presentations, it is from actors to appreciative audiences. When sporting events fill the screen, the communication flow is from skilled players to admiring spectators. Television certainly links people together, but the connectedness is really impersonal and artificial. In the end, instead of enhancing person-to-person life, television can impinge on real relationships.

Have there been times when you've gone to visit a friend who leaves the television on? Little wonder you can't escape the feeling you're not getting undivided attention. Your friend's apparent desire to tune in to two frequencies at the same time depreciates the value of the friendship. You return home wishing you had stayed home.

Too frequently, teenagers are sitting in the same room with their friends and talking without looking at each other. The reason is simple. The TV is on and their eyes are riveted to the screen instead of each other. The avoidance of eye contact may tend to make them feel more comfortable with each other, but it has a negative effect on the development of their social skills. When so much time is invested in watching life parade on by, what is the impact of TV on the art of conversation?

And what has been the effect of television on the quality of life in the family? For most members of the average Canadian family, television is an absorbing and continuous activity. The hours spent watching television on a weekly basis are hours spent not relating directly with each other. A study prepared for the Quebec government says the impact of television-viewing on the family has been underestimated.

The author of the study, Gaston Gauthier, concludes that since the arrival of television, not only have community groups lost members, but "family interaction and individuals' sense of community have been radically changed." Gauthier urged that an agency be created that would allow parents and others to express their concerns about excessive violence on TV directly to the government.[15]

Consider what would happen to family relationships if the television were removed from the house for a month. Isn't it a fair conclusion that family members would have some spare time to spend together?

Whenever eating off TV trays in the rec room replaces sitting around the kitchen or dining-room table, the family loses. Whether the program is the early-evening news or a rerun of "Leave It to Beaver," preoccupation with the TV pre-empts the possibility of family interaction. A family with more than one television set in their home faces another inevitability. Members of the family will tend to separate into different rooms and further preclude communication with each other.

In the realm of relationships, whenever the impersonal impinges on the personal and the artificial pre-empts the real, life takes a step backward. Because relationships are so important to today's youth, tuned-in parents will take every opportunity to be fully present when those instances of spontaneous communication with their teens starts flowing.

PARADING UNRESOLVED PROBLEMS

Last fall, when the autumn leaves were in full colour, I was flying west from Montreal. On the seat next to me was a pleasant young woman in her late teens named Linda. As we cruised over the St. Lawrence River and the Thousand Islands, the bright sunlight glistened on the water below. Looking out the airplane window, I said to Linda, "What a remarkable sight! How's that for beauty?"

Her response caught me off guard. "I wonder how polluted the water is," she said.

What startled me was the finality of her comment. She didn't say, "I wonder if the water is polluted?" Rather, she simply responded out of her perception as a young person that the environment has been damaged. During the next half hour, we discussed the different ways we viewed the world. I realized again that while it's true young people are reflecting many of the status-quo attitudes and values around them, they have perceptions of their present circumstances that are different from the older generation.

Linda's perception of the environment is indicative of how today's youth are seeing their total reality. Although they still have high aspirations, young people of the 90s also have a nagging sense they are surrounded by problems. In their perception of things, they have inherited a world that is marred and scarred.

When you think about it, today's teens have not seen many solutions in their lifetime. The one major exception is the dissipation of the Cold War between the U.S. and what was formerly the USSR, along with an equivalent dissolving of the former fear of a nuclear holocaust. Certainly, young people have seen technological advances, but the difficulties first registered in their early memories still remain unresolved. Whether the problem is famine and hunger, overpopulation, the national debt, drug-trafficking, violent crime, political instability, unending wars, or the dread of cancer, what was still is. And to further complicate matters, more recent concerns such as the depletion of the ozone layer, global warming, the discovery of buried toxic wastes, racial discrimination, and AIDS only compounds their impression that solving problems is not just improbable, but close to impossible. No wonder modern young people are feeling powerless.

It isn't what they perceive to be our social problems that's cause for concern. Rather, it is the increasing weight of these problems on them that's worrisome. A comparison between 1984 and 1992 reveals that the long-standing problems are considered to be much more critical for increasing numbers of today's youth.

For young people, problems in their world are a growth industry. And where do they get most of their impressions about their problem-riddled universe? As if they were hooked up to an intravenous drip in a hospital, young people are fed an unending parade of unresolved problems by various media. In fact, it could be argued that instead of alleviating social problems, the media's preoccupation with bad news contributes to both the creation and the escalation of problems.

The time has come for the media to more consistently make news out of good news, to put as much effort and imagination into telling

SOCIAL CONCERNS		
% Indicating "Very Serious"		
	1984	1992
AIDS	—	77
The Environment	37	69
Child Abuse	50	64
Drugs	46	64
Teenage Suicide	41	59
The Economy	37	57
Racial Discrimination	22	58

good news as they do into communicating bad news. Whether media reflect the culture or create the culture is not the issue. The media have the capacity to beam light into the prevailing darkness, and the moment has arrived for creativity to be given to that assignment. The task will be difficult. But for the sake of young people who are burdened with the problems of the world, and also for the perspective of older people, it will be worth the media's best efforts to turn what is good and beautiful into news that is intriguing and valuable.

GIVING OUT PERMISSION SLIPS

Unless there are a series of stimuli to trigger sudden shifts, attitudes and life-styles in democratic societies generally change slowly, an evolution, rather than the trauma of a cultural revolution. Societies like ours evolve by both the passing out and the taking away of cultural permission slips.

In recent years, we have taken away cultural permission to do certain things. For example, both social pressure and progressive law-makers combined to issue the decree, "Thou shalt not smoke in public." The Blue Box is propelling our social conscience beyond "Don't litter" to "Reduce, re-use and recycle."

At the same time as we take some things away, we are also handing out permission slips. Only a few years ago, it was not permissible for a company to attack another company when telling Canadian consumers about the virtues of their own product. Yet today, we have granted social approval to company after company blatantly putting down its competition.

How did it happen? Culturally, we allowed the ethics of advertising to shift. Instead of adhering to the code of "Advertise on merit," we amended the code to also include "Advertise by de-merit." And the media did nothing to stop the trend. Instead, they looked at their advertiser's bankrolls and sang, "You pay and we'll play your tune." Consequently, auto makers, computer manufacturers, credit-card competitors, pill-pushers, and soft-drink peddlers all follow the new advertising mode of attacking their opposition before they affirm their self-interests. The whole approach is seen by many as morally bankrupt.

But what are the implications for young people? Think about perceiving life from their point of view. The only advertiser's code of ethics today's teenagers have heard and seen in their lifetime is, "Denigrate in order to propagate. Put down in order to climb up." If the mentality of the code could be restricted to advertising, the damage might be contained. But what young people watch over and over in television advertising also sets the standard for their personal code of conduct. If highly regarded and successful companies can put down their competitors, why wouldn't young people also conclude that the way for them to get to the top is to put down whoever gets in their way?

And then there are the politicians. They, too, run down their opponents, often viciously, during elections and in between. Their behaviour is certainly not kept out of sight of television cameras, nor out of sight of teenage eyes.

The moral and ethical foundations of historical Canada were constructed out of Judaeo-Christian concrete. In our past, the forces of religion influenced our thinking and framed our cultural consensus. Well into the 60s, whether or not the subject was sexuality, no matter what constituted a family, or what was considered to be the proper place of prayer in public schools, or what was ethical and what was unethical, Judaeo-Christian assumptions ruled the day. Since that time, other forces and new rules have displaced that former consensus. And the media are among the prime players. If the pulpit was the place of proclamation about what was right and what was wrong in the past, the television screen is the norm-creator and permission-giver in the modern world. As both creators and reflectors of the culture, members of the media also need to consciously grapple with what ingredients they will choose to put into Canada's social structure in the 1990s. Specifically, they will have to decide at what point they will post moral stop signs and around what issues they will proceed full speed ahead. We hope, for the sake of Canada's youth and the rest of us, the leaders and decision-makers in the media will at least slow down long enough to ask the questions.

A comment from a 17-year-old woman from southwestern Ontario illustrates the point:

> *In this generation teens are trying to be less racist and destructive, but it's so hard to be good when TV shows, movies, and the mass media are practically promoting it.*

UNIQUE CULTURAL CONTRIBUTORS

The major characters in stage plays carry a heavy responsibility. The whole theatrical event succeeds or fails on their performance. We contend that the media and television in particular are major players in the modern Canada. Whether TV is the medium for politicians to convey their policies or make their promises in attempts to get re-elected, the vehicle for the sports world to profile their talents and enhance their financial fortunes, a way for the music industry to market and entertain, or the access route for business to promote their products, television plays a lead role. And should they choose, television decision-makers can be unique cultural contributors.

SCREENING THE CANADIAN-AMERICAN MIX

The primacy of television has many implications. The fact that approximately two-thirds of our TV intake is American-made further complicates matters. Our citing the reality of American domination in the television medium does not mean we have an anti-American posture. Western ways, and in particular, the American way has made its presence felt around the world. Certainly, a case can be made that living next to a friendly neighbour who just happens to be a superpower has many advantages for Canada. But it also has problems.

Many people share the opinion that television is central to the question of Canada's cultural autonomy. Journalist John Haslett reasons that:

> *Our cultural sovereignty and sense of identity is perhaps best expressed through the medium of television since it is the medium used by most people for information, news, and entertainment.*[16]

In 1985 noted broadcasting historian Frank Peers introduced other dimensions to the discussion:

Whether broadcasting will help preserve Canada's cultural sovereignty is still unresolved; the question will grow in complexity as technology advances . . . Canada has built the biggest physical system in the world, but in large part has turned it over to the U.S. entertainment industry.[17]

Maybe young people do not consciously link their support for the CBC to the cultural sovereignty of the country, but it might surprise Canadians to know that young people display a surprising loyalty to the CBC. Seven in 10 contend that "the CBC is important to Canada." In fact, our national broadcasting corporation is cherished with a devotion normally reserved for our system of universal medicare.

Obviously, one of the most unique programming slots for the Canadian media has been our national news programs, which have consistently monitored a wide range of global concerns. As a result, we have resisted the intellectual isolationism that characterizes much of the U.S. news agenda. Writing a piece entitled "U.S. Myths Swallowed Whole," journalist Doris Anderson claimed:

They [Americans] believe they are the most open society in the world. In fact, they are one of the most insulated. It's quite possible to be in Hartford, Connecticut, or Phoenix, Arizona, and be as uninformed about what's going on in Europe or the Far East as if twentieth-century communications had never been invented.[18]

Although American news monitors filter what they import from outside the U.S. borders, their prominence in the world means they export their messages to the rest of the world. In Canada's case, the tendency is simply to plug into the American news-feed network and adopt their news as ours. As Keith Spicer, head of the CRTC, noted, "Too much of what passes for Canadian content is the easy, almost automatic quota-filling of news, weather, sports, and game shows.[19] The resulting problem is that a lot of news flows across the border that doesn't apply to the Canadian situation, yet we adopt it as our own.

Prime Minister Brian Mulroney's actions of a couple of years ago is an excellent example. He responded to the concerns of Canadians and shifted some money around in order to declare a war on drugs. Who would argue that the use of illicit drugs ought to be controlled and every measure possible implemented to discourage the devastation drugs generate?

But there are two other factors to consider before applauding the crusade too loudly. First, illicit drug use has been in decline for about the past decade. Only five or six per cent of Canada's teens are repeated users of illegal drugs, and that includes marijuana. What was the source of the concern, if it wasn't "made in America"? Second, a closer look at the prime minister's actions leads to the conclusion he is simply following in the footsteps of the president of the United States, who had decreed his war on drugs. Responsible media will not only offer a critique of political priorities in their assessments, they will also consciously filter what is American from what is Canadian.

We have already noted in this chapter that young people are feeling the weight of our own country's problems without adding more from south of the border. The drug problem, which is a more severe social concern in the U.S., is partly linked to the number of large American cities. In Canada, we do not have the same big-city or inner-city problems. Nor do we have anywhere near the number of guns in the hands of the general populace. The fear that is fostered because big-city crime is a major problem for Americans is only a minor concern for Canadians. Without a doubt, Montreal, Toronto, and Vancouver are places where social dissent can surge and riots can trigger mindless violence. But the devastation recently experienced in Los Angeles is simply unlikely in Canada. So why is there so much fear being cultivated in the residents of *our* cities? Adopting American problems as our own is not only self-denigrating, it is unnecessary.

It is one thing to entertain ourselves with American programming, but surely we have the capacity to inform ourselves with our own reality.

COUNTERING OUR VALUE VULNERABILITY

The images and multimessaging that are projected on the screen are received by young people as choices and alternatives around which to orbit their lives. Think about the range of role models that go on parade. Picture Madonna and all she stands for. Now picture Mother Theresa and reflect on her as a role model. Offering a range of life-style alternatives for today's youth to consider as their own is playing fair. But in our pluralistic society, the media will best serve young people's interests if they also program with balance in mind.

During the early weeks of fall 1991's new television schedule, several prime-time programs dramatized the issue of teenagers losing their virginity. In one script, an 18-year-old male was ridiculed for being a virgin, and it was made plain his sexual innocence should and would end. The story-lines, all referenced toward teenagers, included securing birth-control pills, unsafe sex, and exposure to AIDS. The convergence of the themes triggered public dissent and debate — particularly in the U.S.

The onslaught prompted Michael Weithorn, executive producer of one of the programs involved, to remark, "It is happening all over the dial. I guess this is TV virginity week."

Drawn into the debate because he'd produced another program where teenagers were scripted to sexually consummate their romance, producer Steven Bochco sidestepped the main issue by demoting sexual concerns and responded, "With all due respect, I maintain that virginity, or its loss, is not the only — or even most important — aspect of role modelling. What about ethics? What about honesty? What about taking responsibility for one's behaviour?" Most parents will undoubtedly support family advocate Terry Rakolta, who also got involved in the controversy: "I don't know any mothers who would advise their daughters to do what they want when it comes to sex."[20]

Whatever your perspective on when it's right for young people to be sexually active, and even though Bochco essentially eliminated sexuality matters out of his ethics grid, his point about ethics and honesty deserves to be pursued. This is especially so because of our concern cited earlier about the decline of such values as honesty, forgiveness, and generosity.

Values are not just phenomena that are important to us, they are the internal engines that drive the human spirit. When we express our internal values, they help explain our external behaviour. When we examine the current value orientation of Canada's youth, there is cause for concern.

Values that incite the spirit of individualism dominate what is important to young people. Freedom, having choices, being successful, and living a comfortable life all rally around the current popular chant, "I have rights." To be fair, friendship and being loved also stand alongside what is considered most important. But values that serve the interests of the collective good score low.

Specifically, honesty, forgiveness, working hard, and politeness are considered less important today than in the past. Projecting into the future, we must ask, what does a society become when these virtues are drained from private and public life?

Championing the rights associated with personal freedom and the prerogative to have choices is obviously desirable in a democratic society. However, if those forces are not counterbalanced with an equal commitment to the collective good, the quality of life for everyone is jeopardized. The data are consistent with the prevailing mood. A mere six per cent of 15- to 24-year-olds say they are interested in being involved in politics, and only 13 per cent say "working to correct social and economic inequalities" is a priority. By comparison, 32 per cent designate having "plenty of time for recreation and hobbies" as being important. Cartoonist Ben Wicks captures the situation as he portrays an overbearing executive type scowling across his massive desk at a more timid individual and asking, "Are you, or have you ever been, a concerned citizen?"

Where do the media fit in to this discussion about values? The answer is obvious. The media are one of the primary shapers and conveyors of our current set of values. Because of this, surely they have a responsibility to be more than simply purveyors of information. If relinquishing individual rights is part of what it will take for Canada to have an enhanced future, then the media will resist being manipulated by vested interest groups who incessantly demand life on their terms. If cultivating social consciences and concern for the collective good is a societal need, then that agenda will get positive press. If such desired values as working hard and honesty are diminishing, even though they are considered to be old-fashioned, a responsible media will make some value judgments and intentionally seek to counter our value vulnerability.

SPREADING GLOBAL AWARENESS

People who travel widely are struck by the omnipresence of television. Whether in the homes of the aboriginal people in Australia's outback, in the slums of Bangkok, or in small African villages, with varying degrees of quality, the tube is there. In these modern times, people can have the world brought to them. Social observer Robert Lee has this to say about the phenomenon:

> When Marshall McLuhan predicted that television would create a global village, no one foresaw what an unusual village it would be . . . everybody remained in their huts, watching television. Through the medium of television, they experienced vicariously a reconstruction of experience.[21]

Historically, Canadian journalists have been distinguished by their global coverage. As inhabitants of a lesser player on the world stage, a country next door to a superpower, the media have set their sights beyond the borders and tuned Canadians in to the realities of the international community. As previously noted, young people have absorbed this global view and think Canada should be involved in finding solutions to such issues as illiteracy, human-rights violations, and arms control. In the future we will continue to depend on the media for information about what's happening in other parts of the world. Accurate information will give us a framework to understand and respond to our global neighbours, and thus increase the potential for the expression of social good. But if we suffer information overload or only receive messages of unending despair, we will likely suffer from fatigue, feel powerless, and start tuning out the bigger picture.

Just as obsessive preoccupation with economic recession, plant closings, and unemployment can erode consumer confidence in Canada, so can repeated accounts of famine, civil war, and political instability dampen our enthusiasm for the future prospects of people in the developing world. News coverage inevitably seems to focus on crises, although these are the exceptions rather than the rule. Accordingly, we hear about the 10 per cent who are unemployed rather than the 90 per cent who take home salaries. When it comes to coverage of events in the developing world, the interests of everyone would be better served if there was a balance between communicating the crises and reporting some of the progress. For example, more coverage of post-crisis situations.

When the allotment for global coverage is at the planning stage, giving more priority to profiling other cultures to show their distinctiveness will have a double payoff. Heightened understanding of other cultures will not only give us global insight, it will raise our awareness of the large numbers of ethnically diverse people who now reside in Canada. Being informed about life-styles, favourite foods, and religious practices will better prepare adults in the workplace and young people at school to respond with discernment to the diversity of people around them. Realizing that, in many cases, overpopulation in the world is really a parental strategy to be cared for by one's children in old age will generate understanding instead of judgment. Knowing there are root causes out of people's control that account for the dire circumstances that plague the under-developed nations can generate compassion and prompt responses.

The media are uniquely positioned to be a force for justice in Canada and around the world. That potential is worth extraordinary effort.

MEDIUM FOR THE MIND

Acknowledging Canada's reputation for producing first-class documentaries in what is primarily an entertainment medium prompted one broadcaster to call Canadian productions the "cod liver oil of the broadcasting industry." Even though we know that entertainment is the main purpose of the television medium, we have a sense that although documentaries don't always taste the best, they are good for us.

The pragmatic reality is that, in the television industry, ratings rule. Consequently, producers seek to create what they believe people want to watch so they can sell commercial time to pay the bills. But the medium has potential for so much more.

Despite a report acknowledging that the average child sees 100,000 acts of violence and 8000 murders before the end of elementary school and that TV also contributes to sexual and racial stereotyping, TV can be a tool for good. For example, television can "teach kids academic and social skills . . . and it can spread health messages."[22]

In its present form, however, television is essentially entertainment that is choreographed primarily for the heart. Dramas, sitcoms, movies, serials, and sports tap into the affective domain. Although not completely devoid of ideas, they are first of all written and directed to touch people's feelings. Television, with its technological wizardry, has tremendous potential to turn on people's minds, to energize the cognitive domain. And if ever there was a time for Canadians young and old to think more, the 1990s are it.

Every year, both the federal and provincial governments pour billions of dollars into our educational institutions. Yet, in assessment after assessment, Canadian youth are scoring lower than their predecessors and their international competitors. Why not put some of that money into using television as an educational medium? Sending a video home or assigning the watching of a specific TV program as homework could have positive results.

Calling for real educational reform, Bill Roberts, an executive of TVOntario asks, "National tests and standards are fine, but what about the unique national resource of Radio-Québec, TVOntario, SCN in Saskatchewan, Access Alberta, and Knowledge Network in British Columbia?" Roberts further challenges, "This is the 1990s, and television is an essential educational tool. In an ever more complicated world, television and its related technologies can best inform and inspire. Video has a unique ability to illustrate complex principles and demonstrate subtle distinctions through sight and sound, motion and immediacy.[23]

Investing some educational dollars to use our most advanced technology to produce videos and TV series particularly targeted to the issues and problems of youth simply makes good sense. Not only would educators be given access to culturally appropriate curriculum, some of those entertainment hours could be pre-empted with subject matter for the mind. Youth would benefit if creative writers and producers would address youth issues such as the following:

- The art of decision-making
- Making education choices
- Making career choices
- Moral dilemmas: what's right, what's wrong, and what's best
- Travelling safely and cheaply
- Resolving conflict at home
- What to do and what not to do when you are pregnant
- Becoming a first-class friend
- The importance of reflective thinking

Whether we like it or not, we are becoming more and more dependent on the media. Consequently, providing adequate construction materials for young people to build their lives becomes a concomitant task, and the media has a responsibility to do their part. Elevating the TV medium from one that assumes the audience is present just to *receive* what is sent to one that views the audience is there to *perceive* what is sent will press producers to reformat the medium. T.S. Eliot's alert mind may serve to awaken ours:

Where is the wisdom we have lost in knowledge?
Where is the knowledge we have lost in information?[24]

ENTERTAINMENT FOR COLD WINTER NIGHTS

It would be a mistake to read this chapter and conclude that we're opposed to television. On the contrary, we believe it's a marvellous medium. Certainly the programming is uneven, but think about life without TV. We agree with journalist Hal Boedeker:

> *I am amazed when people tell me they never watch television. Do people boast that they don't listen to music, go to movies or read books? "You're missing out," I want to shout.*[25]

Clearly, entertainment is a joy factor in life. Few sounds in this world are healthier to express or hear than the sound of laughter. Drama that brings tears to tired eyes renews life. Mysteries that tease and intrigue stimulate the mind.

Canadians have a reputation as a serious people. Perhaps we identify too much with the Christian philosopher Pascal who thought that humans have an "instinct which impels them to seek amusement" and this "arises from the sense of their constant unhappiness." It would appear that Pascal's eminent intellectual capacity overlooked Jesus' first miracle, when he turned water into wine so the wedding party wouldn't be a flop!

We could argue that Canadians have a particularly pressing need for entertainment. How else can we endure the long, hard winters! As for Canadian youth, when asked to declare their values, seven in 10 said having a sense of humour was "very important."

THE RESPONSIBLE USE OF POWER

The media and those who work with its powerful tools aren't always balanced in their approach. *Time* magazine's 1991 Person of the Year was Ted Turner. The same Ted Turner who owns a chunk of *Time* and controls CNN. Turner was chosen for "influencing the dynamic of events and turning viewers in 150 countries into instant eyewitnesses of history.[26] Turner and CNN did make a significant contribution in 1991, but still, when journalists create news out of their own news, we have an example of the media becoming an end in itself. It edges toward self-deification. There are dangers when those who have inordinate power perch themselves on the pinnacle of their own creation. The current media mandarins must examine the implications of their cultural power.

BEWARE OF BIASES

We all hold assumptions about life. We all have frameworks and conclusions that assist us to understand what we observe and experience. The people who manage the media are no different. Journalists, editors, and producers all have views of the world that help them make sense of events. Scientist Thomas Kuhn defined the models for how we perceive the world as paradigms. He also warned scientists and others to watch out for "paradigm-induced expectations."[27] Kuhn was aware that, regardless of who we are,

> We adopt sets of categories which serve as ways of managing phenomena. The most fully developed products of this tendency are ideologies, the systems of ideas that rationalize, justify, and sanctify our lives. Nationalism, communism, existentialism, Christianity, Buddhism — all provide us with identities, rules of action, and interpretations of how and why things happen as they do."[28]

Accepting the reality that everyone is predisposed to interpret what they see and experience within the established boundaries of their paradigms, will both enhance our understanding of others and ourselves.

The message to the media is straightforward: be bigger than your personal biases. Acknowledge that your personal perceptions are framed within the boundaries of your working assumptions. Complete objectivity is a myth. Anyone who claims they can interpret and report life's experiences without personal bias shading their perceptions has gone to bed with self-delusion. Once biases are acknowledged and accepted, then one is able to extend to see life from other people's points of view. It is only when more than one side of the story is examined that fairness exists.

The warning to the Canadian public is also straightforward: don't just accept what the media present. Watch and read with a healthy scepticism. Remember that those who tell the story have perceived the story with minds that are cluttered with their subjective views. Look for the biases. Wonder why some details are included while others are omitted. Read between the lines. Widen the lens of the camera to include what has been edited out.

EDIT WITH TRUTH IN MIND

On April 4, 1992, Prime Minister Brian Mulroney was making a speech at a citizenship ceremony to more than 500 people from 85 nations who were celebrating the final stage of becoming Canadians. During his speech, an RCMP officer who was standing at attention beside the podium fainted and collapsed to the floor. The prime minister later quipped, "The only possible thing that could make an RCMP officer weak in the knees was one of my speeches."[29]

The next morning, two of Canada's major newspapers reported their perspective of the story, each using a large front-page photo. The *Toronto Star*, traditionally a Liberal newspaper, showed the RCMP officer collapsed on the floor. The prime minister was pictured behind the podium, his eyes riveted to his notes, still delivering his speech. The *Globe and Mail*, traditionally a Conservative paper, published a picture showing the prime minister assisting the officer back to her feet.

In the one, the prime minister was portrayed as being so self-preoccupied that, at best, he was slow to respond; at worst, he was an unresponsive, uncaring person. In the other, he was shown to be a caring human being. Both photos told the truth, yet conveyed decidedly different messages.

Editors decide which truth they want to tell. They would do well to acknowledge the ideological leanings of their owners and editors, tune in to their own biases, and edit with the total truth in mind.

A look at what is happening in some spheres of our society leads to the conclusion that, rather than clearly defining the true character of some groups of people, the media are feeding into the creation of caricatures. Women, clergy, and teenagers all suffer the same fate.

WOMEN

Although feminists have raised levels of awareness, many advertisers still posture women as sex objects. In recent years, sitcom after sitcom has also been scripted around the dominant theme of sex and more sex.

More recently, the media have cast women in yet another sexual role. Instead of painting women just as sex objects, they are often portrayed as creatures who are sex-hungry and often sex-obsessed. Although programs like "The Golden Girls," "Married with Children," and "Cheers" prompt a lot of wholesome laughter, they fall into the trap of caricaturing women.

Certainly, many programs focus on other subject matter and even occasionally deal with socially complex issues, but the frame that holds the overall picture in place is sex. We're not prudishly calling for sexless scripts, but wish simply to point out that women are being exploited.

After analysing 338 videos, a study by the Quebec Status of Women Council concluded that, "More than half the rock videos broadcast on television are blatantly sexist, and the most flagrant offenders tend to get the most air time . . ." The researchers found that "women are portrayed as submissive and hyper-sexual about 95 per cent of the time in those videos." Group research leader Francis Baby, a professor at Laval University, proceeded to ask, "What impact will this reinforcement of sexist stereotypes have on viewers of video-clips, namely the young people to whom we offer all this as a behaviour model?"[30]

Is it any wonder that some observers share the view of *Toronto Star* writer Lindsay Scotton, who wrote, "Females are not only becoming more assertive, but downright aggressive with guys."[31] Eva, a 16-year-old grade-10 student, says:

> *Girls know what they want . . . the pressure for sex is very high — not necessarily from your boyfriend, but from the other girls around you.*

Adults often look at the younger generation and lament, "What is this world coming to?" In defence of youth, they are not the creators of their world; they are the recipients of a world created by adults. It is adults who write the program scripts and produce the rock videos. Unfortunately, young people often fail to discriminate between what is entertainment and what is real life, between what is caricature and what is character.

RELIGIOUS LEADERS

The televangelists of the 80s who were exposed as immoral in their personal lives and criminal in their activities deserved the ridicule and shame the media heaped on them. The more recent revelations of people who, as youngsters, were physically and sexually exploited in religious institutions in this country is also a wrongdoing that deserves exposure. Physical, sexual, mental, emotional, or spiritual abuse cannot be condoned under any circumstances, and making the public aware can help to reduce further such exploitation.

There are undoubtedly a few more members of the clergy living as swindlers or child abusers but have yet to be exposed. Every profession has its share of deviants. When their indiscretions and sins become public, their professional peers are always embarrassed.

But the fakes and frauds and abusers are the exceptions, not the norms. Unfortunately, everyone in the group or profession is stereotyped, which amounts to collective character assassination. Think about the less than appealing way members of the clergy are sometimes shown in the entertainment media. Reflect on how ministers are portrayed in movies as they officiate at weddings. With their squeaky voices they can be heard uttering inane phrases. In casual conversation they come off as social misfits. A good example was last season's final episode of "Cheers"; one minister was portrayed as being senile and the other as a drunk. Other programs have shown spiritual leaders as wimps, not the sort of people you would see as stimulating dinner companions. The consequences of such caricaturing are lamentable. Too many good people suffer.

In recent years, the negative imaging that has generally characterized members of the clergy has also had exceptions. Mother Theresa in real life and Father Mulcahy in "Mash" have helped bring some balance into the picture. What will the future bring? The media decision-makers will decide, and what they decide will have an impact.

TEENAGERS

Have you noticed how teenagers are often labelled and, therefore, stereotyped in newspaper headlines? Consider what goes through adults' minds about teenagers when they read actual headlines such as:

4 Teens Arrested in Mob Jewellery Thefts
Robbery at Gunpoint: Teenager Sought
Teen Gone, Foul Play Eyed: Police Hunt 18-year-old
Teen Guilty in Stabbing Death

Responding, with good reason, to public criticism about the leniency of the Young Offenders Act, the federal government moved to change the legislation. Instead of a prison sentence for murder being up to a maximum of three years, the limit was appropriately increased to five years. The blaring newspaper headline that reported the legislative change slurred the whole teenage population:[32]

Teen Killers Now Facing Jail Terms up to 5 Years

The headline creates the perception that we have an abundance of teenage killers. In reality, there was one particularly tragic case that received a great deal of media attention. Can you imagine a bold front-page headline that reads:

Robbery at Gunpoint: Adult Sought
or
Adult Guilty in Stabbing Death

Yet teenagers are repeatedly cast in the same collective light. The adults in the media who write the headlines have a different view of themselves than they have of teenagers. Built in to their perceptions is the assumption that teenagers are a neatly contained subculture. Accordingly, they are relatively easy to label. But consequently, the whole generation is painted the same colour.

This practice of generalizing about teenagers leads to stereotyping. And when that happens, it fosters images for adults and arouses sometimes fierce reactions in teens. Repeatedly, they have told us to tell adult Canadians to treat them as individuals. Over and over again, the same message has flowed from their pens. The statement from a young man in grade 10 deserves serious reflection:

> *I believe that adult Canadians, no matter what teenagers do, will always view us as a whole. Their perceptions of us will remain the same . . . that of rowdy, obnoxious, and a pain to society.*

Should the media choose to do so, they can begin to help change how older Canadians perceive the young people who live around them.

We acknowledge that members of the media are lead players in today's world. We recognize that their role in modern society is complex. But as they go about their business, they need to accept the fact that they have immense power. For the well-being of all Canadians, they need to be careful how they wield it. They should edit with truth in mind. They must, above all, try to be fair.

9

THE ROLE OF
OTHER ADULTS

*L*ifting *the level of life exchanged between young people and adults involves everybody. Certainly, as discussed in the foregoing chapters, the key players are parents, educators, religious leaders, and the media. But other important adults on the team include employers, government leaders, and specialists, such as counsellors.*

The surveys reveal young people's perceptions about how they are viewed by adults in general. And too frequently, the news is not flattering. Teenagers tell us they often feel adults don't regard them as "full persons." Consequently, only one in two teens perceive that adults respect them, and they sense their opinions are neither desired nor valued.

In light of what's taking place, young people understandably feel less than comfortable and significant in the presence of many adults. Youth respond by gravitating toward their friends, not as a social supplement, but as a desired substitute.

Consequently, there is a need for Canadians in general to change the signals they send to teenagers.

MADE IN OUR IMAGE

The 60s were different. The decade might be viewed as profound or profane: a modern renaissance or just a wrinkle in time. But at least one characteristic of those years remains desirable: the people of the 60s were agents of change, and they saw themselves that way. They had ideas. They lived with deep feelings. They believed they could make a difference, and they had an agenda for a better tomorrow. In the end, most of the dreams went down the drain, and many of the advocates for change lapsed into social conformity. But new directions were put into motion, ones that are still being pursued.

In contrast, Canadian young people in the 1990s do not see themselves as agents of change. They are like mirrors on the wall of society. Their attitudes and behaviour mainly reflect the status quo. They have not been able to carve out much of a world that is uniquely their own. Distinctiveness has eluded them.

Nevertheless, adults are sometimes heard to lament, "What is this younger generation coming to? What is going on inside their heads, anyway?" The answer is relatively simple. Young people today are coming to where older adults have led them. They are reflecting what they see around them. Whether the areas of comparison are views on universal medicare, confidence in the prime minister, the legalization of marijuana, hopes for success at work and living the good life, attitudes about sexual matters or religion, today's youth are planning on taking the world they have inherited to where it is already going.

It appears that, in many ways, Canadian youth are under control. Only a few cause society much trouble. The great majority are quiet and rather conventional. They are more inclined to conform than to innovate; more comfortable being quietly passive than radically active.

TOO MANY STRINGS?

But, we must ask, are adult Canadians providing the kind of environments that encourage the healthy emergence of young people? Is it possible that today's youth have been overmanaged and underled? Can it be that while modern youth are being socialized into the likenesses of adults they are not being autonomized — given self-determination — to develop their potential and seek their own destiny?

When young people in their teens and those in their early twenties are asked how they believe older people see them, the situation is disturbing. Only one in two young people between the ages of 15 and 24 perceive that older adults "respect their opinions," and fewer than one in three perceive that they "have confidence in young people" or "understand young people." Even more alarming is the fact that those in their 20s and those in their teens have exactly the same perceptions. The seriousness of the predicament is accentuated by the realization that 75 per cent of teenagers place a high value "being respected."

HOW ADULTS RELATE TO YOUTH			
% Indicating Agreement			
	Canada Average	Age 15-19	Age 20-24
Adults are courteous to young people	72	72	73
Adults respect young people's opinions	50	51	50
Adults understand young people	37	37	37
Adults have confidence in young people	29	29	29
SOURCE: Project Teen Canada 88			

Too frequently, older Canadians fail to treat younger Canadians with basic human respect. They relate to teenagers as if they are still children, and many do the same with adults in their early twenties. For whatever reasons, older adults seem reluctant to let adolescents and young adults grow up. Rather than being welcomed into adulthood with its ensuing privileges and responsibilities, younger Canadians are being blocked from entering the adult world.

When we probe young people on the specific messages they are receiving on the subject of being fully adult, they speak clearly. Collectively, they communicate the following:

In Canada, you are fully adult when you have finished your education, are holding down a full-time job, paying taxes, and are preferably married with at least one child. When all the criteria are met, maybe by the time you reach 30, you are accepted by the older generation as being fully adult.

GUIDELINES FOR ADULTS EVERYWHERE

Helping young people grow up is a desirable adult thing to do. Assisting the younger generation to move toward healthy autonomy is the right role of parents, youth workers, teachers, religious leaders, and other adults whose lives intersect the lives of the younger generation. While some behaviours and attitudes serve the purpose of stimulating youth into wholesome developmental patterns, others are detrimental.

Some basic points need to be kept in mind.

STOP STEREOTYPING

In the 1991 *Maclean's*-Decima poll, the following question was put to a cross-section of Canadian adults: "In your opinion, has the behaviour of young people in the community where you live got worse or better?" The responses reveal built-in biases that are projected toward Canada's young people.[1]

HOW ADULTS VIEW YOUNG PEOPLE'S BEHAVIOUR	
% Responding	
Much worse	14
Somewhat worse	33
Somewhat better	10
Much better	4
Has not changed	38
Don't know/NA	1

What is it that's buried in the perceptions of adults in this country that prompts almost half of them to believe that the behaviour of youth is getting worse? For, in fact, instead of getting worse, today's younger generation are pretty much on a continuum. They are inclined to be reflective and passive. If their behaviour is getting worse, it's because they are following in the footsteps of adults who are leading them into decline.

One of the main reasons for adults' negative perception of teens lies in the overall stereotyping of youth. Specifically, the older generation is inclined to project the behaviour of a very small minority of teens on the entire teenage population. For instance, many adults stereotype teens as drug abusers. Yet, only about five per cent of teens habitually use illicit drugs of any kind.

In the national surveys, teenagers have repeatedly expressed their frustrations about being stereotyped. They don't like being pigeon-holed any more than adults do. Listen to the comments from young people themselves:

My dad thinks that all teenagers are bad asses, you know into drugs, sex and crime. We're not all like that. I mean, sure there are a lot of bad teenagers out there, but there are also a lot of bad adults out there too. —a 15-year-old female in grade 10

We are expected to be mature young adults, but yet, we are still treated and considered to be children. No one wants to take us seriously. People should sit down and realize that not all teens are violent, drug addicts, shoplifters, irresponsible, and unschooled. Trust us, we aren't as bad as you think we are. — a 17-year-old male in grade 12

Most of us are okay. Don't judge the generation on a few isolated cases. — a 17-year-old female from Montreal

Stereotyping of any kind fuels bigoted attitudes and damages human relationships. In order to find an improved future, the stereotyping of teenagers needs to stop. Not only is the practice demeaning, it sets up prejudices and precludes the flow of positive life between the generations.

BESTOW SOME DIGNITY

Too many adults conceive teenagers as people who are somehow less than human. Over the years, when your authors have been asked to speak before an audience about our youth research, we are often introduced with a little joke — a reference to the "terrible teen" years, or something along the lines of "Our speaker tonight has survived to see his children enter their twenties." Even there, in a setting where youth is to be discussed seriously, adolescents are the objects of demeaning humour. It's as if:

HALF CHILD + HALF ADULT = HALF HUMAN

Of course, insightful adults realize that just because teenagers are physically developed, that does not mean the emotional, mental, social, and spiritual facets of their humanity have reached maturity. But that insight needs to be supported with an understanding of what consitutes normal development for adolescents. If preschool children are allowed to go through the stages of normal growth on the way to becoming adolescents, so should adolescents be granted permission to go through further stages of development on the way to becoming mature adults.

Just as a young tree that has only a few years' growth is in every sense a genuine tree, so are teenagers genuinely fully human and complete at their stage of growth. Discerning adults will realize that the stages of development are comparable to the growth rings of a tree. Each stage of growth and development will be understood as a movement toward becoming more mature and more complete.

Accordingly, empathetic adults will at least ponder the implications of the question "What's normal about a normal adolescence?"

With an understanding and acceptance of what *is* normal about teenagers, adults will be in a position to bestow some dignity in their direction. They will see beyond their unfinished state of being and relate to them as complete persons, while knowing there are stages of development still to come.

Adolescents are aching for adults to accept them as they are. They may not always express their inner hopes in sensitive ways, but beneath their exterior, modern youth are crying out for respect and dignity. Listen to their urgings:

We aren't losers. Treat us with respect. We have feelings and brains and we could be treated like we do. — a 15-year-old female in grade 10

I think that teenagers are not thought of as an important part of society and their opinions are not valued. In the future, I hope that will change. — a 16-year-old female from Alberta

SEND "I BELIEVE IN YOU" SIGNALS

Youth today need adult advocates. They need people in their lives who will champion their interests and grant them full-fledged status in contemporary society.

Reviewing an art exhibition that featured Mohawk artists, Quebec journalist Ray Conlogue expressed frustration because of the wide range in the quality of the works. "The result is disconcerting for the gallery-goer," he said, "because many of the artists are not professional in the accepted sense." He judged inappropriate the sophisticated art alongside "adolescent work whose muscled warriors and snarling wolves seem to have been lifted from a Dungeons and Dragons board."

Louise Formel, an art professor at the University of Montreal, explained the unconventional practice: "It's part of the [Mohawk] culture to put professional work beside amateur. It's to encourage the young . . . There is no competition among artists. The work is collectively presented.[2]

Adults need to send the signal to young people that, even though their art has not fully matured, it still has inherent value.

Making room for young people is especially important today

because teenagers and those in their twenties are vulnerable to the "baby-boomer squeeze." A total of eight million Canadians were born between 1946 and 1964. The population bulge has put the "boomers," subsequently labelled "Yuppies," in control of much of the culture. Editorialist Bill Mandel, a boomer himself, admits, "The baby boom is giving society an intestinal blockage. There are so many boomers permanently camped in influential jobs that the next generation can't squeeze past us. We postwar buds are getting to an age that was 'old' when we were young, but we've managed to redefine 'old' so it doesn't apply to us.[3]

In his book, *Age Wave,* Ken Dychtwald observes there are reasons to conclude that:

> *The boomers are the youth generation. They love their youth. They love the youthful vigour and vitality that have always been a part of their lives. In fact, we might expect that, because they love their youth so much, they will do everything possible to take it with them into their old age. In the years to come, entire industries will rise and fall in response to this anti-aging, pro-longevity obsession.*[4]

As noted, today's youth have exceedingly high expectations. Their aspirations are testament to their hope and idealism. However, they will need input and people around them to act as catalysts to this idealism. Young people will not only be energized by older people who believe in them, they will be motivated to excel when they are given opportunities to contribute.

GUIDELINES FOR SPECIFIC ADULTS

EMPLOYERS

Employers are a specific adult segment that can make a difference in the lives of modern youth. As today's teens seek to get into the workplace, or want to start a small business, instead of being pampered, they will be well served when they are empowered.

At least half of the young people still going to school hold part-time jobs. What is disconcerting is that, whereas 57 per cent of adults say they receive high levels of enjoyment from their jobs, only 33 per cent of teenagers make the same claim. How can the workplace experience be enhanced and thereby be made more productive and profitable?

TAKE TIME TO RELATE

Remember that today's youth are social creatures. And just as the force of friendship has implications for the family, schools, and religion, so the drive for relationships affects the workplace. Employers who realize that their personal power is every bit as potent as their positional power will start with a right assumption. Expressing a personal interest in young employees is a management style that works. It will pay big dividends.

Including a few thoughtful questions in a job interview sends signals. "What did you like best about your last job?" and, "Have you decided what you want to do after you finish school?" will send the message that people in that company are more than just commodities. After work has begun, greeting people by their names, enquiring about weekend plans, and talking about their favourite musical groups will add to the quality of life.

Because most teenagers are at the stage where they are working only part-time, their stay at a particular job is most often short term. More than just being costly and frustrating, the prospects of high staff turnover can produce a utilitarian attitude toward part-timers. In these circumstances, it is understandable when employers think to themselves, if people are just here today and gone tomorrow, why bother taking them too seriously, let alone trying to get to know them? A deeper look at the problem will reveal that if people are treated as if they won't be around very long, they won't be around very long.

When the time does come for a young employee to move on, it will be worth the effort to help her or him exit gracefully. A last-shift Coke break with the boss will not only allow for two-way debriefing, it will also be an opportunity to give the teenager a personal send-off — along with the invitation to come back and visit sometime. When people get treated that way, word gets around.

ASSIGN WORK IN TEAMS

Every work situation has both limits and opportunities. If possible, allowing young people to work together rather than deploying them in isolation will be preferred. Being alone equates to loneliness for most young people. In a work environment, the result can be demotivating.

Lester Thurow, dean of the Alfred P. Sloan School of Management at MIT in Boston, counsels that the way of the future is working more in teams. Acknowledging that business is moving in that direction, Thurow still contends that in North America, "we don't intrinsically think teams." Rather, "we convert everything into the Lone Ranger. That's not to say individualism isn't important, but somehow you have got to build a team culture into the operation.[5]

Assigning work in small groups and giving incentives that motivate teamwork will be well received by the younger generation. Certainly there will be individual teenagers who will work better on their own. And obviously, it is not possible or feasible for many jobs to be done in groups, but the principle still remains: it is more effective and efficient to make the dynamics of the youth culture work *for* you instead of *against* you.

AFFIRM AND CORRECT — WHEN DESERVED

The book *The One Minute Manager* recommends a sound strategy for supervising young people in the workplace:

1.   Give clear direction. Let young people know what's expected of them. Give them clear goals. Spell out their responsibilities and how they will be evaluated.

2.   Look for opportunities to affirm; with young people, affirmation is more effective than exhortation. Catch them doing something right and tell them so. Young people are like adults — they respond to positive reinforcement.

3.   Offer specific reprimands. Young people know they have a lot to learn. Correct the errors of their ways by helping them do a better job. Done in the right way, young people will amend their ways and respond appropriately.[6]

Today's youth are ready to accept the rules of the working world. When young people do begin new jobs, the expectations need to be carefully spelled out. Allowing adequate time for on-the-job training will benefit everyone. Young people do not see themselves as finished products. Even when cockiness is exhibited, it is usually just an over-compensation for insecurity. It will be a rare exception when they do not respond positively to fairness. Employers who explain what they want done rather than ordering their young employees to do tasks and how to do them will create healthy and productive work environments.

HUMANIZE DEMEANING SYSTEMS

The business sector has a reputation for being on the innovative edge. Writing job positions for young people that include real responsibility will be innovative. Devising systems that give discretion to young employees and encourage them to exercise their judgment will be revolutionary.

Recently, I went through the ordeal of renewing my passport. The first step was to request an application. Filling in the information on the form was the easy part. Getting the right-size pictures and having the form properly signed by a guarantor required a little more effort. Resolutely, I gathered up the numerous items, including my expired passport, and drove across the city to the right government office.

With a sense of confidence I took a number from the cylinder under the sign and sat down to wait my turn. Before long, I was standing at the counter before a middle-aged woman and proceeded to lay the documents out in front of her. After scanning and shuffling the papers for a few moments, her first words to me were, "Can I please see your birth certificate?" My emotions started to churn as I realized that my birth certificate was at home in a drawer. Undaunted, I produced eight other pieces of ID including two with my photo prominently displayed.

"Sir, I need your birth certificate, it says that here right on the form."

"I understand what it says on the form, but won't my expired passport serve as adequate confirmation of my Canadian citizenship? Look, it signifies that right here."

"No. Your birth certificate is required. We are concerned about security and the risk of issuing fraudulent passports."

"Your concern is warranted, but wouldn't you agree that there is a remarkable resemblance between the picture on my expired passport, the pictures required for the new passport, the picture on my driver's licence, and the face that you are currently looking at?"

"Yes, *sir*, but your birth certificate is required."

"Are you not able to exercise your good judgment in situations like this? Is there anyone in this office who can assist you?"

"The answer is *no*! Next please"

The experience was both irritating and frustrating, but the greater tragedy is that the woman had a demeaning job. The hard-line procedures precluded her from using her judgment. Day after day, situation after situation, predicament after predicament, she became less and less human.

Systems that demean people dehumanize people. They reduce human beings into mechanized robots. They systematically squeeze life out of people who begin their jobs with aspirations to make real contributions.

As employers design jobs that include real responsibility, young people will be motivated to be responsible. They will be stimulated to perform. Instead of dreading the very idea of work, the workplace will generate new levels of life in them.

GOVERNMENT LEADERS

Adults in government are another segment of the population who would be wise to ponder their role among today's youth. The challenges will not be insurmountable, but they will be difficult.

MINORITY SUPPORT

When young people were asked about their confidence levels in government, they were not enthusiastic. A total of 32 per cent said they had either "a great deal" or "quite a bit" of confidence in the provincial governments, while 27 per cent were ready to affirm the federal level. At best then, only one in three youth in the country look to their political leaders and are ready to offer even polite applause.

Approximately the same number believe that "average Canadians do not have any influence on what government does." Coincidentally, three in four also believe that they have "too little power."

Another difficulty is that the government agenda is not getting through to the younger generation. During the same time frame, while 45 per cent said they were interested in the serial slayings in Milwaukee, only 13 per cent expressed the same level of interest in the Spicer Commission.

Every day, all across the country, newspapers and citizens on open-line shows offer all kinds of advice to people in every level of government. Will a few more admonitions in this book really make a difference? Are politicians and young Canadians simply an example of another proverbial two solitudes? If so, neither government leaders nor young people will contribute to an improved future.

The situation is not as bleak as it may seem. There are many adults committed to public life who have an active and abiding interest in how the politics and practices of government affect young Canadians.

There are also young people who aspire to explore the political arena and the challenges that face Canada's political institutions.

Why, then, the general estrangement between Canada's current active leaders and our future potential leaders? We've noted that our schools are the one place where youth is gathered. Yet, only a few students graduate with a positive view of politicians. Those responsible for the political parties, political institutions, and their own political careers would do well to spend some time doing public relations with those who have the ear of Canada's youth — Canadian teachers.

Most students leave school with the basic sentiment that government is to be largely ignored. Students don't believe they can make a difference. What positive images of politicians and public service can be offered to the teaching profession? How can teachers be encouraged to offer constructive analysis of the political and policy agenda? Politicians need to take steps to restore credibility with the educators before there is any hope of building credibility and active interest among the students.

CHANNELLING YOUTH VOICES

One positive step will be for politicians to spend more time visiting students at their schools. Our political climate is changing. Openness and consultation are now beginning to play a role in the development of public policy. The obvious design is to promote a more participative process that will ensure a wider support for a particular policy. In the current political climate, if there has not been a fair opportunity for consultation, whatever the final policy outcome is, it will be judged as unrepresentative and likely be unpopular.

Yet, in their present position, young people are basically ignored in the political process. They are a voiceless generation. They are repeatedly told they have "great potential" and "tomorrow is their time." And just as repeatedly, when young people do speak out, they contend that older adults don't take them seriously. They are made to feel as though what they have to say doesn't really matter — because they are young.

Could politicians concerned about the next generation create channels for the voices of our young people? Can students, who congregate by law at our educational institutions, have institutional input into the formation of policies? Obviously, a grade-12 chemistry student should not be forced to experience the pressure of being treated as a constitutional expert. But what would a system look like that allowed input from student bodies of local schools to be passed on to municipal school boards and then on to national agencies and government decision-makers?

Students could enter the policy process on the basis of a current Canadian governmental standard: consultation and openness. If politicians are ready to meet the public in town-hall meetings, they should also show up at cafeteria forums.

But, teachers giving attention to the virtues of a system and students participating in that system will not be enough. The actors who play out the political drama will have to learn some new lines. The data speaks for itself: politicians are not credible in the eyes of the younger generation.

EARNING RESPECT

Anyone who has spent time behind the scenes on Parliament Hill in Ottawa or in any of the government offices in our provincial capitals knows there are individuals who are making great personal sacrifices to serve in public life. The members of Parliament and those in our legislative assemblies who contribute to the committees they sit on, participate in thoughtful and constructive debate, show concern for their constituents, and conscientiously participate in the life of this nation are to be applauded.

However, for those of us who only catch the TV news or read the quotable quotes in the paper there is not a lot to respect. Too many elected representatives are only posturing as politicians. Their main aspiration is to perform on the evening news. Members of the opposition lash out with predictable pretence and rhetoric. Members of the parties in power lash back in the same mode. And since it is more fashionable to be negative than positive, the best strategy when playing to the media is to make sure the verbal strike is as lethal as social limits will allow. Crafted insults that are nasty but not ruthless and clever comments that are indicting but not vicious are the ones that frequent the airwaves. Tragically, political public expression is reduced to four-second sound-bytes that flaunt ultimatums instead of proposing thoughtful alternatives.

Young people in Canada are not impressed.

Young Canadians need to observe politicians in the public forum. They will respond positively to leaders who personify values both they and older Canadians hold as important. While there will always be moments of confrontation in the life of our nation, a conscious effort to promote legitimate moments of consensus will not only vary the political diet, it will also move the collective national agenda forward.

The positive elements of our political process should not be apparent only to those Canadians who closely follow the details of provincial and national life. Those of us who are busy and caught up in the responsibilities of daily living need to see politicians publicly parade their convictions with compassion, instead of simply pursuing their party's power trips.

A recent example makes the point. In the House of Commons, the day after the white population of South Africa voted to proceed with reforms to end apartheid in their country, a key member of an opposition party stood up during question period and commended the prime minister for his long-standing crusade to impose economic sanctions against South Africa. The affirmation was personal and genuine. The level of dignity in the House of Commons was lifted for a moment. And it even made the evening news!

That sound-byte rose above the daily drone of criticizing and carping that characterizes question period. It is also the style that will build the confidence of a generation essentially disillusioned with today's political process.

COUNSELLORS OF TROUBLED YOUTH

A segment of the younger generation wakes up every morning facing circumstances that make them want to stay in bed. Sometimes society labels this group "high-risk youth." They may be high school drop-outs, runaways living on the street, victims of abuse, chronic drug users, or young people whose families have disintegrated, leaving them with the fall-out. They are troubled youth. Whatever their predicament or dysfunctional malady, these young people often end up as wards of the court, on welfare, and under the supervision of social workers and youth counsellors. In what ways can adults in the helping professions best assist these young people who need extraordinary attention?

SOURCE OF THE DAMAGE

Approximately one in 10 young people are severely down on themselves, and see themselves as failures. They enter their teenage years as damaged goods, and all have stories to tell. When empathetic counsellors and other adults take time to probe and listen, they can determine the reasons these young people end up living in nightmares rather than experiencing their dreams, for, like adults, dysfunctional teens can trace the journey of their demise. Often the temptation is simply to lay blame and to judge those who aren't making it.

Most often, when young people stand at the edge of society, they have been helped to get there. Making it back to what society defines as normal is a difficult journey, and one for which help is needed. However, with careful assessment of what went wrong, and guidance and direction, young people can not only recover, they can grow into new ways of thinking and behaving.

One of the great advantages for young people is that they *are* young. Time is on their side. Seldom are their ways set in stone. Nor are they locked into patterns of pretence and denial. But breaking entrenched habits is an ordeal for the young people crushed by their childhood experiences. Consequently, counsellors and other adults who work with hurting youth will need to limit the level of their expectations. They will negotiate short-term agreements and be satisfied with low-risk achievements. They will increase the demands as they go along.

BUILD POSITIVE SELF-IMAGES

When we look beneath the surface, young people who express external behaviour that is antisocial and disruptive also suffer from internal turmoil and disruption. The intent is not to take young people off the hook for their unacceptable behaviour or to enter a not-guilty plea on their behalf. But most often, young people are victims. Those who are abusive have been abused; those who think they are dumb and stupid have been told over and over again they are dumb and stupid; those who do wrong have been repeatedly reminded that they are always wrong; those whose mouths spew lewd and foul language have listened to lewd and foul language; those who are disrespectful have never been respected.

And when you wrap it all up, troubled youth, with rare exceptions, travel with negative self-images. They think they are trash, second-class creeps, and next to worthless. Unfortunately for young people who live with this debilitating handicap, medical technology has not progressed to the point of being able to perform self-image transplants!

Young people with poor views of themselves are in dire need of affirmation. They desperately need people in their lives who can convert the negative into the positive. People who verbally and nonverbally declare:

You are not stupid.
You are not ugly.
You are not trash.

You are as intelligent as your friends.
You are made of good stuff.
You are a first-class, but struggling human being.

Leaders and counsellors who work under the umbrella of the Alberta Alcohol and Drug Abuse Commission (AADAC) give a specific priority to building up the self-images of troubled youth. Rather than focusing on the damage substance abuse produces, the agency looks at the underlying reasons that drive a person to become involved with drugs and alcohol. The intent is to "get kids feeling good about themselves and competent enough to handle the pressure-cooker of adolescence."[7]

Troubled youth whose self-images are in disarray also need to be protected from their pattern of putting themselves down. Altering this cycle of negative reinforcement is a challenge. An interesting approach is to move into a negotiation mode by giving them a daily quota of self-insults. Allowing a maximum of four personal putdowns a day for a given week can raise their awareness of the problem. Lowering the quota the second week and then again in the third week can begin to help these teenagers replace the old destructive pattern. The big breakthrough comes when they change their behaviour so much they genuinely deserve affirmation and praise from both others and themselves. Doing whatever is necessary to motivate troubled youth to take steps from "I am worthless" to "I have worth," from "I can't" to "I can," will be a great gift.

BUILD TRUST AND GET TOUGH

Who would argue? Young people who have been mistreated need other people to champion their cause. Teenagers who have been wounded need both peers and adults to cry with them and encourage them to begin again. These same young people also need adults to challenge them, to push them into constructive behavioural change, and to get tough with them.

There is one prerequisite. Before well-intentioned adults can confront or get tough with troubled youth, they will need to earn their trust. And teenagers whose only impressions of adults are people who don't deserve to be trusted will take a long time to reach. Counsellors of troubled youth must have an extra measure of patience. If not, they should find another vocation.

SOME CLOSING THOUGHTS

RULES FOR ADOLESCENT RELATIONSHIPS

There is a golden rule for human relationships, one that embraces all ages and, for that matter, all cultures. The principle is simple: *Treat others as you would like to be treated.* Translating the lofty theory into behaviour is not simple; it is perplexing, unpredictable, and often exhausting. But the intent to live that way lifts life to a higher plane and everyone in the situation benefits. Translating the principle into teen-adult relationships, *young people prefer to be treated the way adults prefer to be treated.*

There is another principle that particularly applies to life exchanged between adults and teenagers. In the end, it is essentially an adult challenge, and is inordinately demanding. It calls for adults to *treat teenagers like adults, but expect them to act like children at least two days a week.* Like it or not, adolescents are unfinished products. And in the flow of life, they need more mercy than those of us who are older, those of us who continue to wrestle with what it means to be more and more adult — and more and more mature.

Life between the older and younger generations will really get into orbit when we relax enough to genuinely enjoy each other. Computing the implications that seven in 10 teenagers value humour, seeing it as "very important," will be a good starting point for adults. Across every region of the country, embracing both genders and all of our multicultural differences, the majority of young Canadians have a high appreciation for the sound of laughter. What could be healthier than adults and adolescents laughing together?

On too many occasions, we hear adults confess they are afraid of teenagers. What they are really saying is they don't understand young people and have difficulty relating to them. As adults, if we can first see teens as people rather than regarding them as "just kids," we will take a step forward. As we move on to appreciating their idealism, valuing their ideas, accepting their emotional fluctuations, being amused at their hypocrisy, feeding on their energy, and generally welcoming them into our presence, we will take a giant stride into an improved future.

PROSPECTS FOR PROGRESS

Since the watershed decade of the 60s, Canadians have experienced impressive progress in numerous categories of life. In the past 25 years, technological gains have been staggering. Computers that used to take up hundreds of square feet can now sit on your lap. The level of high school drop-outs has decreased by a third. Ecological awareness is delivering new levels of concern. The philosophy Reduce, Reuse, and Recycle wasn't even around in the 60s, and now, joining the environmental movement represents a more responsible way to live.

But on the more human side of life, where do we stand on the progress scale?

Memories of a long lunch and an experience with a lawyer named Steven still linger. Steven spent his vocational life as a low-profile lawyer. He set up his practice close to the university from which he graduated. He stayed in the same city throughout his entire career. His major moves were from one office building to another when his practice was expanding. Steven was known for his stability. Over the years he was faithful to his clients, and they provided him with a very comfortable living. He networked with his colleagues and built a few significant relationships. Today, Steven is getting ready to live off his investments and his pension. He intends to travel and do those things he never had time for in the past.

Before we had lunch, Steven suggested we tour the courthouse. I was intrigued as we poked our heads into various chambers and courtrooms. Steven talked about some of his experiences, and I enjoyed every word. As we walked along, Steven kept greeting people. He introduced me to his favourite judge and other valued colleagues. Just before we were to leave he whispered, "I want you to see the research library."

The library was an impressive place. The high vaulted ceiling made me feel as if I was in a cathedral. The ornate oak carving around the archway and up the banister reminded me that excellence was not a new idea. What seemed like miles of shelves lined with reference books pressed me into a historical frame of mind.

I was musing as Steven began speaking in hushed tones. "See that room back there, the one with the iron bars that looks like a jail cell? That's where the rare reference books are stored. My, how things have changed," Steven lamented. "When I was a student, books like those were on open shelves. Today, unless we have tight security, lawyers steal them and put them in their private collections."

I was astonished. It was quite a paradox. Rare books had to be kept behind bars to protect them from the same people we trust to preserve our laws and sense of justice. The courthouse and court-rooms, the judges and lawyers, the librarians and the library were evidence of our legal history and the important social cornerstone of justice. The rare-book room, with its security and bars, was evidence that, even with our commitment to laudable ideals, we haven't over-come much of our shameful lack of scruples.

Christopher Dawson says with science and technology being held in such esteem in our society, "progress becomes the working faith of the civilization."[8] That is not to say Canadians have blindly embraced progress as an ideology, but the collective self of modern society simply assumes we are getting better. We need to stop and ask, "What is progress?"

Two in three teenagers believe that "in general, values in Canada have been changing for the worse." University of Alberta economist Bruce Wilkinson writes:

Raising moral and ethical questions regarding today's emphasis upon competitiveness, efficiency, profits, financial success, should not require a defence... The mighty Kodak corporation, for example, is the largest single polluter of the environment in the state of New York. The Nestle corpora-tion... is reluctant to alter their production and promotion of breast milk substitutes in developing lands even though they know these increase infant mortality rates. The tobacco companies continue to promote their cigarette sales, especially in developing lands. Numerous companies sell armaments or components for weapons of war to almost any nation which will buy them. Nike sport shoes selling in North America for $150 are being produced in Indonesia by women paid 58 cents a day. Other companies trim layers of management so that those remaining must work longer hours under more stress, to the detriment of family life and/or health all in the name of efficiency and profits, as if these were the only values in life.[9]

And when we apply the issues of progress to the realm of relation-ships between the older and younger generation, how do we fare?

We must break some of those old cycles and do better. In the 60s Bob Dylan sang, "The times they are a-changing . . ." Times need to change again. Freeing up Canadian youth to pursue their own autonomy, rather than socializing them to accept the status quo, might be scary for those of us enjoying the status quo, but in the long run it will enable young people to articulate a vision for their generation. And who knows, their vision could combine the lessons from the past with the stalemate of the present and move us into real progress in the future.

A PARADIGM FOR THE FUTURE

What can we do with the young people in our lives to encourage their potential? Can we as adults celebrate the unfolding drama in the teenage experience of growing up? If you employ young people, if you counsel them, if you legislate for them, or if you simply know teenagers, then cherish who they are and what they can become. And play a constructive role in their emergence.

POINT THE WAY

Today's youth do not need more parades of adult passivity. Adults who waffle about what they think and believe may be well meaning, but they are not the friends of modern youth. Evasiveness about convictions only exasperates the already muddled mind-sets of the young. Opinions disguised in ambiguity are not gifts. They only add to the existing complexity and confusion.

Adult friends of the young will *point the way*. They will *give direction*. As parents and educators, as employers and youth workers, they will teach, instruct, lobby, and demonstrate what deserves to be emulated. They will take a few risks. With limited frequency and on the right occasions, without being overbearing, judgmental, or condescending, concerned adults will articulate, and even pontificate about what is important to them. They will let the young people within reach of their influence really know who they are and what they think.

LEAD THE WAY

This book has clearly established that today's young people are turning out like the adults in their lives. Accordingly, adults cannot escape the fact that, in major ways, teenagers are embracing what they observe around them. Logic leads to the uncontested conclusion that modelling matters. Pushing the point even further raises a question for adults to ponder: "Does my behaviour deserve to be duplicated?"

In today's world, talk really is cheap. Words are dwarfed by deeds. Doing silences the noise of talking. And adults who hope to serve the best interests of the young will *lead the way* with their living. They will model what matters. They will understand that young people are monitoring their attitudes and actions. They will consciously be aware that youth are looking for images of what they want to become. Adults who have high aspirations for the younger generation will give their young eyes something worth watching.

GET OUT OF THE WAY

The majority of people live with good intentions. Adults don't deliberately plan to deny young people pathways into the future. But, well-intentioned or not, when adults overcontrol, overprotect, and overindulge the young, they stifle their development. Instead of stimulating life in the young, in the end, those excesses slow the maturing process.

The alternative is to *get out of the way* so young people can become autonomous. Instead of standing in the way of emergence, wise adults will give young people room to become their true selves. They will give young people their vote of confidence and propel them into being what they are meant to be.

APPENDIX

PROJECT TEEN CANADA 92 METHODOLOGY

The 1992 national youth survey was entitled *Project Teen Canada 92*. Funded by the Lilly Foundation, it was conducted over approximately a four-month period, from mid-November of 1991 to mid-March of 1992. Bibby and Posterski designed the questionnaire. The survey itself was carried out from the University of Lethbridge under Bibby's supervision, with Reginald Bibby, Jr., serving as senior research associate. The methodology of the 1984 *Project Teen Canada* survey was replicated (see Bibby and Posterski, 1984:201-205).

SAMPLE SIZE

As in 1984, a sample of 3600 teenagers was pursued, a figure that, if representatively selected, makes it possible to generalize to the overall high school adolescent population (about 1.5 million) with a high level of accuracy (within about three percentage points, either way, 19 times in 20). A sample of that size also increases the accuracy of analyses involving various aggregates — such as region, community size, gender, and race.

THE SAMPLING FRAME

Once again, since our interest was in the segment of young people on the verge of becoming adults, the sample was restricted to Canadians 15 to 19 years old in grades 10 to 12 across Canada, including CEGEPs in Quebec. These three grades encompass some two-thirds of those between the ages of 15 and 19. Moreover, about 65 per cent of the remaining one-third not in high school — including, obviously, teens in post-secondary institutions — were there for one year or more. Moreover, concerning the charge that we have missed the drop-outs, clearly some of our participants will drop out while, according to Statistics Canada, as many as one in four current students dropped out at some point in their schooling. The drop-outs have not been omitted. We continue to maintain that to get a reading of secondary students is to get a highly comprehensive snapshot of the latest "emerging generation" as it passes through high school.

SAMPLING PROCEDURES

In pursuing the sample size of 3600 high school students, we again randomly selected individual high school classrooms rather than individual students, because of the significant administrative advantages and minimal negative consequences for a random sample. The design involved choosing one classroom in each school selected. Based on an average class size of perhaps 25 students, this meant that some 150 schools needed to participate (N=3750). On the basis of a projected response rate of about 75 per cent — based on our 1984 experience — the sample was comprised of approximately 200 schools.

The schools were chosen using multi-stage stratified and cluster sampling procedures. The country was first stratified according to the five major regions, with each region then stratified according to community size (100,000 and over, 99,000 to 10,000, less than 10,000). Each community-size category was in turn stratified according to school system (public, separate, private).

Specific communities within each size stratum were then randomly selected, with the number of communities drawn from each province in the Prairie and Atlantic regions based on population. Finally, one school in each of these communities was chosen randomly. The number of schools selected in cities with a population of greater than 100,000 was proportional to their population in their region. The specific grade of the classroom involved was also randomly designated.

THE ADMINISTRATION OF THE SURVEY

Similar to 1984, guidance counsellors or an appropriate substitute at each school were contacted, and asked to (a) choose a classroom which they viewed as representative of the required grade, and (b) personally administer the questionnaire. They were instructed to stress that participation was voluntary, and that anonymity and confidentiality would be honoured. Upon completion of the questionnaires, counsellors were asked to place them in the pre-paid postal envelope provided "in full view of the students," and to seal the envelope in their presence.

THE RESPONSE

Questionnaires were returned from 180 of the 193 designated classrooms — a return rate of 93 per cent (see Table A1). The remaining 13 schools either declined to participate (five) or did not respond to requests to do so (eight).

A total of 4190 questionnaires were received, with 226 of these discarded primarily because they had been filled out by students younger than 15 or older than 19. The number of usable questionnaires thus totalled 3964. The 1984 total was 3530.

REPRESENTATIVENESS

As Table A2 shows, in its final, weighted form, the sample is highly representative of Canadian high school students, 15 to 19. We again would point out that the minor variations that do exist seem to reflect methodology rather than differences between the population and the sample. Marital status for 35- to 59-year-old adults is only a crude estimate of the marital status of the parents of teenagers, containing more single people.

In sum, the sample is both sufficiently large and representative of Canadian teenagers 15 to 19 to permit generalizations to the high school population with a very high level of accuracy. On most items in the questionnaire,

TABLE A1: School Participation in the Surveys by Region: Actual Numbers					
	RECEIVED	REFUSALS	NOT REC'D	TOTALS	%
1992					
British Columbia	20	0	1	21	95
Prairies	36	0	1	37	97
Ontario	58	4	2	64	91
Quebec	44	0	3	47	94
Atlantic	19	1	1	21	91
Yukon-NWT	2	0	0	2	100
Unknown	1	0	0	1	–
TOTALS	180	5	8	193	93
1984					
British Columbia	14	5	1	20	70
Prairies	33	6	4	43	77
Ontario	46	12	6	64	72
Quebec	39	2	8	49	80
Atlantic	20	2	2	24	83
TOTALS	152	27	21	200	76

the national results should come within about three percentage points of the results of other surveys probing the teenage population, 19 times in 20. For specific details of the 1984 survey, including tables documenting representativeness, see *The Emerging Generation*, pp. 201-205.

THE PROJECT CANADA AND PROJECT TEEN CANADA 88 SURVEYS

The book makes extensive use of Bibby's *Project Canada* adult surveys of 1975, 1980, 1985, and 1990. These surveys are all national, consisting of samples of approximately 1500 cases each. Conducted by mail with return rates of roughly 65 per cent, they have yielded high-quality data. The samples are highly representative of the Canadian adult population, and are of sufficient size to be accurate within approximately four percentage points, 19 times in 20. Methodological details can be found in Bibby's *Fragmented Gods*, pp. 273-279.

We have also made some use of our 1988 national survey of Canadian young people between the ages of 15 and 24. This survey, carried out for the Canadian Youth Foundation, involved face-to-face interviews with 2033 people. The two of us constructed the interview schedule, with actual data collection carried out by the Gallup organization. The data are high quality, the sample very representative of Canadian youth. This sample included about 800 high school students. As indicated, in some places we make use of the entire sample, in other instances only the teens, 15 to 19, in high school. A complete methodological summary is found in Posterski and Bibby, *Canada's Youth: Ready for Today*, Ottawa: Canadian Youth Foundation, 1988, pp. 54-55.

```
┌─────────────────────────────────────────────────────────────────┐
│                                                                   │
│      TABLE A2: Characteristics of the High School Teenage (15-19) │
│                Population and Teen Canada 92 Sample               │
```

		Teen Pop.*	Weighted Sample
REGION	British Columbia	12	12
	Prairies	17	17
	Ontario	37	37
	Quebec	25	25
	Atlantic	9	9
	Yukon-NWT	< 1	< 1
COMMUN. SIZE	100,000 & over	53	54
	99,000-10,000	15	14
	under 10,000	32	32
GENDER	Male	48	48
	Female	52	52
SCHOOL SYSTEM	Public	79	81
	Separate	15	15
	Private	6	4
PARENTAL MARITAL STATUS**	Married	85	78
	Divorced	5	16
	Widowed	3	4
	Never Married	7	2

*Population estimates derived from Statistics Canada, varied publications.
**Population data: marital status of adults ages 35-59.

TABLE A3: Sample sizes of categories used in analyses: 1992*

REGION	B.C.	477	RACE	White	3237
	Prairies	676		Black	80
	Ontario	1475		East Ind-Pak	85
	Quebec	994		Native	81
	Atlantic	358		Oriental	186
	Yuk-NWT	11			
GENDER	Male	1829	LANG	Francophone	783
	Female	1986	(Que)	Anglophone	203
COM SIZE	100,000+	2136	ATTEND	Weekly	700
	99-10,000	574		Never	923
	<10,000	1281			

*This information is provided to give interested readers some idea of the sub-sample sizes. The 1984 N's are very similar. Further information can be obtained from the authors.

NOTES

1 FIVE OLD PATTERNS THAT ARE CHANGING

1 *The Gallup Report*, August 2, 1991.
2 Canadian Press, Vancouver, June 21, 1991.
3 William Glasser, *Reality Therapy*. New York: Harper and Row, 1965, p. 7.
4 *The Gallup Report*, November 28, 1991.
5 Anthony Kerr, *Youth of Europe*. Chester Springs, Pa.: Dufour Editions, 1964, p. 168.
6 Brenda Nielson, "Teens Find Own Niche in School Peer Groups," *Lethbridge Herald*, April 6, 1992 For a discussion of such variations in the mid-1980s, see Myrna Kostash, *No Kidding: Inside the World of Teenage Girls*. Toronto: McClelland and Stewart, 1987, p. 55.
7 Associated Press, February 2, 1992.
8 *The Gallup Report*, January 25, 1992.
9 *Globe and Mail*, April 11, 1991.
10 *Globe and Mail*, April 2, 1992.
11 See Marc Eliany, "Alcohol and Drug Use." *Canadian Social Trends*. Spring, 1991, p. 21.
12 *The Gallup Report*, June 13, 1991.
13 Eliany, *op. cit.*, p. 25.
14 Statistics Canada, 1991.
15 Canadian Press, Toronto, April 2, 1992.
16 *Globe and Mail*, April 2, 1992.
17 *The Gallup Report*, January 16, 1992.
18 *Globe and Mail*, June 22, 1992.
19 Canadian Press, April 9, 1992.
20 Faith Popcorn, *The Popcorn Report*. New York: Doubleday, 1991, p. 43.
21 Jean Dumas and Yves Peron, *Marriage and Conjugal Life in Canada*. Ottawa: Statistics Canada, 1992.
22 Canadian Press, December 23, 1991.
23 United Press International, April 12, 1992.
24 Dumas and Peron, op. cit., 1992.
25 Cam Stout, "Common Law: A Growing Alternative," *Canadian Social Trends*. Winter, 1990, pp. 18-19.
26 Associated Press, May 24, 1992.
27 Reginald W. Bibby, *Mosaic Madness*. Toronto: Stoddart, 1990, p. 65.
28 Canadian Press, Ottawa, May 10, 1992.
29 Janelle Holmes and Eliane Leslau Silverman, *We're Here, Listen to Us!* Ottawa: Canadian Advisory Council on the Status of Women, 1992.
30 Associated Press, March 30, 1992.
31 *Globe and Mail*, March 13, 1992, A7.
32 Canadian Press, Ottawa, May 11, 1992.
33 *Globe and Mail*, March 13, 1992, A7.

34 Associated Press, January 26, 1992.
35 *The Gallup Report,* February 13, 1992.
36 Derived from Carol Strike, "AIDS: Into the 90s," *Canadian Social Trends.* Winter, 1991, pp. 23-24.
37 Canadian Press, February 20, 1992.
38 *Lethbridge Herald,* January 14, 1992.
39 Canadian World Almanac, 1990.
40 Reginald W. Bibby and Donald C. Posterski, *The Emerging Generation: An Inside Look at Canada's Teenagers.* Toronto: Irwin, 1985, pp. 122-123.
41 See, for example, Rodney Stark and William Sims Bainbridge, *The Future of Religion,* Berkeley: University of California Press, 1985.

2 FIVE NEW PATTERNS THAT ARE EMERGING

1 Canadian Press, Toronto, May 11, 1992.
2 Column of January 11, 1990.
3 Jillian Oderkirk, "Canadians Travelling Abroad," *Canadian Social Trends.* Autumn, 1991, pp. 2-7.
4 Reginald Bibby, 1990, op. cit., pp. 80-81.
5 *The Gallup Report,* January 20, 1992.
6 *The Gallup Youth Survey,* January 16, 1992; movie stars: February 12, 1992 and February 19, 1992.
7 *Globe and Mail,* April 2, 1992.
8 Canadian Press, March 26, 1992.
9 Ted Fergurson, "Fifth Column," *Globe and Mail,* April 2, 1992.
10 Canadian Press, November 28, 1991.
11 Mordecai Richler, *Oh Canada! Oh Quebec!* Toronto: Penguin, 1992.
12 Canadian Press, Ottawa, April 8, 1992.
13 *The Gallup Report,* February 24, 1992.
14 See Southam Literacy Survey, 1987; Canadian Literacy Survey, 1991.
15 Canadian Press, February 5, 1992.
16 *International Comparisons in Education.* Edmonton: Alberta Chamber of Resources and Alberta Education, 1992.
17 *Calgary Herald,* March 16, 1992.
18 *Montreal Gazette,* December 4, 1991.
19 United Press International, November 28, 1991 and *The Gallup Youth Survey,* January 1, 1992.
20 *The Gallup Report,* June 6, 1991.
21 See, for example, Holmes and Silverman, op. cit., 1992, pp. 19-21.
22 Canadian Press, Ottawa, February 3, 1992.
23 Canadian Press, Ottawa, February 20, 1992.
24 Interview on CBC's *The Journal,* July 1, 1992.
25 *The Gallup Report,* July 29, 1991.
26 *The Gallup Report,* April 27, 1992.
27 Canadian Press, Barrie, February 13, 1992.
28 Canadian Press, December 15, 1991.
29 Stephen Waldman, *New Republic,* reprinted in *Globe and Mail,* January 25, 1992, D5.
30 Popcorn, op. cit., pp. 43-49.
31 David Cravit, "Testing Brand Loyalty in Canada," *Globe and Mail,* April 24, 1991.

32 John Naisbitt and Patricia Aburdene, *Megatrends 2000.* New York: William Morrow and Company 1990, p. 307.
33 Canadian Press, Toronto, April 7, 1992.
34 *The Gallup Report,* January 10, 1991.
35 Reginald W. Bibby, 1990, op. cit., p. 9.
36 *Globe and Mail,* October 16, 1989.
37 Popcorn, op. cit., p. 86. For an overview on the "just society" emphasis emanating from the Trudeau era, see Thomas S. Axworthy and Pierre Elliott Trudeau (eds.) *Towards the Just Society: The Trudeau Years.* Toronto: Viking, 1990. An excellent exposition and critique of the multiculturalism policy and programs is provided by Augie Fleras and Jean Leonard Elliott, *Multiculturalism in Canada.* Toronto: Nelson Canada, 1992.
38 *The Gallup Report,* March 12, 1992.
39 Naisbitt and Aburdene, op. cit., p. 31.
40 *Canadian Living,* January, 1992, pp. 63-66.
41 CBC's *Morningside,* May 4, 1992.

3 TWO DISTINCT DEPARTURES

1 Francophones and anglophones have been operationalized in terms of the language in which the questionnaire was filled out (i.e., French or English), checked against languages in which proficiency is claimed. The small number of individuals who said that they spoke neither official language were excluded from the linguistic analysis. For a discussion of the difficulty of dubbing people as francophones and anglophones, see Alan Freeman, "Credentials," *Globe and Mail,* July 2, 1992, A19.
2 Stout, op. cit., 19.
3 Dumas and Peron, op. cit., 1992.
4 Reginald W. Bibby, *Fragmented Gods.* Toronto: Stoddart, 1987; Jean Francois Lisée, "Qui Nous Sommes: Anatomie d'une Société distincte." *L'Actualité,* January, 1992. For a succinct overview of the decline of the Church in Quebec, see Hubert Guindon, "Quebec and the Canadian Question." In M. Michael Rosenberg, William B. Shaffir, Allan Turowetz, and Morton Weinfeld (eds.), *An Introduction to Sociology.* Second edition. Toronto: Methuen, 1987, pp. 670-677.
5 Cited in Mordecai Richler, *Oh Canada! Oh Quebec!* Toronto: Penguin, 1992, p. 12.
6 *The Gallup Report,* March 5, 1992.
7 Peter Black, Thompson News Service, February 26, 1992.
8 Canadian Press, Montreal, June 18, 1992.
9 Samuel Clark, "Social Movements," in James T. Teevan (ed.), *Introduction to Sociology: A Canadian Focus,* Third Edition. Scarborough: Prentice-Hall, 1989, pp. 407-410.
10 Marcel Rioux, *Quebec in Question.* Toronto: James, Lewis and Samuel, 1971, p. 78.
11 Raymond Breton, "French-English Relations." In James Curtis and Lorne Tepperman (eds.), *Understanding Canadian Society.* Toronto: McGraw-Hill Ryerson, 1988, p. 576.
12 Gregory Baum, "Quebec's Cultural Convergence," *Compass* 6, 1992, p. 27.
13 *Gallup Report,* July 15, 1991.
14 *Gallup Report,* August 13, 1991.
15 For a superb overview of the historical difficulties of women in Canada, see Alison Prentice, Paula Bourne, Gail Brandt, Beth Light, Wendy Mitchinson and

Naomi Black, *Canadian Women: A History*. Toronto: Harcourt, Brace, and Jovanovich, 1988.

16 Royal Commission on the Status of Women in Canada. Ottawa: Information Canada, 1970.

17 Metta Spencer, *Foundations of Modern Sociology*. Fifth edition. Scarborough: Prentice-Hall, 1990, p. 275. For an excellent overview of work carried out by academics on gender relations in Canada, see Marlene Mackie, *Gender Relations in Canada*. Toronto: Butterworths, 1991.

18 Holmes and Silverman, op. cit., pp. 38, 47.

19 Mackie, op. cit., 133-134.

20 Researchers continue to document the same pattern. See, for example, Edward S. Herold, *Sexual Behaviour of Canadian Young People*. Markham: Fitzhenry and Whiteside, 1984; Philip Blumstein and Pepper Schwartz "Intimate Relationships and the Creation of Sexuality," in Barbara Risman and Pepper Schwartz (eds.), *Gender in Intimate Relationships*. Belmont, Calif.: Wadsworth, 1989, pp. 120-129. Wendy Dennis's recent journalistic account sees similar tendencies, while at the same time maintaining that the difference in definitions is diminishing: *Hot and Bothered: Men and Women, Sex and Love in the 90s*. Toronto: Key Porter, 1992.

21 Carol Gilligan, *In a Different Voice*. Cambridge, Mass.: Harvard University Press, 1982.

22 For expositions of his work, see Lawrence Kohlberg, "The Development of Children's Orientations Towards a Moral Order: I. Sequence in the Development of Moral Thought," *Vita Humana* 6, 1963; Kohlberg, *The Philosophy of Moral Development*. New York: Harper and Row, 1981.

23 See, for example, Linda K. Kerber, "On A Different Voice: An Interdisciplinary Forum. Some Cautionary Words for Historians," *Signs* 11, 1986, pp. 304-301; Ann Colby and William Damon, "Listening to a Different Voice: A Review of Gilligan's 'In A Different Voice,' " in Mary Roth Walsh (ed.), *The Psychology of Women: Ongoing Debates*. New Haven: Yale University Press, 1987, pp. 321-329 and Barbara J. Risman, "Intimate Relationships from a Micro-structural Perspective: Men Who Mother," *Gender and Society* 1, 1987, pp. 6-32.

24 For research on gender and religion see, for example, Hart M. Nelsen, and Raymond H. Potvin, "Gender and Regional Differences in the Religiosity of Protestant Adolescents," *Review of Religious Research* 22, 1981, pp. 268-285; Merlin B. Brinkerhoff and Marlene Mackie, "Religion and Gender: A Comparison of Canadian and American Student Attitudes," *Journal of Marriage and the Family*, May, 1985; Patrician A. Yeaman, "Prophetic Voices: Differences Between Men and Women," *Review of Religious Research*, 28, 1987, pp. 367-376. Leslie J. Francis, and Laurence B. Brown, "The Influence of Home, Church and School on Prayer Among Sixteen-year-old Adolescents in England," *Review of Religious Research* 33, 1991, pp. 112-122; Timothy F. Hartnagel, "Feminism and Religious Behavior: Greeley Revisited," *Review of Religious Research* 33, 1991, pp. 153-168.

25 Leona Flim, *Lethbridge Herald*, May 10, 1992.

26 For recent examinations of the continuing importance placed on the appearance of women, see, for example, Diane Barthel, *Putting on Appearances: Gender and Advertising*. Philadelphia: Temple University Press, 1988, and Naomi Wolf, *The Beauty Myth*. Toronto: Random House, 1990.

27 See, for example, Holmes and Silverman, op. cit., pp. 16-17.

28 Ibid., pp. 11-14.

29 *Gallup Report*, October 10, 1991 and *Project Canada* survey series.

30 Canadian Press, London, April 2, 1992 and *Gallup Report*, May 30, 1991. A valuable overview of a wide variety of abuses experienced by women, including sexual assault, domestic violence, and harassment is offered in Walter S. DeKeseredy and Ronald Hinch, *Woman Abuse*. Toronto: Thompson Educational Publishing, 1991. Recent examinations of domestic violence include Merlin B. Brinkerhoff and Eugen Lupri "Interspousal Violence," *Canadian Journal of Sociology*, 13, 1988, pp. 407-434; Eugen Lupri, "Male Violence in the Home," *Canadian Social Trends* 14, 1989, pp. 19-31; and Murray Straus, and R.J. Gelles *Physical Violence in American Families*. New York: Transaction Books, 1990.

31 W.I. Thomas, *The Child in America*. New York: Knopf, 1928.

32 Canadian Press, London, April 3, 1992.

33 *Gallup Report*, December 13, 1991.

34 See, for example, Marlene Kadar, "Sexual Harassment as a Form of Social Control." In Arlene Tigar McLaren (ed.), *Gender and Society*. Toronto: Copp Clark Pitman.

35 Canadian Press, Calgary, May 6, 1992.

36 Associated Press, June 14, 1991.

37 See, for example, Martin Meissner, Martin, Elizabeth Humphreys, Scott Meis, and William Scheu, "No Exit for Wives: Sexual Division of Labor," *Canadian Review of Sociology and Anthropology* 12, 1975, pp. 424-439; Pat Armstrong and Hugh Armstrong, *The Double Ghetto: Canadian Women and Their Segregated Work*. Toronto: McClelland and Stewart, 1978; Isabel Bassett, *The Bassett Report*. Toronto: Collins, 1985; and Arlie Hochschild, *The Second Shift*. New York: Avon Books, 1989.

38 Meg Luxton, "Taking on the Double day," *Atlantis* 7, 1981, p. 12.

39 *Globe and Mail*, September 30, 1991. Obviously, not all men are wanting to "work together" to solve the problems; some are reacting strongly to change. See, for example, Susan Faludi, *Backlash: The Undeclared War against American Women*. New York: Crown Publishers, Inc., 1991, and Marilyn French, *The War against Women*, New York: Summit Books, 1992. For other men, the times call for a re-examination of who they are; a recent popular example is Robert Bly's *Iron John: A Book about Men*. New York: Vintage Books, 1990. Gloria Steinem has recently stressed the need for women to experience change not only structurally but personally in her *Revolution from Within*. Boston: Little, Brown and Company, 1992.

4   WHAT THE TRENDS SAY ABOUT LIFE IN CANADA

1 Alan King, *The Health of Canada's Youth*. Ottawa: Department of Health and Welfare, 1992.

2 Clearly there are some young people who are suffering severely. This often overlooked minority is described well in Marlene Webber's ethnography, *Street Kids: the Tragedy of Canada's Runaways*. Toronto: University of Toronto Press, 1991.

3 Edward Lang, "The Language of Business," *Canadian*. Toronto: Canadian Airlines International, August, 1991.

4 Canadian Press, Calgary, March 2, 1992.

5 Dumas and Peron, op. cit., 1992; *Globe and Mail*, April 24, 1992.

6 Canadian Press, Ottawa, December 3, 1991, and Alastair Lawrie, "Why Are Canadians Such Tightwards?" *Globe and Mail*, October 26, 1990.

7 Canadian Press, Ottawa, February 6, 1992.

8 *Gallup Report*, April 6, 1992.

9 Canadian Press, Ottawa, January 4, 1992.

10 Suzuki, "Reflections" column, December 21, 1991.

11 Waldman, op. cit.

12 Allan Bloom, *The Closing of the American Mind.* New York: Simon and Schuster, 1987, p. 34.

13 Canadian Press, Toronto, August 1, 1992.

14 *Toronto Star,* October 29, 1991, A1 and Statistics Canada, as reported by Canadian Press, Ottawa, March 23, 1992.

15 *Toronto Star,* November 10, 1991, A1, A7.

16 David Suzuki, op. cit.

17 Cited in Bibby, 1990, op. cit., p. 12.

18 *Maclean's,* May 27, 1991, p. 43.

19 *Vancouver Sun,* July 15, 1989.

20 Canadian Press, Vancouver, May 11, 1992.

21 Canadian Press, Vancouver, December 19, 1991.

22 "What Canada Thinks," Canadian Press, May 24, 1992.

23 *Globe and Mail,* June 15, 1992.

24 Reginald Bibby, *Globe and Mail,* June 27, 1991.

25 *Lethbridge Herald,* March 12, 1992.

26 Canadian Press, Calgary, June 16, 1992.

27 Bibby and Posterski, op. cit., pp. 179-180.

5 THE ROLE OF THE FAMILY

1 Kathleen Harris and Phillip Morgan, "Fathers, Sons, and Daughters: Differential Paternal Involvement in Parenting," *Journal of Marriage and the Family,* 53, August 1991, pp. 531-532.

2 Ibid., p. 540.

3 Ralph LaRossa et al., "The Fluctuating Image of the 20th Century American Father." *Journal of Marriage and the Family,* 53, November 1991, p. 987.

4 Harris and Morgan, op. cit., p. 532.

5 Vivian Smith, "Fathers' New Roles Aren't Easy to Rehearse," *Globe and Mail,* June 18, 1992.

6 John Gardner, cited in *Excellence.* New York: Harper & Row, 1961, p. 121.

7 "Proud Parents Happy to See Son Leave Home," *Toronto Star,* April 1, 1989.

8 Susan Littwin, *The Postponed Generation.* New York: William Morrow & Company, 1986, p. 17.

9 Jean Dumas and Yves Peron, "Marriage and Conjugal Life in Canada." Ottawa: *Statistics Canada,* 1992.

6 THE ROLE OF EDUCATION

1 *Report of the Royal Commission on Education in Ontario.* Toronto: Baptist Johnson, 1950, p. 167.

2 *National Association of Secondary School Principals Newsletter,* September 1989.

3 Ibid.

4 Reginald W. Bibby, *Mosaic Madness.* Toronto: Stoddart, 1990, p. 70.

5 Michael Valpy, "From Vertical Mosaic to Ethnic Pudding," *Globe and Mail,* December 29, 1990.

6 Bibby, op. cit., p. 157 and 91.

7 Edward De Bono, *Handbook for the Positive Revolution.* London: Penguin, 1991, pp. 116-17.

8 Marc Tucker, "On Education and the Economy," *Educational Leadership*, March 1992, p. 19.
9 John Naisbitt, *Inside Guide*. Spring 1988, p. 33.
10 Donn Downey, "McKenna Attacks Education System," *Globe and Mail*, April 7, 1992.
11 Aldo Santin, "Canada's Prosperity 'In Danger'." *Winnipeg Free Press*, April 30, 1992.

7 THE ROLE OF RELIGION

1 "What We Heard," a report from the federal government Royal Commission on New Reproductive Technologies, 1991, p. 26.
2 Henri Nouwen, *The Way of the Heart*. New York: Ballantine Books, 1981, p. 48.
3 Michael Warren, *Youth, Gospel, Liberation*. San Francisco: Harper & Row, 1987, p. 116.
4 John Westerhoff, *Will Our Children Have Faith?* Minneapolis: Seabury Press, 1976, p. 98.
5 Stephen Jones, *Faith Shaping*. Valley Forge: Judson Press, 1980, p. 48.
6 Miriam Durkin, "Teenage Skeptics," *Calgary Herald*, January 18, 1992.
7 James Fowler, *Stages of Faith*. San Francisco: Harper & Row, 1981, pp. 117-211.
8 Ron Graham, *God's Dominion*. Toronto: Key Porter, 1990, pp. 11-12.

8 THE ROLE OF THE MEDIA

1 Miro Cernetig, "Inuit Fall Victim to Flabby Lifestyle," *Globe and Mail*, May 19, 1992.
2 "More Kids Turning Out Television, Study Finds," *Toronto Star*, April 15, 1992.
3 Quentin Schultze et al., *Dancing in the Dark*. Grand Rapids: Eerdmans, 1991, p. 252.
4 Michael Pfau, "A Channel Approach to Television Influence," *Journal of Broadcasting and Electronic Media*, vol. 34, no. 2, 1990, p. 208.
5 Robert Mason Lee, *One Hundred Monkeys, The Triumph of Popular Wisdom in Canadian Politics*. Toronto: Macfarlane Walter & Ross, 1989, p. 25.
6 Schultze, op. cit., p. 252.
7 Schultze, op. cit., p. 251.
8 Pfau, op. cit., p. 208.
9 Dorothy Lipovenko, "Barbara Frum: Private Acts of Kindness," *Globe and Mail*, April 6, 1992.
10 Robert Hawkins, "In Search of Television Viewing Styles." *Journal of Broadcasting and Electronic Media*, vol. 35, no. 3, 1991, p. 376.
11 Rick Salutin, "Cross Currents," *Globe and Mail*, January 17, 1992.
12 William Zinsser, *On Writing Well*. New York: Harper Collins, 1990, p. 55.
13 David Rutherford, "Worshipping at the Altar of False Images," *Toronto Star*, May 13, 1992.
14 Jerry Foresburg, professor of communications, Trinity Western University, personal interview, May 21, 1992.
15 Conway Daly, "Family Life Affected by TV," *Globe and Mail*, May 20, 1992.
16 John Haslett, "Cross Currents," *Globe and Mail*, January 29, 1992.
17 Sheelagh Wittaker, "Canadian Programs are the Cod Liver Oil of TV," *Canadian Speeches*, vol. 4, no. 1, March 1990, p. 54.
18 Doris Anderson, "US Myths Swallowed Whole," *Toronto Star*, April 6, 1992.
19 Keith Spicer, "Broadcasting Helps Keep Canada Alive and Well," *Canadian Speeches*, vol. 4, no. 5, August/September 1990, p. 82.

20 Dennis McDougal, "Win, Lose or Trauma: TV Teen Virginity," *Toronto Star*, September 19, 1991.

21 Lee, op. cit., p. 178.

22 Karen Peterson, "Grading TV, 'C', with Need for Change," *USA Today*, February 26, 1992.

23 Bill Roberts, "Channelling the Power of Educational TV," *Globe and Mail*, June 18, 1992.

24 T.S. Eliot, "Choruses for the Rock," *Selected Poems of T.S. Eliot*. London: Penguin, 1948.

25 Hal Boedeker, "Have you Hugged Your TV Today?" *Toronto Star*, February 5, 1992.

26 "Prince of the Global Village," *Time*, January 6, 1992.

27 Thomas Kuhn, *The Structure of Scientific Revolutions*. Chicago: University of Chicago Press, 1962, p. 53.

28 C. Trungpa, *Cutting through Spiritual Materialism*. Boulder and Longdon: Shambhala, 1973. Cited in *Mindfulness*, by Ellen Langer. Don Mills: Addison Wesley, 1989, p. 11.

29 Jim Wilkes, "PM Came Calling — But So Did Nature," *Toronto Star*, April 15, 1992, and Peter Tym, photo, *Globe and Mail*, April 15, 1992.

30 André Picard, "Study Assails 'Sexist' Rock Videos," *Globe and Mail*, April 15, 1992.

31 Lindsay Scotton, "Turning the Tables," *Toronto Star*, March 16, 1992.

32 "Teen Killers Now Facing Jail Terms up to 5 Years," *Toronto Star*, November 27, 1991.

9 THE ROLE OF OTHER ADULTS

1 "Sex, Politics and Dreams," *Maclean's*, January 7, 1991, p. 33.

2 Ray Conlogue, "Spirituality Prevails over Politics," *Globe and Mail*, January 27, 1992.

3 Bill Mandel, "Roll Over, Beethoven," *San Francisco Examiner & Chronicle*, June 4, 1989.

4 Ken Dychtwald, *Age Wave*. Los Angeles: J.P. Tarcher Inc., 1989, p. 20.

5 Margot Gibb-Clark, "It's Not What You Do — It's How You Do It," *Globe and Mail*, May 17, 1991.

6 Ken Blanchard and Spencer Johnson, *The One Minute Manager*. Berkeley, 1982, pp. 27, 38 & 53.

7 Sherri Gallant, "AADAC Steers Clear of Scare Tactics," *Lethbridge Herald*, November 16, 1991.

8 Christopher Lasch, *The True and Only Heaven*. New York: W.W. Norton & Company, 1991, p. 43.

9 Bruce Wilkinson, "Trade Liberalization, the Market Ideology, and Morality: Have We a Sustainable System?" From a paper presented at York University, 1991.

INDEX